UNDER A RED SKY

HAYA LEAH MOLNAR

UNDER A RED SKY

Memoir of a Childhood in Communist Romania

FRANCES FOSTER BOOKS
Farrar Straus Giroux / New York

Distributed in Canada by D&M Publishers, Inc.
Printed in February 2010 in the United States of America by
RR Donnelley & Sons Company, Harrisonburg, Virginia
Designed by Jay Colvin
First edition, 2010
1   3   5   7   9   10   8   6   4   2

www.fsgkidsbooks.com

Library of Congress Cataloging-in-Publication Data
Molnar, Haya Leah.
    Under a red sky : memoir of a childhood in Communist Romania /
Haya Leah Molnar.—1st ed.
        p.   cm.
    ISBN: 978-0-374-31840-6
    1. Molnar, Haya Leah—Childhood and youth—Juvenile literature.
2. Family—Romania—History—Juvenile literature.   3. Romania—
History—1944–1989—Biography—Juvenile literature.   I. Title.

DR267.5.M65A3 2010
949.803'1092—dc22
[B]
                                                    2008055562

In memory of my parents, Stefanie and Gyuri Zimmermann,
and for my family—past, present, and future

Contents

AUTHOR'S NOTE

Under a Red Sky is based on events that happened to my family from the late 1950s until we left Communist Romania in 1961. The story is filtered through my memory as a child of a time and place that no longer exist. Today, Romania is still very much on the map in Eastern Europe, but the country has undergone a major recovery—economically, culturally, and spiritually—from being under the thumb of a long line of tyrannical Communist rulers. Much of this book is based on my family's oral history, documenting some of the horrific events that took place during World War II in Romania. Before the war, there were 800,000 Jews living in Romania and Transylvania. Nearly 400,000 perished in Nazi concentration camps and pogroms incited by fascist Romanian groups such as the Legionnaire Iron Guard. I grew up listening to my family's stories of this time the way other children grow up hearing fairy tales, and while the dialogue may not be exact, the essence of what was said is true.

I owe a debt of gratitude to two books in particular, which confirm the historical background upon which one of my grandmother's stories is based: *Balkan Ghosts* by Robert D. Kaplan and *The Holocaust in Romania* by Radu Ioanid.

With the exception of my immediate family and some well-known political figures, the names of the characters in this book have been changed to protect their privacy. Some characters, though not major, appear as composites of several people; some of the events happened in different time sequences. In brief, this is not a journalist's rendition of historical events but my personal story about growing up in Communist Romania.

UNDER A RED SKY

WHAT CAME FIRST—BUCHAREST, ROMANIA—NOVEMBER 1957

GRANDPA YOSEF TAPS on our bedroom door. Mama helps me dress in the early morning silence, her index finger crossing her lips, urging me to keep quiet so I won't wake up Tata—my father—who is snoring lightly in the bed next to mine. I am sleepy but excited. Mama has agreed to let me go with Grandpa to Bucharest's old outdoor farmers' market for the first time.

In the dining room Grandpa has set out for me a plate with two slices of buttered crusty bread and a cup of tea with a wedge of lemon. Next to it is a small bowl filled with sugar cubes. I pop a sugar cube in my mouth, tucking it behind my two front teeth with my tongue, the way Grandpa Yosef has taught me, and sip my tea. Grandpa sits with me sipping his tea and dragging on his cigarette, its tip glowing in the early morning light.

"You were a lovely baby," Grandpa says, surveying me from across the table. "You are growing more beautiful every day." I make a face at him between bites, and he smiles back. "Just as long as you know that beauty is only skin-deep, you'll be all right. Raw intelligence isn't enough." I roll my eyes still heavy with sleep at him, but he goes on, ignoring me. "You'll need common sense, wisdom, and luck. I hope you will have luck. Luck is the most important thing of all." He stops abruptly and looks at his watch. "It's almost five. We have to go, or there won't be anything left at the market for us to buy."

I run to the entrance hall closet. Grandpa holds my coat as I slip each arm in. He bundles me in my muffler and makes sure that my wool hat covers my ears. "Let's go," he says, taking my hand.

It is chilly outside. A satchel made of strong white netting hangs out of Grandpa's overcoat. His pants pockets are stuffed with bits of string, small pieces of rope, and carefully folded sheets of newspaper. "Only fools or foreigners go to the market without their wrapping," he says, handing me a hard candy in cellophane. "Save it for later, in case you get hungry while we wait in line."

We walk hand in hand to the tram. Grandpa's hands are rough except for his smooth gold wedding band, which is loose enough for me to twirl around on his finger but too tight to slide past his gnarled knuckle. Grandpa is wearing his usual hat, with the brim turned down just enough to cast a shadow over his eyes. He calls it his Humphrey Bogart hat. I've never seen a movie with Humphrey Bogart because he is an American movie star and we are not allowed to watch American film propaganda, but Grandpa says that Mr. Bogart is a great actor. Of course he would know, since Grandpa used to own the best movie house in all of Bucharest. His Humphrey Bogart hat is one of his reminders of life before the war.

The sun has not yet risen, but a hint of purple as deep as the skin of a plum is turning pink at the horizon. The tram is approaching from the distance. Electric sparks light up like fireflies above a spiderweb of wires. I am fascinated with how smoothly the tram glides into the station on its thin metal rails. The doors open, and we climb up into the car and find seats. I wonder silently how come Grandpa never complains that he's no longer being driven around Bucharest like a rich man in his fancy horse-drawn carriage.

"Who shopped for you before the war?" I ask him.

"The cook's helper, shhhhh," he whispers, his eyes roaming the tramcar to make sure that our conversation isn't overheard. Everyone looks half asleep. Grandpa sighs and gazes out the window.

"Yes, but did the cook's helper buy what you needed?" I press on. "How did she know what to buy if *you* weren't there?"

"She didn't." Grandpa smiles. "I do a far better job than she ever did." He winks at me as if that's our secret. "I'm friends with all the farmers. That's why I always get the best goods at the best prices. Unfortunately, there isn't much to buy nowadays."

"Why not?"

"Because the farmers aren't producing as much as they used to," Grandpa continues, his eyes still scanning the car to make sure that no one's listening.

"Why aren't the farmers producing?"

"Because there's not enough money in it for them and because there's no love in working for someone else," Grandpa answers in a lowered voice.

"I don't understand," I whisper back, tugging at his coat.

"It's better that you don't," Grandpa says curtly, but then he tries to explain. "There was a time not that long ago when farmers sold their goods and the profit was theirs to keep. Now that they work for the Party cooperatives, they only get to keep a small percentage."

I have no idea what *profit* and *percentage* mean, but I under-stand that the farmers aren't happy because the Communist Party is now in charge.

THE SUN HAS JUST RISEN when we arrive at the market. It is a gray, chilly day that smells like snow may arrive sooner than expected. There are only a few farmers' stalls, with lots of people in gray over-coats milling about. Everyone is intent on finding out what's for sale. Grandpa grabs my hand and gets in a line without checking the stall first. We are fifth in line, and lots of people are hurrying behind us.

"Why are we standing here, Grandpa?"

"To buy something." Ashes fall like snowflakes from the tip of his cigarette as he takes a deep drag.

"I know that," I whisper back impatiently. "*What* are we going to buy?"

"I don't know. We'll find out when we get to the front of the line." Grandpa looks anxiously past the people ahead of us. "We'll take whatever they're selling, just as long as it's something we can eat. Your grandma is counting on us."

We wait for what seems like forever. The people in front of us are buying so many things, I am worried that nothing will be left for us. Then I set eyes on the farmer. He is a giant of a man wear-ing a black fur hat and a heavy khaki vest with brass buttons. His shrewd gray eyes are topped by a set of huge bushy eyebrows. He recognizes Grandpa instantly.

"Mr. Yosef, sir, how are you?" The farmer smiles at both of us, revealing a gold front tooth.

"Can't complain," Grandpa answers. "So what have you got today, Ion?"

"Oh, we've got new potatoes and some onions," Ion says, point-ing at the baskets in front of him, rubbing his hands together, and blowing air into his fists to warm up. "I've also got peas," he con-tinues as he uncovers another basket filled with green pods.

I notice that some of the potatoes have sprouts growing out of them. The onions are small, but their scent is so strong I can smell them without putting my nose up close. I love the pea pods. Each is like a little boat holding its treasure of green pearls within. If Grandpa decides to buy these, I know that I'll have my work cut out for an entire afternoon since Grandma Iulia always asks me to shell them for her. Ion checks me out while Grandpa is scrutiniz-ing the produce. I can feel his eyes upon me, so I hide behind Grandpa.

"Who is this young lady with you, Mr. Yosef?" Ion asks.

"This is my granddaughter, Eva." Grandpa pushes me forward gently. "Eva, say hello to Comrade Ion."

"Hello," I whisper, looking down.

"What a pretty young lady you are." Comrade Ion smiles and bows, taking my hand in his giant one and brushing his lips against my fingers. "*Sărut mâna, domnişoară*—I kiss your hand, young lady." He looks me over as if I were intentionally trying to charm him. I am mortified. No one has ever kissed my hand before! I've seen men greet my mother, my aunt Puica, and Grandma Iulia like that. But it has never occurred to me that someday a man might kiss my hand in greeting.

Grandpa rescues me. "Yes, Eva is as smart as she is lovely. That's why I want her to learn to shop properly." Grandpa takes out his matches. He opens the matchbook cover and glances at Grandma Iulia's wish list, scribbled on the inside flap.

"How can I possibly help you, young lady?" Ion addresses me as if I were already a grownup.

"Hmm." I consider his question, then blurt out, "I would like a chicken. Please."

"A *chicken?*" Ion whispers and laughs, his narrow eyes widening.

"Yes, a chicken," I repeat.

The people in line behind us stir. There's a short, uncomfortable silence before Ion answers me with conviction. "Well, how can we disappoint such a charming young lady on her first day at the market? Mr. Yosef, sir, would you mind paying for your potatoes and vegetables now?" Ion speaks softly, his eyes looking directly into Grandpa's. "Can you wait until I'm done with my other customers and come back later?"

"No problem," Grandpa is quick to answer. "We'll check in with you in about an hour."

Grandpa takes my hand and starts walking decisively away.

"Grandpa, I'm hungry," I tell him the minute we leave Comrade Ion.

"Eat the candy I gave you."

The sticky sweetness immediately fills my mouth with saliva and delicious orange flavor. We walk around happily hand in hand. Everyone nods in recognition when they see Grandpa. His gait has an assurance that few men carry, but his shoulders are slightly rounded. His head is bent in resigned contemplation; his dark brown eyes are moist and kind; his nose is big. He is clean-shaven. The hair he has left on the sides of his head has turned silver, but the top of his head is bald and shiny. What I love about Grandpa is that he exudes a quiet calm that's missing from everyone else in our house.

We stop at the sugar and flour stall. The line here is shorter.

"Grandpa, we've already got sugar and flour at home."

"That's true," he replies, unfolding a brown paper bag from his pocket. "But you never know when they're going to sell it again, and we don't want to run out."

The lady who is serving us fills the bag with great care, making sure not to spill even a single grain of sugar.

"How much longer do we have to wait for the chicken?" I ask.

Grandpa glances at his watch and looks in the direction of Ion's line. "Just a little longer," he says.

"I'm hungry."

"I know. That's why we're waiting," he says, smiling at me.

"But, Grandpa, how do we know that he's got a chicken?"

"We don't know, but we have to have faith."

"Faith?" I cry. "Grandpa, I want to *know*!"

"The only way you will know is if you have faith and patience."

"But, Grandpa, what if he's lying?"

"Did he look like he was lying to you?" Grandpa's face turns serious.

"No, but what if—"

"There are no what-ifs. We just have to trust him and hope that we'll get a chicken." Grandpa's voice is calm, but the grip of his hand feels tighter around mine.

"But what if he sold the chicken to someone else?" I imagine the aroma rising from a bowl of steaming chicken soup. My mouth waters in anticipation of the moment of that first sip of broth, which I've experienced only a handful of times since I was born. "Maybe he'll take the chicken back to the farm for his own family," I say, tugging at Grandpa. "Or he might sell it to someone else."

"Oh, my sweet, how you love to make up stories!" Grandpa says. "There can be no doubt. Ion will have a chicken for us."

"You have no doubt?" I ask in astonishment.

"None whatsoever," Grandpa says, throwing his cigarette butt on the ground and stepping on it.

When the line finally disperses, Grandpa and I approach Ion's stall as unobtrusively as possible. The farmers are packing up their baskets all around us. Ion motions to us to follow him behind a small building that houses some makeshift offices and the toilets.

"This way," he says, and points with his chapped fingers. He leads us to a wooden shed. He takes an old metal key out of his pocket and unlocks the rusty padlock. It is very dark inside. Ion pulls on a string, and a bare bulb lights up. I adjust my eyes and see that we are standing on a dirt floor covered with sawdust. All the way in the back of the shed is a mound of hay, and perched on it is a white chicken with a red crest on top of her head and eyes that are as shiny as amber jewels. The chicken is clucking softly.

"You wanted a chicken?" Ion motions toward the bird with a flourish. "She's yours," he says, beckoning me to come closer.

I climb the straw mound carefully, so as not to scare the chicken.

"Go ahead," Ion tells me. "You can pet her."

I put my hand out and barely touch the bird's feathers. They are softer than anything I have ever felt before.

"I brought two chickens from the farm," Ion confides, "one for my brother, Petrică, who now lives here in the capital. Petrică picked his up at dawn, before the market opened. He didn't want anyone to see it and get into a fight over it." Ion points at my chicken. "This one I was saving for whoever will pay top price."

Grandpa nods. "How much?"

"Being that you have this beautiful young lady with you, Domnule Yosef, I mean Comrade Yosef, I'll take whatever you can offer. Within reason, of course." Ion chooses his words carefully.

"I'll give you everything I've got on me," Grandpa tells him, opening his coat and taking three loose cigarettes out of his shirt pocket. He gives one to Ion, who places it between his lips without taking his eyes off Grandpa. In turn, Grandpa looks at Ion and takes his matchbook out again, ignoring Grandma Iulia's wish list on its inside cover. He strikes a match, shielding the flame with his hand for Ion to light up. Ion takes a deep drag on his cigarette and winks at me, his eyes smiling. Grandpa runs his hand across his chest, feeling for the small sewing needle with which earlier that morning he had pinned all his cash to the inside of his shirt pocket. His stiff fingers withdraw a bunch of folded lei bills. Without counting them, Grandpa hands over the entire wad of money. Ion takes the bills, also without counting them, and places them carefully inside his vest pocket, where they make a huge bulge.

"I'm sorry that I don't have more." Grandpa's voice trails off, sounding genuinely regretful.

"No problem, Mr. Yosef. No need to apologize. You're not like all the rest." Ion nods toward the now empty marketplace. "They take so much pleasure in haggling, they forget that farmers have to live too. They assume that we're lucky because we have food. Let them try to pay their bills while fulfilling the Party's cooperative quota! If this is all you can afford, Mr. Yosef, I'll take your word. It's enough," Ion says, watching me squat by the chicken and run my fingers through her feathers. "Besides, it's a pleasure to see Miss Eva here so happy on her first day at the market."

"You've made my entire family happy, Ion. We've got seven more mouths to feed at home," Grandpa says, handing Ion the extra cigarette and shaking hands. Ion ties the chicken's legs with a thin piece of rope. The bird does not resist as he places her in a straw basket and covers her with a cloth.

We do not take the tram back. We walk home. Grandpa is afraid that someone on the tram might hear the chicken clucking and try to rob us. I am hungry and exhausted but too happy to complain.

GRANDMA IULIA GREETS US at the door and follows us into the kitchen, her slippers making a flapping sound. Grandpa Yosef unpacks the potatoes, onions, and peas. He hands her the sugar and the flour. Grandma carefully takes stock of everything.

"That's all?" Her question hangs in the air.

"Almost." Grandpa's voice is serious, but he winks at me.

"What *else?*"

"Take a look." Grandpa motions to the straw basket on the kitchen floor. Grandma's eyes widen as she slides the cloth off the basket. "Oh my God, Yosef, it's a *chicken!*" she cries.

"Of course it's a chicken, Iulia. But this is not just any chicken. This is Eva's present, because she charmed Ion into selling it to me."

Grandma is not interested in the details of the sale. She lifts the basket with great care, places it on the kitchen counter, and examines the bird closely. With her left hand she holds down the chicken while she feels for the body fat under her wings. She touches the bird from the top of her red crest down to her scrawny legs and her sharp, pointy toes. It is clear that Grandma is figuring out how to make the most out of my chicken, but her eyes are still incredulous. The chicken ignores Grandma's excitement and fills the kitchen with soft clucking sounds.

"Yosef," Grandma says, "you'd better get ready to slaughter this bird. And please do a better job than you did the last time. I can still see that poor thing running around without her head, splattering blood all over my kitchen. It took Sabina half a day to clean the mess off these walls. Who can have an appetite after such a thing? I didn't touch a bite from our last chicken."

I tiptoe to the pantry, open the door slowly so that it won't squeak, and slide in. The pantry is my hiding place, tucked away from the hustle and bustle of the house. I pull out a wooden stool from under a shelf and sit down in the cool darkness, where I can stretch my legs and think.

"Don't worry, Iulia." Grandpa's voice drifts in from the kitchen. "I will be as swift and merciful as a *shochet*." In the damp of the pantry I wonder what a *shochet* is, but I stop short of blurting out the question.

"God forgive us," says Grandma, "we've been reduced to having to slaughter our own chickens! My parents must be turning in their graves, may they rest in peace." Even though I can't see Grandma Iulia from my hiding place, I know that, right about now, she is shaking her finger at Grandpa.

"I know," Grandpa Yosef says. "Once upon a time I corrupted you by marrying you and made you change your parents' kosher ways." His voice holds a hint of sarcasm.

Grandma shoots back, "You have no respect, Yosef."

"Sure I do, but I'll be the first to admit that I'm no *shochet*. You expect merciful butchers from the Communists, Iulia?"

"Just be swift," she pleads.

"I will," Grandpa promises, "and I will have mercy in my heart and say a prayer just for you."

"*Now* you're praying? Where were *you* when we had a chance to get out of this godforsaken country? Don't pray for me, pray for the poor chicken." Grandma sniffs.

"I'll say a prayer for the chicken *and* for you. I'll ask God to help us get out of here so that you can have your kosher chickens once again. Do you feel better now?" Grandpa laughs.

Grandma Iulia doesn't respond.

"Don't hang around here," Grandpa tells her. "You make me nervous."

I SIT IN THE DARK of the pantry for a long time and listen to the clucking of my chicken drift in from the counter. I can't imagine my beautiful bird with her soft white feathers and her glowing amber eyes transformed into a bowl of chicken paprikash with dumplings and chicken soup as well. I wish I had never asked for a chicken.

Grandpa's footsteps approach. The pantry door squeaks as I push it open a crack. A shaft of light enters the dark space.

"What are you doing in here?" Grandpa asks, carrying the basket with my chicken in both his arms.

"Thinking."

"What about?"

"Nothing." I sigh, then add, "My chicken."

Grandpa places the basket down and lifts me up.

"Your chicken is a great, great present," he says. "Thank you."

"Not anymore," I answer, glaring at him. "You're going to kill her!"

"You can't eat a live chicken," Grandpa says, "but I promise to slaughter her as mercifully as a *shochet*."

"I don't feel like eating chicken anymore. What's a *shochet*?"

"When you're hungry, you'll eat almost anything, especially delicious chicken. A *shochet* is a butcher who is trained to slaughter with mercy and prepare meat according to our laws."

"Why don't we have a *shochet*?"

"The Communists don't allow it."

"Oh. Grandpa?"

"Yes?"

"I hate you having to slaughter my chicken."

"I know, me too. But we have to eat."

"Can I say goodbye to her?" I ask.

"Why, certainly," he answers, sitting me down on the kitchen counter. "I won't slaughter her today, just so you can have an extra day with your chicken."

"Grandpa, you can't hide the chicken from Grandma. She'll hear the clucking and be angry that you didn't kill her yet."

"Don't worry, Grandma won't mind."

"Yes, she will. What are we going to tell her?"

"I don't know. We'll think of something," he murmurs.

"Can I pet my chicken?"

"Of course," he says, lifting the bird out of the basket and placing her on the counter next to me.

"I don't like her legs tied up," I whisper as I run my fingers through the feathers.

"She doesn't either," he whispers back as I wrap my arms around my chicken and feel her chest heave with clucking sounds.

Grandpa sighs. "We'll hide her in the pantry until tomorrow afternoon. Here, help me put her back in the basket," he says. "Open the handles wide and I'll lift her." The chicken flutters her wings as I open the basket.

"Look, Grandpa!" A perfect white egg is nestled amid the straw at the bottom of the basket.

"Now, that's special," Grandpa says. "You know, I think she did that just for you."

"Do you think so?" I can't take my eyes off the egg.

"Absolutely. That's the freshest egg you've ever seen. Watch." Grandpa walks across the kitchen and holds up the egg against the light from the window. "Can you see the yolk?" he asks, pointing at the shadow beneath the shell.

"It's round like the sun." I am in awe.

"It certainly is. We'll tell Grandma Iulia that this chicken's earned herself an extra day of life. You can have the egg for breakfast tomorrow. Okay?"

"Maybe she'll lay another egg, Grandpa," I say, hoping to save my chicken from her fate.

"God knows, anything's possible." Grandpa answers with a straight face, but his eyes are full of laughter.

THE CHILD

MY MOTHER CALLS ME EVA, after the first woman in the Bible and also to carry on the initial *E* for Grandpa Emile, Tata's father, who died in Auschwitz.

Grandpa Yosef also calls me Eva, but once in a while when the two of us are alone, he refers to me as his Leah, the name he gave me in memory of my great-grandmother, his mother-in-law.

Grandma Iulia calls me Evushka, a Romanian endearment.

Aunt Puica, my mother's younger sister, calls me Evişoară, also a Romanian endearment, but only when she is in a good mood, which is seldom.

Uncle Natan, Mama's older brother, refers to me as "the Little Girl."

Uncle Max, Aunt Puica's husband, the only one to whom I'm not blood-related, calls me "the Child."

My father is hardly ever home, so he seldom has a need to address me.

I am the only child in a family of seven adults who live together under one roof along with Sabina, our live-in maid. Before the

Communists took over, Grandma had an entire staff—a maid, a cook, a washerwoman, a gardener, and a footman. Grandma says Sabina is now the one extravagance she refuses to live without. Everyone in our household contributes to Sabina's upkeep without an argument—one of the few things they *don't* argue about.

Each member of the family, with the exception of Sabina, feels that he or she is my one and only true parent. Every one of my parents loves me, but they don't all love each other.

"You took forever to be born and almost killed your mother," Aunt Puica tells me with great gusto. "You are *living proof* of why I won't have children, so you'll have to do. Your mother was ashen after losing a ton of blood from laboring with you for over thirty-two hours." Seeing that I am watching every word that's coming out of her mouth, Aunt Puica does not hold back the gory details of my birth.

She continues with a smile. "She looked like one of the cadavers I used to autopsy in nursing school. I was so convinced that she would die, I even checked her breathing while she lay there after the delivery, to make sure you hadn't killed her. I promised myself then that no baby is ever going to do that to me. Max can whine all he wants. You're all the children he's ever going to get. Men! After your mother busted her butt to give you life, I called your father to let him know that his wife had just given birth to a baby girl. When he heard that you were not the boy he had hoped for, he hung up without saying a word. What else can you expect from that Hungarian son of a bitch?"

I don't know why Aunt Puica despises Tata so much. I am too young to argue with her but feel guilty for not defending my father. Besides, I am afraid that she may be telling me the truth.

"Of course," she continues, "that didn't stop you from looking just like him, a miniature Gyuri—with that same jaundiced monkey face, those huge shit-brown eyes, and a shock of hair as black as a raven's feathers. What made it worse is you had soft facial hair too. Thank God your monkey hair fell out within a week of your birth and your eyes turned out to be blue. You look a whole lot better now," she says, patting my cheek, the gap between her two front teeth showing as she smiles.

Uncle Max comes to my defense, his eyes looking over the paper. "Puica, stop upsetting the Child. Eva was the most beautiful baby ever born in all of Bucharest. I was green with envy the first time I saw her pink, wrinkly face. She was so radiant, I wished she were mine."

"Imbecile liar," my aunt blurts, pounding his back with her fist and coughing uncontrollably between drags on her cigarette.

Uncle Max knows better than to argue with his wife, especially while she's having a coughing fit, so the details of my birth are settled.

ÆT THE DINNER TÆBLE

EVERYONE IS ON A DIFFERENT SCHEDULE. Mama and Tata (when he's home) come and go throughout the day at different times, as do Uncle Max and Uncle Natan. My grandparents, Aunt Puica, and Sabina are always at home with me.

The day Sabina came to us she appeared seemingly out of nowhere like an illustration in one of my fairy-tale books. Her egg-shaped face is marked by deep wrinkles and warts; her eyes bulge slightly like a frog's. Her hair is completely hidden beneath a white cotton turban that's tightly wrapped around her head. At night before going to bed in her tiny room under the eaves, Sabina unravels her turban, exposing a thin braid of graying hair neatly coiled like a long mouse tail around her head. During the day she wears layers of multicolored peasant skirts that brush the floor with every step she takes. Her apron is always spotless and ironed. The bow, tied neatly at the back of her waist, bobs up and down as she moves. I have never seen anyone wear such an outfit, so on my first encounter with Sabina I duck under her skirts, curious to see the view from beneath her large tent. To my surprise, Sabina whirls around and is clearly embarrassed. I am too stunned for words, because she isn't wearing anything underneath!

"What are you doing, Miss Eva?" she asks, startled.

"How come you're not wearing underwear?" I blurt.

"We don't have toilets on the farm where I come from. How do you expect me to go to the bathroom with bloomers on in the fields?" she asks, laughing.

"I don't know," I answer. "How *do* you go to the bathroom?"

"I just pull up my skirts like this." She demonstrates, opening her legs and squatting. "That's how I do my business," she explains.

"You can pee without sitting on the toilet?" I ask, stunned.

"Certainly." She smiles. "You wouldn't have time to go to the toilet if you worked in the fields."

From that moment on Sabina and I become good friends. I am so curious about the world she came from that secretly I lock myself in our bathroom, take off my undies, pull up my skirt, and try to pee standing in our bathtub. It isn't any fun since I get my legs wet and then have to scrub the tub after myself, before Mama has a chance to find out.

Despite my questions about the farm, it's clear that Sabina feels the past must be left behind. She never speaks about her family, her friends, or her life before joining us unless asked a direct question. She has a thick accent that I have trouble understanding at first, but eventually she and I forge an alliance with few words because we have something in common. As the Child, I am adored by all, while Sabina, the Maid, is ignored by all. We are both outsiders looking in on the lives of others.

"Sabina! Set the table, please," Grandma Iulia calls from the kitchen.

Within minutes our dining room table is dressed in a white tablecloth and the china and silverware magically appear in their proper places. My grandparents and I eat our lunch together. Then Grandma's voice is heard again. "Sabina, please clear the table."

The tablecloth is lifted, revealing the dark, heavy oak grain of our dining table. Half an hour later Grandma's voice sounds the dinner bell again. "Sabina, set the table for Max," and then, "Set the table for Natan," followed by "Set the table for Stefi," and so on. This ritual repeats itself in order to accommodate everyone's schedule until one day Grandma Iulia puts an end to all of this commotion and our life changes.

"I'm sick and tired of 'Set the table and clear the table'!" she declares one evening over tea. "What do you think this is, a restaurant? From now on, lunch will be served between the hours of two and four p.m. And I warn you, you'd better show up if you want to eat. After four p.m., Sabina will clear the table and the kitchen will close for the evening. You're all welcome to help yourselves to a light supper as long as you do your own dishes. Does everyone understand this?" Grandma's words hang in the air as eight pairs of eyes watch her in silence. Clearly this topic is not open for discussion. Encouraged by our response, she concludes, "And from now on, Eva will set the table so that she can learn how to do it properly." I look up at Sabina to see her reaction. She is leaning against the dining room wall; I can't tell what she's thinking, so I tug at her skirts and she grasps my hand and squeezes it. I'm relieved, because this means Sabina will teach me.

The next day everyone in the household has mysteriously synchronized their watches. They all appear on time for lunch, which is served promptly at 2:00 p.m. I set the table under Sabina's supervision, and now forks and knives can be heard clicking against the porcelain plates. Aunt Puica dishes an enormous helping of mashed potatoes onto Uncle Max's plate. My mother's left eyebrow goes up like the tight bow of an arrow.

"What are you ogling at?" Aunt Puica snaps. "You're welcome to serve your own husband."

"My husband can help himself," Mama snaps back.

Uncle Max coughs uncomfortably.

"I will not have any arguments at this table," Grandma Iulia warns while Grandpa Yosef winks and smiles at me.

"Thanks for the food," Uncle Natan says from behind his thick glasses. He pushes back his chair and leaves the table, grabbing the newspaper from the top of his nightstand, which is located at the end of our dining room. He lies down on his cot and buries his head in his newspaper as if an invisible wall has just descended between him and the rest of us.

The phone rings. Both Tata and Aunt Puica get up to answer it at the same time. Aunt Puica reaches it first. "It's for me," she says, waving my father off with one hand and pulling the phone into her bedroom. She shuts the door with the black phone cord stretching tightly between the foyer and her room.

"Tell your darling little sister not to monopolize the phone," Tata whispers to Mama. "Beard will be calling to let me know when he needs me at the Studio."

A little later, both Uncle Max and Uncle Natan have gone back to their offices for the afternoon shift. Grandma and Grandpa are taking a nap in their bedroom. On her way out to teach her afternoon ballet class, Mama taps on Aunt Puica's door. Her knock is ignored as the black phone cord is pulled tighter into Aunt Puica's bedroom. Mama sticks her head into our room. "Sorry. I tried to get her off but couldn't. You're on your own with the phone, Gyuri. I'm late for class."

Tata glances at his watch and goes back to reading a thick hardbound book in French. I pretend I don't notice him and continue to flip the pages of my comic books. The black clock on our Biedermeier chest is marking time. Tata looks at his watch again and goes into the bathroom. I hear him running the water. He emerges clean-shaven, looks at his wristwatch again, and goes out into the foyer.

Tata's loud knock is followed by Aunt Puica's shrill voice. "Can't you see I'm on the phone? You'll just have to wait your turn."

"You've been on the goddamn phone for nearly an hour." My father's voice is raised but controlled. "I'm expecting an important call from the Studio."

Aunt Puica's curly head pops out her bedroom door; the phone receiver is still glued to her ear. "I bet you're expecting a very important call from the Studio, from one of your lady friends," she says, smirking.

"You bitch," my father mutters under his breath as he returns to our room. I want to duck under my covers, but I am too afraid to move.

Aunt Puica slams the phone down and appears in our doorway. "What did you call me?"

Tata looks up from his book and answers calmly, "I was wrong to call you a bitch. I should have called you a viper with a forked tongue. Get out of my room, viper!" he says in a soft voice, glaring at her.

Aunt Puica remains standing in our doorway, red-faced and speechless.

"You heard me," Tata says in a controlled voice, then shouts, "Get out!"

"Max is going to kill you," Aunt Puica hisses.

Tata gets up and confronts her at the door. "Oh yeah? Let him try. Get out, viper, before I throw you out. It's a wonder no one has murdered you yet."

Aunt Puica's bedroom door is slammed shut so hard the walls quiver. As I scurry toward the kitchen pantry, I notice Grandpa's face peering from behind the lace curtain of the French door to his bedroom.

It's nighttime. I'm tucked in bed behind our bookshelf room divider. Tata has gone off to the Studio and won't be back for the night. I hear loud voices from the foyer. "If that Hungarian son of a bitch ever dares to threaten my wife again," Uncle Max shouts, "I swear to you, Stefi, I'll take a knife to his throat!"

"Puica had better stop monopolizing this phone," Mama shouts back. "We pay for half of it and we hardly ever use it." Her tone turns to indignation. "Gyuri would never threaten anyone unless he was provoked."

"You're as blind as a bat!" Uncle Max shouts back. "One day you'll wake up and see that your sister is right."

"My sister had better stay out of my life!" Mama slams the door behind her as she enters our bedroom. I hold my breath and hope that Mama doesn't notice I'm still awake.

ABOUT BUTTERFLIES AND FLOWERS

I'M SITTING ON A BENCH swinging my legs. It must be lunchtime because my stomach is making grumbling sounds, but I'm not hungry. I think about going back home, but I don't want to see any of them. Dragonflies are making wide pirouettes in the hot summer air, displaying iridescent wings. Couples stroll hand in hand, too absorbed with each other to notice a six-and-a-half-year-old girl by herself. A dog lifts his leg and pees on his worn leather leash while his mistress tugs and grumbles. Students from the local middle school hurry by on their way home for lunch recess. Their gait is full of purpose, their black-and-white checkered uniforms are in stark contrast with the red silk scarves tied in square knots around their necks. I know this means they're Pioneers— part of the Communist Youth Organization. They march past me, shoulders pulled back in self-importance. Next year I will be in first grade and walk through the park with a backpack filled with heavy books, just like them. Eventually, I will become a proud Pioneer and wear the red kerchief around my neck. I wonder what school will be like. It's probably a lot better than staying home and listening to the grownups fight. I wish I could stop them from being so mean to each other. The park is so peaceful.

A bee just landed on a marigold. I'm not afraid of bees. Bees make honey, and I love honey. I lie down on the bench, my eyelids heavy. A white butterfly flutters by as I fall asleep in the hot afternoon sun. Hushed voices full of dread pull me out of my sleep.

"How did she get here by herself?" Mama's voice is echoed by Grandpa's "Thank God she's all right," and then Mama says, "This better not happen again," to which Grandpa answers, "Then all of you will have to stop fighting." Mama is now shaking my shoulders. The whole world is swirling as I sit up. The lines from the slats of the park bench are still pressed into my cheek.

"We were so worried about you," Mama says, continuing to shake me as if I hadn't woken up. I rub my eyes. She looks relieved, but her lips are pursed in anger.

"I wanted to go to the park," I try to explain. "I'm all right."

"You can't just take off by yourself," she scolds, grabbing my hand. I can feel the full force of her anger as she starts walking me home, her grip hurting my arm. Grandpa's feet are shuffling behind. When we get back, Grandma Iulia and Sabina are both waiting by the door with worried faces. Mama pushes me into the bathroom and says, "Go wash your face and hands. It's past three o'clock. You must be starving."

The water feels cool on my cheeks. I dry my hands and then go into the dining room. The table hasn't been set. That's my job. I set the table and go back to our room, where I find Mama waiting. She's sitting so straight on the edge of her bed, it looks as if she just swallowed a stick. Her posture is exactly the way she said mine ought to be in order to *walk properly*, except Mama is sitting.

"I never, ever want this to happen again," she starts. "Do you understand?" she asks, holding my chin and making me look into her eyes. I nod, deciding not to cry. "I thought I made it clear that you are not to go to the park without an adult. I don't want to have to worry about your safety. Do you understand?" I nod again, but Mama doesn't see me. "Isn't it bad enough that even adults nowadays can't go for a walk in the park without being afraid to have a simple conversation overheard?" She is half talking to herself and keeps asking, "Do you understand me?" over and over. Then, as if seeing my face for the first time, she gives up. "Let's go and have lunch," she says, getting up.

Everyone is already seated at the dining room table except for Tata, who's still off filming somewhere. The room is completely silent. I can sense their eyes following me as I walk around to my chair, which is between Mama's and Grandpa's seats. Grandpa pulls my chair out and places two large phone books on it so that I can reach the table comfortably. The chair makes a scraping sound as Grandpa pushes it forward. "Sabina," Grandma calls from the head of the table, "please bring in the soup."

I love the smell of the vegetable soup as the steam rises from my bowl. Grandpa Yosef breaks off the end of the baguette and hands it to me. The crusty end is my favorite part. I dunk the crust into my soup and let it soak up the delicious broth. We all sip in silence, our spoons clicking against the porcelain bowls. Grandpa slurps his broth with great satisfaction. There is a sense of relief in the room as Sabina gathers the bowls and then comes back from the kitchen with a platter of steaming frankfurters and a cauliflower casserole dish.

"Where's my knife?" Uncle Max asks.

Aunt Puica tells him, "Take mine," then stops abruptly. "I don't have a knife either." She looks bewildered at the empty spot next to her plate. I pick up a frankfurter with two fingers and bite into it. They all stare at me.

"Eva, did you forget to set the knives?" Grandma Iulia demands.

I shrug and keep nibbling at my frankfurter.

"Sabina," Grandma Iulia says, "go get some knives please."

Sabina pulls out the sideboard drawer, searching for the knives. "Madam," she says, "the knives are all gone."

There's lots of commotion as everyone gets up from the table in search of the missing knives. I stay in my seat and keep nibbling.

Aunt Puica's puzzled voice drifts in from the kitchen. "They're not in here either."

"Where have all the knives gone?" Uncle Max's question hangs in the air.

"Eva, do you know?" Grandpa Yosef's voice is gentle. I nod, still playing with my food. "Show me," Grandpa says. I slide off the phone books and walk to the sideboard. I open the doors to the shelves where our table linens are stored. I take out a tablecloth heavy with the hidden silverware and place it on top of the sideboard. Grandpa unfolds it, revealing all of our knives tucked in its folds.

"What's this all about?" Uncle Max asks.

"I didn't want you to stick a knife into Tata's throat," I whisper, without looking up at him. Everyone watches me in silence as I set the knives in their proper places at the table. When each of them has a knife and I'm back in my seat, Uncle Max taps his fork on his glass to get everyone's attention and addresses the room as if he were making an announcement over a loudspeaker:

"From now on, no one is to speak about anything in front of the Child," he says, his cheeks flushed as his glance catches mine. "Except about butterflies and flowers."

THE HOUSE

WE LIVE ON A QUIET, tree-lined street, wedged between two of Bucharest's loveliest parks. Grandpa Yosef found the two-family house and rented the second-floor apartment shortly after the Communists nationalized all private property, including Grandpa's businesses and the several houses he owned before the war.

A Russian family with no children lives in the ground-floor apartment. I've been given strict orders by Aunt Puica never to converse with *the Russians*, as if that explains everything. They own a gray cat with yellow eyes that is always perched on their stoop, but the cat is off-limits too.

"Having the Russians downstairs is far from ideal," Grandma Iulia reminds us every chance she gets. "But it's a whole lot better than having to live with strangers *inside* our home. That would be like sleeping with the devil!"

No one dares contradict Grandma Iulia, even though I know that there are days when my parents desperately want to move out and secretly talk about looking for better quarters. Mama and Tata never act on this dream, primarily because they know that, as soon as we leave, the Communists will place strangers in the tiny bed-room the three of us share. This would put our entire family at great risk from informers and the Securitate, Romania's secret police.

"Look at what's happened to Fanny." Grandma Iulia's voice in-terrupts the slurping sounds around the dinner table. "Her son and daughter-in-law moved out, and now my poor sister has to share her stove and her toilet with a couple of hicks from Bucovina, with such heavy provincial accents, Fanny says she's not even sure that they're speaking Romanian. The wife fries everything, so Fanny's entire house now reeks of onions, garlic, and bacon fat!" Grandma wrig-gles her nose in disgust. "My sister's clothes smell so bad that, no matter how many times she does the wash, she can't get the cooking stench out. Fanny's frightened that these people will denounce her for making slurs against the Party. She says she bites her tongue three times before she opens her mouth in her own home."

My parents are well aware that neighbors, colleagues, even friends and family members—especially children—often *do* be-come informers, intentionally or unintentionally. They roll their eyes at Grandma's tirades, but it's clear they're in agreement with her, because they are so careful about every word that crosses their lips outside the house. At home, they let loose as if we're safe. We all know that moving out has grave consequences, which is why virtually all families in Bucharest stick together, tight quarters or not.

Still, Grandma Iulia never misses an opportunity to drive home her point.

"If *they* hold a grudge against any of you," she says, shaking her soup spoon at us without explaining who *they* are, "they can report you for saying something against the Party, and the Securitate is sure to pick you up in the middle of the night. Whether their accusation is true or not, you're *guilty*. And may I remind you, from the place where the Securitate takes you, trust me"—Grandma stops in midsentence to make sure that her message has sunk in—"you will never return. You will disappear from the face of this earth just as if you had never been born."

We live in fear of the Securitate knocking at our door, day or night, and I am so tired of it that sometimes I wish I had never been born. Of course, I don't let any of them know just how exhausted I feel, since I am the only one in the house who can make every one of them smile.

MY GRANDPARENTS share the largest bedroom. The other adults hardly ever enter this room, which is one of the reasons why I love it so much. It is my sanctuary and also the only place in the house where I feel that my voice is fully heard. It is a dark, quiet room that faces the back alley. Despite its location, this room is proof of lovelier times. Unlike the bedroom that I share with my parents, which contains makeshift furniture, my grandparents' room has a bedroom set made of beautiful blond fruitwood. There is a queen-size bed with a graceful curved headboard. A stack of books and a glass of fresh water are always on Grandma's night table. The full-length mirrors on her armoire gleam, reflecting little rainbows off the bevels. Inside, she stores her precious monogrammed linens, always ironed and folded. She tucks dried lavender in the drawers, and everything smells like spring.

Grandma has trouble sleeping. She often reads through the night, every novel she can get her hands on. After breakfast, I find her rubbing her red, teary eyes, which have swollen from straining to read by the light of the bedside lamp. Grandma is fluent enough in German and French to read books in these languages as well as in Romanian. She also speaks Yiddish, but only with Grandpa, when they're trying to keep a secret from me. Grandpa Yosef doesn't read anything except the papers, but he loves the movies and knows the names of all the stars: who played in what movie, what role, in what year.

The two of them seldom argue except about the past, and then it is mostly Grandma arguing *with* the past.

"I hope you're happy now, Yosef," she starts in on him. "If you had listened to me before these Communist snakes nationalized everything including the skins on our backs, you would still be wealthy." She sighs.

Grandpa replies, "And if my grandmother had wheels, Iulia, I too would be a bicycle." This comment doesn't make Grandma smile.

"Remember the day," she goes on, ignoring his remark, "right after the war when you came home with a briefcase full of money?" Grandpa Yosef sits on the edge of their bed, waiting for her words to spill out. Grandma hardly catches her breath. "Didn't I tell you, now's the time to get out? If you had listened, we would all be landowners in the land of milk and honey. Instead, thanks to Lazăr, your genius of a brother, you took all of our money and sank it in this country that's overrun by Communist parasites who have nationalized everything. *Nationalized!* It's highway robbery and now we're stuck *forever*. I hope you're happy, Yosef. It serves you right, and if you're miserable you have only yourself to blame." At this point Grandma's finger is shaking in the air, her face flushed. "Too bad that I was stupid enough to come along for this lousy ride! I should have left that day, just as I threatened." Grandma pulls out a handkerchief that's tucked under her cardigan sleeve and blows her nose gently. She takes stock of Grandpa as he waits for her tirade to subside. "I'm sure you would have followed me, Yosef. Perhaps on a bicycle."

Grandpa never argues with Grandma when she gets going like this. Instead, he lets her unwind until she falls into a hard silence. On one such occasion, I saw him sitting on the edge of their bed, stroking her head. "You're right, Iulia," he said, trying to calm her and tucking in a stray strand of her silver hair. "You're *always* right, but what can I do *now*? I'm grateful that you stayed. There's no use crying over the past."

Grandma Iulia always has the last word. "What do you expect me to cry about, Yosef, the *future*?"

UNCLE NATAN has a presence no one can ignore. He is tall and as thin as a rail. He wears his belt tightened to its last hole so that his pants pucker in the front, making him look even thinner. His belt buckle digs into his ribs every time he coughs, his body convulsing uncontrollably. Despite this, he lights a new unfiltered cigarette before he finishes his last, which is why his fingernails have yellowed. His thick glasses magnify his blue eyes so that they bulge like the eyes of a fish out of water, gasping for breath.

We all know that Grandma Iulia favors him—Uncle Natan is her firstborn and only son—but since he is also the only bachelor in our midst, he has been relegated to sleeping on a cot in the dining room. Even Sabina has her own tiny room on the attic floor above the pantry, yet Uncle Natan's presence is a fixture in the dining room. After meals he hides behind his paper, smoke billowing from his cigarette toward the cracks in the ceiling. Everyone forgets that he is here because he rarely engages in conversation.

UNCLE MAX is the first to leave for work in the morning and the first to get home for lunch. Every day except Sunday, I hear his familiar I'm-home whistle announcing his impending arrival from as far as two blocks away. Aunt Puica bounds out of bed in a panic the moment she hears him and rushes to her dressing table, where she pinches her cheeks until they blush appropriately in the mirror. She dashes a touch of red lipstick across her puckered lips and runs a sharp comb through her tangled curls. She accomplishes all of this in a flash while barking orders at me.

"Max is coming! Evişoară, get off your butt and grab his slippers." She marches into the dining room, the belt of her fuchsia silk robe flying past me as I place his slippers by the door.

"Sabina, Sabina!" Aunt Puica's voice rings through the house like an alarm. "Master Max will be here any minute. Have you set the table?"

After lunch, Aunt Puica and Uncle Max retire to their bedroom, a small room that Grandma Iulia refers to as the Bat Cave. All of their windows have black curtains so that Aunt Puica can sleep in for as long as she likes. While Uncle Max is at work, Aunt Puica smokes until the room is in a fog, reads thick romance novels with complicated titles, and talks incessantly on our new telephone. The room is so crowded with large pieces of furniture that even I have trouble moving about. Their ornately hand-carved bedroom set is dark-stained walnut and was imported from Italy—a wedding present from my grandparents before the Communist takeover.

"I'm a lot smarter than your mother," Aunt Puica loves to remind me. "I made sure that *I* got a dowry. Your mother was happy to get her hands on that stubborn Hungarian mule, and conveniently forgot about *material things,* as she likes to call the *finer things* in life. Pretty stupid, if you ask me," she mutters before striking a match to light her cigarette.

Aunt Puica's wedding portrait hangs opposite her bed. The white of her veil frames a radiant face. Looking at that photograph, you would never suspect the depth of rage waiting to surface from the smiling bride.

My aunt's favorite scent, Chanel No. 5, lingers in the stuffy room. "Too expensive for little girls," she says, offering me a whiff of the bottle cap.

MY PARENTS AND I occupy the second largest bedroom because there are three of us. Our room has private access to the bathroom that all eight of us share, a door to the only terrace, and natural light that streams in every afternoon. Opposite my parents' bed is a new armoire, its corners adorned with hand-carved tulips.

"Not the best quality," Mama says, "but the best we could afford after saving from two salaries for four years." Next to the armoire is the Biedermeier chest of drawers. It is quite beautiful, and, Mama says, it is museum-quality. A small oil painting is perched on top of the chest, leaning against the wall. It is a portrait of a woman with flaming red hair who looks the way I imagine courage might look, if it had a human face. The painting is a reproduction of a famous Degas portrait that my cousin Mimi has painted. Mimi is an artist well known enough to be allowed to travel abroad. Tata, however, loves to remind Mama that it certainly doesn't hurt Mimi to be married to the director of the National Museum. "We're artists too, Stefica, but we're hardly allowed to travel past the Cişmigiu Gardens in Bucharest," he says, smirking. Sharing center stage on top of the Biedermeier chest are an ebony mantel clock with brass fittings and a hand-painted porcelain vase. The roses and lilac blossoms depicted on the tall vase look so real, I can almost smell them.

My narrow bed is separated from my parents' bed by a book-case that serves as our room divider. The back of the bookcase faces my bed. The shelves face my parents' side of the room and are packed with art books and a thick, leather-bound volume of the complete works of William Shakespeare. Mama has sewn a curtain out of a sheet and hung it at the foot of my bed to fill the gap between the bookcase and the wall. "Now you have your own little room," she says, drawing the curtain after tucking me in. The light from the bedroom filters through the yellow material with its blue cornflower pattern. Wedged against the bookcase is my night table, a heavy iron safe decorated with Roman soldiers in full armor—helmets, shields, and spears. The lid of the safe is so heavy, I have to ask for help each time I want to lift it open. The underside of the lid houses the safe mechanism, lots of wheels and gears, all in need of oil. Stored inside this safe is my most important treasure, a collection of dog-eared comic books that Tata's artist friends have smuggled in from France.

On warm summer evenings Tata lays out a thick green army-issue blanket on the cold floor of the terrace and fluffs my pillow. He covers me with a soft cotton blanket and surveys the night sky before returning to our room.

"Look at these stars," he whispers, gazing up at the moonless expanse. "These very same stars shine over other countries," he says, turning to me and pointing to a cluster of bright stars directly above my head. "Far away from here," he whispers. I don't know if he's referring to the stars above or to other countries. Both feel equally remote to me.

"Is it different in other countries?" I ask.

"Very," he answers before returning to our bedroom. "In other countries the stars do not rise in a red sky." I want to ask him what he means by "a red sky," since all I can see above is the black night shimmering with countless stars, but his voice stops me. "Good night. Go to sleep now."

"I want to say good night to Mama," I tell his shadow standing against the yellow light of the bedroom.

My mother's silhouette appears in the doorway. She sits down next to me on the blanket and tucks her legs in.

"Tell me about when I was born," I ask just before drifting off.

"You were the most wanted child in the world," she whispers, stroking my head. "The doctor said I could no longer get pregnant. I had lost too many babies during the war. He said that I had a *hysterical* pregnancy, that I wanted a baby so much, I was imagining being pregnant. But I knew that he was wrong, so here *you* are."

"Did it hurt?" I ask.

"Did what hurt?"

"When I came out," I answer impatiently.

"Sure it hurt."

"How bad?"

"Bad enough for me to pass out until the pain woke me up again." She laughs, then adds quickly, "You are worth it. I named you Eva because you are my one and only girl, after Eve, the very first woman in the world. But you were given another name as well by our neighbors, your godparents."

"Mama, who are they?"

"They were a very religious old couple from Cluj, your father's hometown. They took us in when you were a tiny infant, when no other Hungarians would lease a room to a young Romanian woman from Bucharest with a newborn. They were childless, so they asked me to allow them to give you a name. So I did."

"How come?"

"They were kind, good people, and it was a *mitzvah*."

"What's a *mitzvah*?" I ask.

"Shhh, go to sleep," she whispers. "It's a good deed, just like what they did for us."

"What name did they give me?"

"I don't know. I let them take you to their temple, but I didn't go to the naming ceremony. They were so happy and very grateful when they returned with you."

"Can't we call them up on the telephone and ask them my name?"

"I don't think so," Mama answers. "Those people are long gone. They were very old."

"You *really* don't remember the name that they gave me?"

"No, I don't. I'm sorry. It didn't seem to matter at the time. It was more important to just let them give you a name, to do the good deed."

I drift off to sleep hoping that someday I will find my lost name.

THE ORPHANAGE

BEFORE I ENTER FIRST GRADE, I spend most afternoons jumping rope and playing hopscotch by myself in our large front yard. First, I jump rope while counting to one hundred. Then I do it again to two hundred, this time twirling the rope horizontally beneath my feet. When I am finally exhausted, I draw a hopscotch grid with white chalk on the yard's gray pavement, throw a pebble in one of the squares, and hop one-legged around the grid, alternating between winning and losing since there is no one to play with.

Next door, however, there are lots of other children. Our yard abuts a state-run orphanage, whose courtyard is at the top of a six-foot wall that separates our property from theirs. The wrought-iron fence that keeps the orphanage children from falling into our yard is topped with black arrowheads that slice the air between our two worlds. The liberated squeals of the children next door, when they are let out from what I imagine to be stone-cold corridors, sound like a flock of birds taking off. The boys and girls are about my age, and they wear gray checkered uniforms. The boys' hair is cut so short, you can see their scalps. My mother claims it's for protection against head lice, but all the girls have shoulder-length hair just like mine, except theirs is pulled back with white headbands, while mine is kept off my forehead with a bobby pin.

The day is overcast. The orphan kids next door are out in the yard. Their shrill voices are jarring, but I ignore them and go about my usual routine—jumping rope and playing hopscotch. When I tire, I lean against the wall and gaze up across the yard to watch the other children. They're standing in a circle, clapping and singing a familiar Romanian nursery rhyme, while a boy runs around the outer perimeter of the circle waving a white handkerchief: *"Mi'am pierdut o batistuţa, mă bate mămica, cine are să mio deie, îi sărut guriţa.*—I've lost my little hankie, Mama's going to beat me, whoever finds it and returns it, I'll reward with a kiss on the mouth." The boy drops the hankie behind one of the girls' backs. She swishes around to pick it up, her braids flying above her head, but a breeze breaks the heavy stillness of the air and floats the hankie down into our yard. All of their eyes are suddenly upon me. "Pick it up! Pick it up!" they shout in unison, clutching their hands into fists around the black bars of the fence.

I press my back against the yard wall and feel its hardness as I glance at the white patch of cotton that has just landed at my feet. I don't know what to do. "Pick it up, and bring it back!" the girl with the braids screeches. I step forward into the hopscotch grid on my right foot, my left leg dangling in the air. I bend down and retrieve the white handkerchief just as if I were picking up a hopscotch pebble. I break into a run out of our yard and stop abruptly by the orphanage gate. I wait for the boy to come and retrieve his handkerchief, but instead he pulls me into their yard, right into the middle of their circle. "She's *it*! She's *it*!" he cries.

"You've got to kiss *her!*" All the orphan kids are singing at the top of their lungs and twirling around me so fast that I cannot see straight. My ears are pounding as the boy plants a big, wet kiss on my cheek before I grab my jump rope and run breathlessly home.

AFTER THE HANDKERCHIEF INCIDENT, I try to ignore the kids next door, but the girl with the braids does not ignore me. One day, after the others have gone inside, she stays behind and places her face between the fence bars.

"What's your name? Mine is Eugenia," she volunteers.

"Eva," I answer, not wanting to continue the conversation.

"That's pretty," she says without taking her eyes off my jump rope.

"Uh-huh," I mumble.

"Can I test your jump rope?"

I really don't feel like sharing, but I go to the wall and throw my rope up through the fence bars. Eugenia catches it and starts to jump as if she's been doing it her whole life.

"Can you keep count for me?" she yells breathlessly.

I count to one hundred and Eugenia isn't even breaking a sweat. At one fifty she stops abruptly and throws back my rope.

"Thank you very much," she says, running into the orphanage building.

I wonder how come no one seems to have missed her all this time. I bet if she were living at home with her family someone would have noticed that she was gone, the way my mother and Grandpa Yosef did when I went off by myself to the park.

"Grandpa," I ask at breakfast the next day, "why are the children next door orphans?"

"Because their parents are either dead or not able to care for them," Grandpa answers, looking at me.

"Right. But why?"

"Why?" Grandpa considers my question while fogging his reading glasses and wiping them with the corner of his shirt. "Sometimes parents die and there are no other family members who can take the child in," he says, placing his glasses, which are still somewhat greasy, back on the tip of his nose. He scrutinizes me above their frames. "Other times the parents are alive and want to care for their child very much, but they can't."

"Why *can't* they?"

Grandpa looks tired. "I don't know. Circumstances dictate the situation."

"What circumstances? What does *circumstances* mean?"

"It's just another way of saying *life*, what happens in life, Eva. Suppose both parents are ill or . . ." Grandpa sighs.

"Or?"

"Or in jail."

"Why would they ever go to jail, unless they were really bad people?" I ask, swinging my legs under the table.

"Not everyone who goes to jail is a bad person." Grandpa looks straight at me, and my legs stop swinging automatically.

"Did you ever know anyone who went to jail who wasn't a bad person?"

"Of course." Grandpa smiles.

"Who?"

"I've been in jail, Eva, and so have many other innocent people."

"But *why*?"

"Because people who are in power don't always do the right thing."

"Oh" is all that I say because now my mind is racing back to Eugenia, whose braids fly in the air while she skips across the orphanage yard and who can jump rope to over one hundred and fifty counts. I wish I knew why *she* lives in the orphanage, but I'm afraid to ask. Are both her parents dead? Or are they rotting in some Communist jail, living only for the moment they can come home to reclaim their daughter? What will happen to Eugenia if the Party decides that her parents are guilty?

ALL EYES, ALL EARS, NO TONGUE—SEPTEMBER 1958

TODAY IS MY FIRST DAY OF SCHOOL, and I'm as excited as the day when I went to the market with Grandpa Yosef for the first time. It's 6:00 a.m. and I'm already up. My new school uniform is laid out on the chair next to my bed. The uniform is a black-and-white checkered cotton smock that is worn over my regular clothes like a coat, but it buttons at the back. Mama carefully starched and ironed its round white collar until it was so stiff that it leaves red marks against my neck. There's also a pinafore that wraps around my waist and ties at the back with a bow. It has wavy shoulders that remind me of butterfly wings. On regular school days we are to wear a black pinafore, but on special days and holidays, we get to wear a white one. Since the first day of school is a special occasion, Mama's been notified in advance that I'm to wear the white one. The notice also specified a white headband to keep my hair off my face, white knee-high socks, and polished black shoes. Finally, my teeth must be brushed thoroughly, and my nails must be cut and spotlessly clean. Each student's appearance will be inspected by the teacher. I'm nervous, but I'm ready. Eventually I will become a Pioneer and get to wear a red silk scarf. But I won't be eligible for that until second grade.

I'm not hungry at breakfast, but Mama insists that I take at least a few bites of bread with butter as I gulp down my hot chocolate. After I've brushed my teeth and smiled at myself in the bathroom mirror to make sure they're white, Mama parts my hair precisely in the middle and braids it into two tight pigtails. She folds each pigtail in half and secures the ends with bobby pins that stick into my scalp. Then she ties two small white bows around the bunches and hands me the white headband. I slide it over my forehead and tuck in a few stray hairs. Everything feels tightly pulled back. I barely recognize myself in the armoire mirror. I have been transformed into a student.

I'm itching to get going, but Mama pulls me down to sit on the edge of the bed next to her. "I have something important to tell you before you take off," she says in a serious voice I do not like. "Never, ever, repeat anything you hear in this house to anyone, especially any talk about before or after the war or about the Party. None of our conversations are to be discussed outside this house, not even with the other kids in school," she adds, looking at me intently as if I've already done something wrong.

"But, Mama, I don't know any of the kids yet," I argue. "I have no idea what we're going to talk about."

"Say nothing," she continues. "There are children who have gotten their parents in trouble just because they repeated things that they shouldn't have heard at home. Surely those kids didn't mean to cause any harm to their parents, but they did. What innocently came out of their mouths became a weapon the Securitate used as evidence against the parents. These kids now live in orphanages like the one next door because their parents are in jail and there's no one who can care for them. We don't want to have that kind of thing happen to us, do we?"

Mama's left eyebrow arches as I shake my head vigorously. It occurs to me that Eugenia, the girl with the flying braids, might be one of these children. Mama surveys my face and nods in approval. "Good. If anyone wants to know anything about what we discuss at home, you come and tell me first. Just play dumb and tell them you know nothing. Understood?" I nod again, and she gives me a big hug and kiss. "You'd better run now. Your tata's going to take you this morning."

MY FATHER IS WAITING for me in the foyer and offers me his warm hand as we walk out into the street. He seems happy, whistling a familiar tune and taking great strides past the old houses down our block. I have a hard time keeping up with him because his legs are very long and he walks quickly.

The school is a big red-brick building. In the lobby there is a giant framed print of a historic monument. "Stand right here next to this picture," Tata tells me. "I'm going to take a photo of you in front of Trajan's column." I lean against the wall and look up. I'm dwarfed as my eyes follow the length of the picture all the way to the vaulted ceiling.

"Look back at me and smile," Tata says as his camera starts to click.

BEFORE I KNOW IT I'm standing in line in front of the classroom door along with many other boys and girls. The girls are all wearing the exact same uniform as I am, and the boys are wearing gray trousers, white shirts, and ties. Tata whispers in my ear, "Just listen to the teacher, do as you're told, and you'll be all right." He offers me his cheek, which I barely have time to brush with a kiss before he waves goodbye and I enter the classroom.

"Attention, everyone. Children, pay attention!" Comrade Popescu commands. Our teacher is a trim woman with steel blue eyes and a razor-sharp voice. "I want every one of you to line up according to your height, the shortest in the front and the tallest in the back." We scramble as we look at each other to determine who is taller than whom, and we start to giggle. Comrade Popescu strikes a wooden ruler against her desk with a thud. Our sudden silence is interrupted by a fly buzzing right above my head and by someone whispering in the back of the room. "I didn't say you could talk while you do this. Silence!" Comrade Popescu says, striking her ruler like a thunderbolt.

Once we're seated according to height—the shortest in the front, the tallest in the back—Comrade Popescu reads our names off attendance cards in alphabetical order. Even though I'm sitting in the front row because I'm short, I am the last one on the roll call. "Zimmermann, Eva!" My name reverberates in the room. I raise my hand quickly and answer "Present!"

Comrade Popescu distributes pencils and notebooks. She outlines all the different subjects that we will be studying throughout the year: the Romanian alphabet, basic grammar, calligraphy, arithmetic, history, and geography. Each subject will have its own homework assignment to be completed in its own separate notebook and handed in the next day. We will be graded on neatness and penmanship as well as content. Attendance and behavior will count equally. Whoever does not advance according to the curriculum will be left back to repeat the grade until he or she gets it right.

"Those of you who understand what I've just said, raise your hands!" She surveys our stiff, outstretched arms. "Good," she mutters. She speaks slowly to no one in particular, as if all of us were one person. "Stack your notebooks on your desks, and place your pencils and erasers in your pencil holders. Now I want you to stand with your shoulders back and your faces forward. If you slouch, you will be detained in this room instead of going to recess with the rest of the class. You will exit the room single file in the order that you've entered it. Does everyone understand this?"

We listen in silence, still seated, until Comrade Popescu raises her voice and repeats, "Are all forty of you deaf and dumb? Do you not understand? Answer me, 'Yes, Comrade Popescu, we understand,' and stand up immediately!"

We shout, "Yes, Comrade Popescu, we understand!" Then we stand and march toward the door. Comrade Popescu is waiting as we walk past her single file into the yard. I'm close to the door when I notice a notebook on one of the desks nearby, its white pages turning with the breeze from the yard. I place my hand on the page to caress its smooth whiteness and quickly close the notebook when I feel the sting of Comrade Popescu's ruler on my knuckles. "I didn't tell you to touch anything," she says in a calm voice. I nod and step into the blinding light of the courtyard, where my eyes well up and my head swims backward.

WHAT THE COMMUNIST PARTY MEANS TO ME

COMRADE POPESCU is droning on. "Religion and superstition are one and the same thing." This makes me uncomfortable because it reminds me of Tata, who sneers whenever the subject of religion comes up. "The Communist Party"—Comrade Popescu's voice sounds as if she's speaking from the bottom of a wooden barrel—"is our savior because it defines our economic existence and our ideological reality. All comrades can participate in the decision-making process because each and every one of us is a Romanian and a member of the Proletariat. We are all workers, united and equal in the eyes of the Party. Your homework for tomorrow is to write a short composition entitled 'What the Communist Party Means to Me.'"

I've been waiting for the recess bell, but instead the church bells down the street start to peal, making the windows and wooden desks vibrate.

"Please remember that you will be graded on your penmanship as much as on the content of your composition," Comrade Popescu continues as she crosses herself automatically at the ringing of the church bells. If religion is just superstition, I wonder, why does the Party allow the church bells to ring? I decide at that moment that when it comes to religion and the Communist Party, nothing makes sense.

At recess everyone is jumping around in the yard. A bunch of girls are playing hopscotch on the chalk squares drawn on the gray asphalt. Another group of kids are jumping rope and singing a tune I know, but I don't hum along. Instead I stand alone, leaning against the cool bricks of the building, and watch everyone else play. There are lots of questions in my head, questions I know I cannot ask because the answers may lead to trouble for me and my parents, the way Mama warned me on my first day of school. But I really do want to know why Comrade Popescu crosses herself when the church bells ring. What does the Party have against religion, and why does Tata believe in math and science instead of God?

School turns out to be a lot more demanding than I expected. When Mama comes home from work, she spends at least two hours every night going over homework assignments with me. I dread doing this, not because the homework is so difficult, but there's so much of it, I have no time left for any reading—and that's the best part about going to bed at night.

"Don't complain, Eva. You started first grade after you turned seven, so you got to play for an extra year. When I was growing up, first grade started when we were six." I roll my eyes, but Mama ignores me as she continues to check each answer in my math assignment.

Everyone in the class is terrified of Comrade Popescu, yet despite my fear of her, I find her lectures interesting. I love listening to her stories about Romania's past, about how we were once ruled by the greatest civilizations on earth—the Greeks, the Romans, and the Ottomans. Throughout our history, Comrade Popescu tells us, Romanians have survived invasions by many tyrants, including the Mongols, the Tatars, and the Huns—all savage tribes that pillaged the land, raped our women, and oppressed our people. She goes on to explain that even though our conquerors brought with them a lot of suffering, they also enriched our culture with many contributions.

"Do any of you know where black Kalamata olives, stuffed grape leaves, and feta cheese come from?"

Claudia, a girl with a huge white ribbon in her hair, raises her hand.

"Yes?" Comrade Popescu motions to Claudia to speak.

"All of these products come from our Cooperative Farmers' Market," Claudia replies.

The look on Comrade Popescu's face is of utter disgust as she corrects Claudia. "Yes, of course. However, I didn't ask you *how* we purchase these products in modern times. I asked you *where* they originated from, culturally. You must listen carefully before you answer a question. Does anyone know from which country we inherited these foods?" We are silent. "Very well," she continues. "Kalamata olives, feta cheese, and stuffed grape leaves all came from our Greek ancestors. They also brought with them baklava, our sweet pastry. But more important, they brought with them the way we reason, the way we think; philosophy, mathematics, and our love of theater all come from the Greeks. Anyone care to guess which food that we consider the most basic Romanian fare was brought to us by our Roman conquerors?"

There are no raised hands.

"What's the matter with you all? Didn't your parents teach you to take any chances? I said you may guess, so take a guess." She is still met with silence. "Very well, then," Comrade Popescu continues. "Our *mămăligă* came from the Romans. In Italy they call it *polenta*. However, they do not serve it as we do, with feta cheese. They fry it or bake it. You see, we combined two culinary traditions, the Greek feta cheese and the Roman polenta, to make our very own Romanian *mămăligă cu brânză*—polenta with cheese. The point I'm trying to make you understand is that our conquerors enriched us in many ways. We became more inventive, more versatile, because of them. Perhaps in spite of them," she adds.

When she speaks about our ancestors, Comrade Popescu's blue eyes turn greenish. Her face relaxes and becomes almost kind, and her voice loses its edge. It is easy to see how much she loves many of the places that she is describing, how proud she is of the Romanian people.

"To the northwest is Transylvania, where my father comes from," she says, pointing with her ruler to that area of the map. "This part of the country was once under the Austro-Hungarian empire, which is why most of the population there speaks Hungarian and German in addition to Romanian." Her voice trails off as if she's lost her train of thought, and then she asks, "Do any of you know what we received from the Soviet Union, our Communist ally?"

My hand goes up as if it has a mind of its own.

"Yes?" Comrade Popescu motions to me.

"The color red?"

Everyone in the class starts to snicker, but Comrade Popescu isn't smiling. Instead she ignores my answer entirely and continues, "I'd like you all to think deeply about what makes each of you Romanian. Tonight's homework assignment is to answer the following question: What constitutes a true Romanian and how is our country influenced by our relationship to the USSR? I'm well aware that we have not discussed the Soviet Union yet, but I'd like to get your thoughts just the same. You are to write no more or less than one page. Any questions?" Comrade Popescu scans our blank faces, and since no hands are raised, she tells us to go home, think about this some more, and come back with our thoughts on the subject.

I'M SO EXCITED about this assignment that I run home and tell Tata all about it, hoping to impress him with my new knowledge of history. But instead of giving me praise and help with my homework, Tata gets upset.

"What kind of a loaded question is Comrade Popescu asking you about the USSR?" he booms into the thick air of our bedroom. "You tell her you have no idea what *Mother Russia* has to do with any of this. And don't call it *Mother Russia*," Tata says, waving his finger at me. "It's absolutely unfair of her to ask you anything about Russia without first teaching you the proper, *approved CURRICULUM*." Tata utters this word as if it were the most important thing in the universe, as if it weighed a ton. "You ask Comrade Popescu to define *her* relationship with the Soviet

Union and watch her squirm when she gets into trouble with the almighty Party!"

Tata stops for a moment and looks at Mama, who's sitting in bed propped against her pillows, knitting a sweater. "Is Eva's teacher crazy to ask a bunch of first graders such a politically charged question, Stefi?" Mama doesn't say anything, but her ball of yarn rolls off the bed, its red string of wool looking much like one of the borderlines drawn on Comrade Popescu's map of Romania. "Am I right, Stefi, or not?"

Mama looks up and sighs. "You're right, Gyuri, but I think you're overreacting. I don't believe that Comrade Popescu is trying to trap the kids into anything. I think she just wants to see what they come up with, that's all."

But Tata goes on as if he never even heard her. "Well, we shouldn't allow Eva to elaborate on such subjects. They're way over her head. It's too risky, Stefi. Do you have any idea what the consequences will be if Eva's innocent answer gets her in trouble?"

"It's not *over* my head," I blurt out, "and I don't think it's risky because—" Tata's cold stare stops me in midsentence.

My mother sighs. "Eva's not going to say the wrong thing, Gyuri. She's smarter than that."

Tata glares at my mother. I wish I had never told them about this assignment. I don't want to contradict Tata, but now I'm really scared because I can't go back to school and face Comrade Popescu with a bunch of questions instead of answers. What does he mean that all of this is "over my head"? I know very well that Romanians have no choice but to follow whatever the USSR dictates, even if those policies change from one day to the next. Does Tata think I'm stupid or something? I believe the Romanian history Comrade Popescu is teaching us shows that we've survived many tyrants. I think that maybe the USSR is just another tyrant like the rest of them, but I'm not going to tell anyone, because I'm afraid this is a dangerous thought, the kind that Mama warned me would get us all into trouble if I spoke it out loud. But I don't believe for a second that Comrade Popescu would punish me for thinking it.

Tata is so beside himself, he's pacing up and down on the terrace. I excuse myself, saying that I'm going to get a slice of bread and jam from the kitchen, but instead I run to my grandparents' bedroom. Grandpa Yosef is snoring in bed, and Grandma Iulia's side is empty. She must be in the kitchen. I start to tiptoe backward toward the door, but Grandpa Yosef's voice stops me.

"Eva, is that you?" he asks with his eyes half open.

"Yes."

"What's the matter?" How does Grandpa always know when something is wrong?

"Nothing," I lie, and then immediately blurt out my predicament about the school assignment. "Tata says Comrade Popescu's wrong to be asking us loaded questions about our relationship with the Soviet Union. He says it's over my head, but it's *not*, and I don't know what to do. I've got to have an answer by tomorrow, Grandpa, or I'll get in trouble for sure." My words tumble out as Grandpa sits up, his eyes wide open now.

"That's easy." Grandpa chuckles. "Tell your teacher a Romanian is a person who's born in this country. That covers just about all of us. You can't go wrong with that answer. As far as the Soviet Union is concerned, tell her you're looking forward to learning all about it when you have the honor of becoming a Pioneer. *She's* the teacher." Grandpa winks at me. "You let *her* do the hard work and point the way, and that's that."

I run back into our room and tell my parents what Grandpa Yosef just advised, and they both look at me with blank faces. "That's a good answer," Tata finally concedes, and Mama's shoulders relax as she continues to knit.

THE BOY UPSTAIRS

ON HIS FIRST DAY OF SCHOOL, Andrei doesn't say much. I don't blame him, since it's already November and he's missed the beginning of classes and doesn't know anyone. Comrade Popescu assigns him a seat in the row next to mine, directly to my right. When he finally opens his mouth to answer one of her questions, everyone snickers because of his provincial accent. Andrei brushes his hair off his forehead with the rough knuckles of his hand, but he doesn't respond. Comrade Popescu warns us that the next student who laughs at Andrei will be detained after school.

"Our comrades from the provinces are more Romanian than any of you," she says with great passion in her voice. "Peasants are the true proletariat, the backbone of this country. They put food on your table and you'd better be thankful. I dare you to make fun of Andrei's accent again." She surveys all of us with her razor eyes, caressing her ruler. Suddenly, there is complete silence in the class. Still, Andrei is speechless for the rest of the week.

After school we walk home together, because Andrei's family has moved upstairs from us on the attic floor right next to Sabina's room! I don't know what his parents do for a living, but it's clear that they are poor since they can only afford to live in servants' quarters. They have two tiny bedrooms, one for his parents and the other for Andrei. They all share the bathroom in the hall with Sabina. Andrei is lucky because he has his own room, but I wouldn't want to live up on the third floor, where the ceiling is so low his father has to slouch to avoid hitting his head. The heat is stifling up there.

WHILE WE WALK HOME from school, we don't talk to each other, except to say goodbye. When we finally get home, Andrei bolts up the stairs two at a time, his heavy-laced ankle boots making thud noises. I am curious about what it's like to live in the country with cows that moo and chickens that cluck and lay eggs just like mine did, but it's difficult to ask Andrei about any of these things, since he clearly doesn't want to open his mouth. Then one evening after supper our phone rings and Aunt Puica answers it.

"It's Andrei's mother," she whispers. "She wants to know if it would be all right for him to do his homework with you." She turns before I've had a chance to answer and speaks loudly into the receiver. "Yes, of course, Mrs. Ionescu, tell Andrei to come down. Eva will be happy to help him with math."

I can't believe Aunt Puica just did that! I wish Mama were home because she would have asked me how I felt about it before saying yes. But it's no use arguing with Aunt Puica.

Andrei seems as nervous about us getting together as I am, and it is clear that this was not his idea either. He really is stuck in math since he's missed two months of school. Instead of just giving him the answers to the assignment, I teach him how to do the calculations. He works very hard on each problem, and finally we compare

answers. Andrei's smart. He gets nine out of ten right, without peek-
ing. After that, Andrei begins to talk to me in his funny provincial
accent, and I smile but I make sure not to laugh. I notice his eyes
are very blue. His hair is coarse and the color of wheat.

"Back home"—Andrei speaks slowly, struggling to pronounce
each word the way we do in Bucharest—"we used to go to church
every Sunday, but we haven't done that since we've arrived here.
I really miss it. Where do you go?"

"We don't," I confide.

"You don't go to church? What are you, a kike?"

"I don't know what a 'kike' is," I tell him, but I'm sure that it's a
bad word. I once saw Tata get red in the face after seeing a man spit
on the ground and call another man a "kike."

Andrei just stares at me as if *I'm* the one who moved to Bucharest
from the provinces, but he doesn't offer an explanation.

"I've never been to a church, but I once saw a baby boy baptized
in the monastery yard up in the country where my mother and I
spent the summer," I tell him, trying to prove that I'm not completely ignorant. "The priest wore a giant silver cross and a tall black
hat. He looked like a chimney sweep with a beard." I giggle, but Andrei isn't laughing, so I continue quickly. "He held the baby by his
feet and dunked him in well water. The baby started wailing and
turned really red. The priest couldn't chant the prayers because the
baby was so slippery, he almost wiggled out of his arms."

Andrei finally laughs, and I am relieved. "Yeah, I've been to a
few baptisms, they're all the same," he says, pausing. "Is it true that
they don't approve of religion in Bucharest? My parents told me
that I shouldn't talk about our Lord Jesus Christ in school. They
say the Party is much stricter about this in the capital. We never

had a problem with it back home." Andrei lowers his eyes and fidg-
ets with the pencil between his fingers. "Please don't tell anybody."

"Oh, don't worry, I won't say a word," I reassure him. "I know
how to keep a secret. Besides, I don't even know who Jesus Christ
is. My father doesn't believe in God, and Mama doesn't talk about
religion."

"What does your father believe in, then?"

"I don't know." I shrug. "Nothing, I suppose. I think he believes
in science and math. What's a kike?" I ask again.

"What do you guys do at Christmastime?"

"You mean, in winter?"

"Of course, that's when Christmas happens." Andrei looks confused.

"Well, Grandpa Yosef always gets a beautiful pine tree. I love
the way the house smells when he brings it in. Mama and I make
decorations for it. We put cotton balls on a string to make it look
like snow, and we wrap colorful paper chains around the tree. Last
year, my cousin Mimi gave me three beautiful glass balls, a red, a
blue, and a gold. We hung them on the branches. Grandpa gets
dressed up in his Santa Claus outfit and pretends that he's travel-
ing all the way from the North Pole. Then we clip candles onto
the branches, that's my favorite part, but we have to be very careful
and watch the flames so that the tree won't catch fire. That's it. We
blow out the candles and go to bed."

"You don't go to church or exchange presents?" Andrei asks.

"No. The Christmas tree is our present."

Andrei's face shows that he doesn't quite understand this. I can
tell he's worried that I might give him away by telling the kids in
school that his family is religious, but of course I won't, since I

promised. Andrei missed the class when Comrade Popescu taught us that all religion is just superstition for ignorant, uneducated people. I suspect Tata agrees with this view despite the fact that he hates the Party. I don't want to offend Andrei, and I remember Mama's warning not to tell other children what I overhear at home, so I don't share these thoughts with him.

THE CLOCK THAT STOPPED

"IF GOD IS ALL-POWERFUL," my father says, his eyes twinkling with delight, "could He create a mountain that is so big that even He could not move it?" I look at Tata, not knowing how to answer, but just from the twist of his smile I know that this is a trick question.

My father believes in scientific proof. "If you can't see it, hear it, touch it, or smell it, it's probably only your imagination," he tells me. "Thank God, the Party doesn't preach religion on top of their propaganda."

"What does *propaganda* mean?" I ask.

"Never mind. *Never* utter that word again."

Tata looks ridiculously serious as he says this, and it makes me nervous, so I start to giggle.

"You hear me, Eva?"

THE MOST CONSTANT sound in my life is made by the swinging pendulum of the mantel clock that my father keeps on top of the Biedermeier chest of drawers in our bedroom. Tick tock, tick tock.

I am so used to it that, for the most part, I don't notice it. Tata found the clock upon his return home from a Russian labor camp. It was one of a handful of other objects that once belonged to his parents. He was thirty-one years old at the time, having spent the previous eight years in various *lagers*, concentration camps: four years in Nazi work camps, and then four more years after the war as a prisoner of war in the Russian gulag. I've only been told the historical facts, not the personal details.

TATA IS HOME this Sunday, having just completed a film shoot on location. He is taking advantage of his rare free time by cleaning out the two drawers that Mama has allocated to him in the Biedermeier chest. Under a bunch of folded socks is a tin box filled with old papers and photographs. I am not allowed to touch any of my father's belongings, but I watch as he fishes out a dog-eared postcard and reads it in silence. I ask him what it says since I don't read or speak Hungarian. His face hardens before he answers, "It says *goodbye*."

"Who says goodbye?"

"My mother. Your *other* grandmother." He points to a faded signature beneath a few carefully scripted lines in black ink.

"Why?" I have a feeling I shouldn't be asking this, but I can't help it.

"My mother knew it was unlikely that we would ever see each other again." Tata's voice is barely audible.

I don't know what to say. Tata looks at me, as if suddenly remembering that I am here. "Someone must have found this postcard on the train station platform and placed it in our mailbox," he tries to explain. "See, it doesn't even have a stamp," he says, pointing to the spot where the stamp is clearly missing. "This postcard waited in our mailbox for four years, Eva, from April 1945, when my parents were deported to Auschwitz, until late in 1949, when I came home from Russia." Tata looks up at me. "A small miracle," he says, forcing a smile.

"How come you are so sure that they died in Auschwitz?" I'm pushing my luck. "Maybe they're still alive somewhere and you don't know it."

"Don't be ridiculous, Eva," Tata says, his smile fading. "I know. Believe me, I know." I notice that the muscles on his forearms are twitching.

"Have you searched for them?" I am relentless.

"Look," Tata answers, raising his voice slightly, "I'm one hundred percent sure." The tone of his voice lets me know that this conversation has ended. "Why don't you run along and play in the yard?" he says, turning back to his tin box. "They're dead. Believe me." His voice trails off as I skip out of the room. "Dead."

IN THE AFTERNOON I tell my mother about Tata's postcard and she gets upset. "Why in the world did he ever show you *that*?" she asks. "Promise me never, ever to ask your father about the war or about what happened to his parents in Auschwitz. It depresses him, and you must respect that."

"But why, Mama? Grandpa Yosef and Grandma Iulia talk about the war all the time," I point out.

"My parents weren't deported to a concentration camp in cattle cars like your father's parents. None of us were murdered, thank God," she adds, looking at me helplessly. "Promise me you won't bother Tata about any of this anymore. Promise?"

"Okay, I promise, only if you tell me about Tata and the war."

"I know almost nothing," my mother answers, "because he doesn't like to talk about it, but he did take me to see the house in Cluj, where he used to live before the war."

"What was it like, Mama, was it beautiful?"

"It was empty," she says, clearing her throat. "The walls had turned yellow beneath the torn blue wallpaper. Your father pointed to where the dining room table had stood. It was the only polished patch of oak flooring in the room. He showed me where the crystal chandelier had bounced rainbows off the ceiling. A giant hole with a tangle of disconnected electrical wires gaped at us, like a decaying tooth. It was getting dark, but we were too exhausted to move. We dropped to the floor and fell asleep in each other's arms. When we awoke, the house was pitch black. Tick tock, tick tock, tick tock. The sound of a clock beckoned through the empty house. Your father rose to his feet and searched for the clock through the thick darkness." Mama's voice trails off as she gazes across the room at the clock on our Biedermeier chest. "We never figured out who wound it."

THAT EVENING I ask my parents if I can sleep on the terrace. The wide-open space of the sky above feels so good in contrast to my narrow bed behind the bookcase. There is a slight breeze, and the sky is filled with stars. I fall asleep quickly and dream a dream so clear, it doesn't feel like a dream at all.

The night turns to day as my father's mother, Grandmother Hermina, visits me. I recognize her the moment she appears, even though we've never met. She is young, beautiful, and vibrantly alive. I am aware that she died before I was born, but her presence is quite real. Grandmother Hermina knows instantly who I am, just as I know

her. She takes my presence in and murmurs, "Your father is all right."
She repeats this to herself more definitively, "Your father is all right."
Her words penetrate the space between us until they light up my con-
sciousness so deeply that I wake up.

What does Grandma Hermina mean by "Your father is all right"? Tata is not *all right*. He's always worried about something or other. He's not nice to me, and none of that is *all right* by me. I try to think through my dream logically, but it doesn't make sense. Yet in my heart I know that what Grandma Hermina has just told me is as true and as real as the stars that hang in the night sky above me.

This dream stays with me until a few days later I ask Grandpa Yosef about it, and he thinks for a while before answering.

"Dreams always reveal a hidden truth. The problem is not with the dream but with the *interpretation*."

"What do you mean, the *interpretation*?"

"Just that—*what the dream means*."

"But, Grandpa, I don't understand what Tata's mother meant when she said 'Your father is all right,' because I don't think he is."

"Aha, now I see." Grandpa smiles. "Try looking at it from your Grandmother Hermina's point of view."

"How can I? It's *my* dream!"

"Of course it's your dream, but since your grandmother visited you and spoke to you, she obviously has her own mind, so why not consider what she's saying?"

"I don't understand what you're talking about, Grandpa."

"Try to see it through her eyes, if only for a moment. Before she died, did she think that her son was all right? If you were a mother, Eva, and now I know I'm asking you to really use your imagination because you are far too young even to think about being a mother, but let's just suppose you are much older and you have a son who is somewhere in a concentration camp where millions of people are dying." Grandpa stops abruptly and looks at me before continuing. "And you don't know if your son is still alive. What would your dying wish be?"

My words spill out. "I'd want him to live!"

"Precisely." Grandpa takes in a deep breath.

"Grandpa, I know what Grandma Hermina was trying to tell me. She saw me sleeping and she realized that Tata is alive, that he's *all right*!"

Grandpa Yosef nods. "Your grandma Hermina probably never rested until she visited you."

"But, Grandpa, why didn't she just visit Tata?"

Suddenly, the creases around Grandpa's eyes are deeper than I've ever noticed. "God is merciful and wise. He gave your grandmother Hermina a gift that would not tear her apart. She had suffered enough while she was alive."

"It was only a dream, Grandpa."

"Dreams are as real as life, Eva, because they contain seeds of the truth. Just like you can't see the seeds from a plant because they're buried in the ground, you can't always see the meaning of dreams right away. But just as surely as a plant grows, the truth of dreams eventually emerges. Most dreams are hidden in plain sight, waiting for us until we are ready to discover their meaning and heed their message."

While Grandpa tries to explain these things to me, I wonder— *how could a dead person come and visit her sleeping granddaugh-*

ter? I agonize over this, but I do not question Grandpa Yosef further, since he clearly believes in miracles. And even I know that miracles are events you do not question.

I PROMISED MY MOTHER not to bring up Tata's parents to him again, but I can look at our clock ticking away on top of the chest to my heart's content. Grandpa Emile's thin pencil markings keeping track of the dates on which he wound the clock can still be found etched on its back panel. How could *things* survive yet *people*, who are irreplaceable, perish?

The clock is the first thing my father looks at when he gets home from a film shoot. He goes through the ritual of winding it every thirteen days. He begins by opening the back panel and slipping his hand into the small space that houses the mechanism and the brass pendulum. It is only during these moments, when Tata is barely aware of my presence, that I feel him connect to a past that has included a family other than my mother and me. His fingers search for the metal key stored in the clock's base. He inserts the key in place and starts to wind, holding his breath and counting each turn of his wrist in his head. *One . . . two . . . three . . . four . . . five.* Exhale. He is careful not to overwind. When he is finished, Tata secures the clock's crown, making sure that none of the brass fittings on the ebony surface are loose. Finally, he shuts the door to the inner mechanism as if he has just left another realm; then he dusts the clock before returning it to its central place on top of our chest. For a moment, he listens to the back-and-forth movement of the pendulum while gazing at the three brass cherubs playing a lyre on the clock's front panel. He completes his ritual by checking to see that the clock's hands are synchronized with those of his Russian-issue wristwatch. Then he turns around and is back in our little room as if nothing out of the ordinary has happened. In the two weeks that follow, the clock resumes its ever-present background sound of our daily life.

TATA'S FRIENDS

MY FATHER INSPIRES GREAT LOVE and loyalty from a small but important group of friends who gather regularly in our bedroom. Most of them work closely with him at Romania's government-owned film studio, where Tata is the leading cinematographer. They call him Zimmy, short for Zimmermann, his last name. His friends are film and theater directors, actors, artists, writers, poets, and composers—all of them part of Bucharest's talented elite.

The one exception is Victor, a short man with thick, black-framed glasses, who survived all of the *lagers*, including the Russian POW labor camp. While all of these friends are close, none are as close to Tata as Victor. The two of them talk, laugh, smoke cigarettes, and drink *ţuică*, strong Romanian plum liquor, often until daybreak. As the evening wears on, their laughter grows louder, their stories more colorful. These get-togethers usually take place on an evening when my mother has rehearsals, though Mama regards Victor as family.

• • •

"HEY, VICTOR." Tata's voice booms from the other side of the bookcase. "Remember when we got that shipment of aspirin in the labor camp in Siberia and you decided to dispense it to the entire prisoner population? You tried so hard to convince us that you had discovered the magic cure-all for every disease known to man." Tata laughs. "Hey, guys, no breakfast? Why not pop one of Victor's Vitamins instead? It's guaranteed to bore an even bigger hole in your stomach than you've already got."

I crawl to the bottom of my bed and peek from under my covers. Victor is waving his shot glass at Tata. "Look who's talking about holes in his stomach. You had a hole in your *head*, Zimmy, carrying a volume of Shakespeare around as if it were the Bible. Here's to you, Mr. Hamlet"—Victor raises his glass—"may you make up your mind if you want *to be or not to be!*"

"Watch your mouth, Herr Doctor." Tata's words are slurred from the liquor. "You're mocking the greatest writer the world has ever known. You're not fit to lick Shakespeare's boots."

"Your performance is impressive tonight, Mr. Hamlet," Victor snaps. "Shakespeare has no need for boots, because he's dead. And he isn't God."

"He's dead to you, you idiot, because you don't read! As far as Shakespeare being God, he comes in a close second, if there is a God," Tata answers.

"Your Mr. Shakespeare nearly got us all killed," Victor continues. "Need I remind you that your best friend, Yoni, would still be alive today if he hadn't run back for *your* Shakespeare? It took us weeks to plan our escape from hell, and Yoni blows it by running back to retrieve a book!" Victor's rant now sounds like machine-gun fire. "He paid with his life, poor schmuck, for your immortal 'auteur'—he got it square in the head over an *English* book!" Victor uses his hand as a gun. "Bang!" Then his voice goes flat. "Yoni's gone. And the rest of us are running for our lives like a bunch of rats straight into the arms of the Bolshevik bastards who deported us to Mother Russia." Victor's voice trails off. "Zimmy! Are you listening? We're just ghosts who refused to die, cigarettes still warm after they've been stubbed out on frozen Russian soil." When my father doesn't respond, Victor stops. "Hey, Zimmy my friend, you look like you don't feel well. Do you want me to get you an aspirin?"

"Don't be funny," Tata whispers. "I wish you wouldn't keep ranting like this. Every time you have a drink in you, your tongue gets loose about the camps." Tata grabs the Shakespeare off the shelf from the other side of our bookcase, and I slide under my covers. "How *could* I forget? This book was so important to Yoni, it cost him his life."

"Too high a price," Victor answers flatly.

"Look," Tata mutters, tapping the Shakespeare volume, "it's got Yoni's dried blood on some of the pages." Tata leafs through the book. "I also risked *my* life for it when I ran back to get it after Yoni died. Only I got lucky. I lived. Why? I have no clue. I certainly don't deserve that privilege any more than Yoni. Maybe he was luckier." Tata's voice is controlled. "Don't kid yourself, Victor. Yoni didn't run back to retrieve the book for me. He wanted the Shakespeare for himself. You can think what you want, and you can blame me if it makes you feel better, but Yoni and I are not the only two crazy people in the world who love Shakespeare so much we'd risk our lives for a book. You forget what's important, Victor," Tata says, dropping the Shakespeare on the bed with a thud. The room turns silent except for the sound of our clock.

"Nothing's as important as your *life*, Zimmy. *You* ought to know that better than most."

"I'm not sure anymore," Tata says, half talking to himself. "What's life without books, art, or music? Or without the people you love?"

"Don't get maudlin and poetical on me," Victor snaps. "I remember how terrified you were when that Nazi bastard played Russian roulette with your life. You almost shit in your pants when he waved his gun in your face. I bet you would have sold your mother just to stay alive, but they had already finished her off." Victor's laugh is a dry bark.

"Don't bring up my mother, you drunken fool! What's wrong with you?"

"Zimmy, we're all capable of terrible things, but at least *I* admit it."

"You talk too much," Tata snaps. "Come on, Victor, you're out of here," he says, helping his friend up. "Next time, less booze and more Radio Free Europe. Maybe we can catch the BBC news on Thursday night. Go home, Victor. I love you, but I need to sleep."

TATA'S FILM DIRECTOR PARTNER, whom Tata refers to as Beard, is his closest friend and collaborator at the film studio. Beard earned his nickname by risking jail for growing a beard. The Party considers growing facial hair a subversive activity. Beard plays cat and mouse with the authorities by shaving before every official meeting with Party members. The moment the meeting is over, however, he starts to grow his beard again. Everyone is aware of this, including the Party officials, since Beard bribes them with free tickets to the film premieres. They laugh, enjoy the free movies, and refer to Beard as an "eccentric artist."

On cold winter nights after they finish work at the Studio, Tata and Beard show up at our house and hide themselves in our bedroom so they can discuss the day's shoot without being overheard by the rest of the crew. When Mama is home, she brings in a tray with tea and lemon and a few slices of *cozonac*—Romanian coffee cake—and goes out to the dining room to spend time with my grandparents. Tata never asks me to leave our bedroom because my curfew is 8:00 p.m. I'm tucked in bed in my makeshift little corner, and they forget I'm there. Most of the time, I read and ignore their conversation, but there are times when I pretend that I'm asleep and I listen.

"We can't have a wide-angle shot of the lawn chairs with a single chair sticking out of line," Beard tells Tata. "The Artistic Content Committee will claim that we're advocating dissent and capitalist individualism."

"Nonsense," my father argues. "They're too stupid to think that. Don't be paranoid, Beard. In order for them to cite individualism, they need a brain capable of interpretive powers. You give these imbeciles way too much credit." Tata taps his pipe into the ashtray. I can smell the fresh tobacco from his pouch before he lights up.

"They're not *all* stupid, Zimmy," Beard retorts. "Some have brains, and I guarantee that every one of them is mean-spirited. That's a lethal combination."

Tata doesn't agree. "Why not throw their argument right back in their faces? We'll tell them that it's all in their filthy, small, Bolshevik minds. They're seeing things in the film that simply aren't there." Tata smiles. "Art is subjective, after all."

"Yeah, but it's a dangerous game to play, because *they* hold all the cards, Zimmy. They can put us out of business."

"You have no idea how much I detest these clowns," Tata grumbles, his teeth clicking on the stem of his pipe.

"Yes I do," Beard says. "Your precious chair scene can stay in the film for now, just to keep you happy. We'll take another look at it when we do the final cut. Okay?"

Tata's answer is an unintelligible string of Hungarian curses.

Tata's conversations with Beard often sound like heated arguments to me, but Mama says neither makes a move without the other. Even in his personal life Beard relies more on my father than on all of his wives combined. Beard is in between wives, but he's in love with Renée, a Belgian puppeteer, who came to Romania for a children's theater festival. I only met Renée once, when she showed me how the strings of a puppet work.

"Refrain from getting married," Tata advises Beard. "An official marriage certificate from the Communists will only complicate your life, and it will leave you in debt again after you divorce."

"You know I'm crazy about Renée," Beard whines.

"You are crazy. Why must you make it a habit to get married to every pretty woman you meet?" Tata asks. "Renée doesn't even live here. Be happy that you can still get laid without first obtaining permission from the Party. Do me a favor, Beard: don't get married again and don't make babies. Buy some condoms from Victor. He just got a shipment in from France."

Beard sighs in response, but both of them know that Tata's lecture is useless. When it comes to women, Beard can't help himself. He is willing to marry every woman who's ever caught his eye because he thinks all women are beautiful. "No wonder they're all crazy about you," Tata says.

A COUPLE OF WEEKS LATER, Beard shows up early for one of his visits and waits for Tata in our room. I am thrilled because Beard is fun. He looks just like a picture Tata has shown me of Albert Einstein — the wild mane, minus the silver-white. Whenever Beard visits, he turns on the radio and tunes in to a classical concert. He loves music, and he once told me that, when he was a young boy, he wanted to become an orchestra conductor. As the music on our radio soars, Beard stands in the middle of our bedroom in his baggy pants and starts to conduct. His eyes are closed, and his face twitches in rhythm to the music.

Sometimes his arms move slowly and gracefully, while at other times he is punching the air with his fists and his wild mane gets wet with droplets of sweat. As the music fades, Beard stops and plants a kiss on my cheek.

"Did you miss me?" he asks. "Close your eyes and open your hands. Renée has sent you a present from Belgium."

My eyes are shut tightly. I'm secretly hoping that Renée has sent me a puppet, but the object that Beard places in my hands feels smooth, like a box.

"Open your eyes," Beard says. In my hands is a turquoise plastic box with two arched handles.

"Want to see what's inside?" Beard asks, snapping the catch open.

It's a toiletry kit filled with the most amazing things! There is a bar of lavender soap, hand lotion, a toothbrush and a tube of toothpaste, a comb, a hairbrush, and even lip pomade.

"Renée asked that I give you a big hug and kiss for her," Beard says, taking me in his arms.

This is the best present I've ever received! I run to the bathroom and brush my teeth for the second time that day, this time with Belgian toothpaste that tastes like mint. Then I hide all of my most important possessions in my new toiletry box. My collection of stamps, my dog-eared French comic books, and my satin hair ribbons—all fit inside. I place the box on my nightstand and run back to give Beard another hug.

When Tata arrives, Beard starts to cry about how much he misses Renée, and he concocts an elaborate scheme to escape to Belgium.

"I don't know why you aren't deliriously happy." Tata laughs at Beard. "Most men would kill for such a sweet deal. You can keep the embers of passion glowing between Renée's visits, because, as the saying goes, absence makes the heart grow fonder. You don't have to deal with the jealous husband since he's in Belgium and what he doesn't know won't hurt him. You don't have to buy her presents, because she's got more money than you. Plus, she's got access to all the goods in the free world, so if you ever need anything all you have to do is ask. What more do you want? She's mad about you, and she doesn't want your baby."

Beard replies miserably, "I want to hold her every night for the rest of my life, preferably in Belgium."

"You're as crazy as you look, Beard," Tata says, dragging on his pipe. "Assuming you can get out of here alive, your romance will sour the minute you're an unemployed *ex*–film director in the

West. What the hell do you think you're going to do for a living over there, make strings for Renée's puppets?"

"I'll think of something, Zimmy. Stop making me feel hopeless."

"You'll feel even more hopeless when Renée's jealous husband blows your brains out and leaves your hair as the only evidence of your existence." Tata laughs again.

"Haven't you ever heard of divorce, Zimmy?"

"No. When I make a commitment, it's for life."

"Like you've never had another woman since you got hitched, Zimmy."

"Hey, there's a difference between a roll in the hay and marriage. Marriage is a huge decision, not to be made in haste or taken lightly."

"Oh yeah? How long did it take you to propose to Stefi, Zimmy?" Beard inquires, though it's likely he already knows.

"A month."

"*That* long?"

"A month is a long time when you're in love with the right woman."

"I know. I've been pining for Renée for three years!"

"Man, you've got it bad," Tata says, patting Beard on the back.

Tata has to go out on an errand, and Beard falls asleep sprawled on my parents' bed. I am so taken with his unruly hair that I start to braid it, careful not to wake him. When Beard finally opens his eyes, he has no idea where he is. I spy on him from behind the bookcase as he wobbles, disoriented, to the bathroom. I hear the water running as Beard washes up, then a loud burst of laughter. Beard emerges from the bathroom with his wild mane all twirled and woven into dozens of tight braids that I've fastened with colored laundry pins. He grabs my arms, grinning from ear to ear, and plants an itchy, bearded kiss on my cheek.

"Never mind that Renée doesn't want babies. *I* want babies, who'll make my hair stand up just like you did." Beard laughs, putting his black leather jacket on. He rushes out with the laundry pins still in his hair.

DANCING

MAMA'S HAIR has a mind of its own. In the morning with the light streaming in from the terrace, I catch her still asleep, her chest rising and falling rhythmically, her thick, chestnut hair spread out like wings flying in all directions.

Mama tries to tame her curls every time she looks in the mirror. "This is not a fitting coiffure for a ballet dancer," she mutters after running a comb full of brilliantine and water through her mane and then pulling it into a tight bun at the back of her neck. "That's better," she says, tucking in a loose strand.

I love Mama's curls, but she tells me she would much rather have straight, fine hair, like mine. "So much lovelier in every way," she says as she surveys me from head to toe. "You are lucky to take after your father. I would have killed for a body like yours, a dancer's body, perfectly proportioned, just like Leonardo's drawing of the Vitruvian Man." Mama takes one of my father's art books off the shelf and opens it to a drawing of a man with multiple outstretched arms and legs that make him look like an octopus.

"I don't look like that!" I say, horrified.

"Of course not." Mama laughs. "Leonardo is just showing the best proportions for a person, and you've got them. See, your head is one eighth the length of your body." She demonstrates, taking a tape measure and counting the centimeters from the top of my head to my chin. "Perfect," she murmurs. "Not only the proportions, but look at your dancer's feet! Point your toes, Eva."

I point my toes and look up. My mother is delighted. "This curvature of your feet is called your *cou-de-pieds*. Now let's see how high you can lift your legs." Mama lets me use our bureau for balance. She lifts my leg all the way up to my ear. "Tell me when it begins to hurt," she says.

"Ouch."

"That's great! Can you imagine what you could do with a little proper ballet training? Not everyone has such a natural advantage. I had to compensate for my short legs and height, and I sweated for the slightest improvement." Mama is under five feet tall but looks much taller.

MY FIRST MEMORY of walking *properly*, as Mama calls it, is when she places a book on the crown of my head and tells me to walk across the room with my head held high and my spine straight, without dropping the book. I walk in slow motion, minding each and every step, until I reach the other end of the room. The book wobbles when I gaze at her sideways for her approval. "Good," she says, "but don't look at me. That's how you'll lose your balance. You must look straight in front of you and never take your eyes off where you are going. Always walk as if this book were still on top of your head, and keep your neck long and your shoulders down. It should feel as if your head is suspended from an invisible hook in the sky, but your feet must be planted on the ground."

That's the expression that Grandpa Yosef and Grandma Iulia use when they're talking about Mama. "Stefi's feet are planted on the ground," they say proudly, but my mother points out that she's gotten to where she is today by dreaming of whatever she wants and by having enough discipline and persistence to work hard to get it.

Mama's face lights up whenever she talks about dancing, but I've never seen her dance except in photographs. Unlike Tata's war photographs, where he looks like a prisoner, Mama's photos taken during that same period in Bucharest show her wearing exotic costumes. Her lips are outlined to make them look bigger, the arches of her thick eyebrows are drawn with dark pencil, and her high cheekbones are accentuated with rouge. Her body is animated as she dances; her neck is long and her torso spirals up.

"By the time the war was in full swing, my parents had no choice but to give in and accept my dancing." Mama smiles at the recollection. "I was the only one in the family who was still getting paid for working. The rest of them were all doing forced labor for the Nazis. My evening dance recitals meant there was food for everyone at our table."

I'm curious about her dancing, and I wish I could have seen her on the stage. "How come you don't dance anymore?" I ask her.

Mama ignores my question. "I always decided on the topic and the content of my performances. I choreographed, staged, and promoted an entire one-woman show. All of my performances sold out, but unfortunately, the show had to close after two months because of the blackouts and air raids."

"Did you ever dance through an air raid?"

"Of course not. We had to run into the shelter as soon as the alarm sounded, but despite that, I did a lot of dancing during the war."

"I don't understand why Grandma and Grandpa didn't want you to be a ballerina, if you did so well."

"Your grandmother tried to drum it into my head that girls from *good families* in Bucharest did not take to the stage. Only whores and desperate women became actresses, Mother told me, and being a dancer was just one step removed from being one of those women in her eyes."

"You didn't care?"

"I cared. There are times when you just have to be deaf to what others say and do whatever makes you happy. I loved dancing too much to give it up."

"If dancing makes you so happy, how come you don't dance anymore?" I ask again.

Mama's face has an edge of hardness as she answers. "I had to make some tough choices, but it all worked out fine."

"What worked out fine?"

"Life. In life you often have to make choices that don't feel good. Soon after I married your father I had an offer to go to Moscow and study at the Bolshoi Ballet, but I turned it down."

"You were going to be a ballerina with the Bolshoi?" Even *I* have heard that the Bolshoi is the best ballet company anywhere.

"If I had gone to Moscow, I would have had to be separated from your father for two years, maybe more. That was not an option."

"Why didn't Tata go with you?"

Mama's unexpected cackle is infectious. I start to laugh with her, even though I don't know what's so funny. "Your father would not be dragged back to Russia if it were the last place on earth. Not even for me!"

"Why not?"

"Eva, do you realize how often you ask *why*?"

"Why?" I repeat, and crack up.

"Because your father was a prisoner in Russia for four years, that's why. He couldn't bear to go back there, and I couldn't bear to live without him in Moscow. The truth is, he probably couldn't bear two years without me either, but he would never admit it."

"Why?" I ask, cracking up again.

Mama ignores my laughter. "Your father told me I should go to Moscow, but I knew he didn't mean it. He made it very clear that he didn't want to impede my career. But he also told me that if I chose *not* to go, he never wanted to hear about it again, regardless of what happened between us. The choice was mine. Once I made my decision, I had to live with it and never bring up the subject again. That was the deal."

"Are you sorry, Mama?"

"Of course not, you silly goose," Mama says, hugging me. "I wouldn't have had *you*, and I would have been miserable without your dad."

"It's not my fault that you don't dance anymore!"

My mother puts her hands on my shoulders as if she were about to shake me, but instead she is very still and looks straight into my eyes. "Everything I did, I did for myself. A dancer's career is short. Most dancers are finished by the time they're thirty-five. When I teach, I touch many, many lives, and when I choreograph, I get to see my dreams come alive onstage."

"Yes, but don't you miss dancing, Mama?"

"I miss it all the time." She sighs. "But I regret nothing."

I KNOW that the money my mother earns is important by the way she gives it to Grandma Iulia on payday. Grandma Iulia takes the folded bills and puts them into her checkered apron pocket. "Thank you, Stefi," she says to Mama, her thin lips getting a little tight at the corners, before she retreats into the kitchen. The kitchen door swings lightly behind her, but it stays open long enough for the aroma of whatever is cooking in there to waft into the foyer. Mama lingers for a moment, looking at the swinging door. One day the phone rings just as Mama gives Grandma Iulia the money. I grab the receiver before she has a chance to answer it.

"May I speak to Stefania Mihail?" a man's voice asks politely.

I hand my mother the phone. She speaks directly into the mouthpiece. "This is Comrade Stefania Mihail. To whom am I speaking?" Mama's voice sounds so official, I hardly recognize it, even though I am looking straight at her face.

Later I ask her why she is using a strange name, and she says, "It's my professional name. That's what people call me at work, Stefania Mihail."

"But, Mama, I've never heard you use Mihail before. How did you ever come up with that name?"

"It was my first husband's name. The one I was married to before I met your father."

"You were married before Tata? What happened to your first husband?"

"He died," Mama answers as if that explains everything.

"Why?" I ask, but I really mean *How?*

"People do, you know."

"Do what?" I ask blankly.

"People die. Look, I really don't want to discuss this. I'm very happy to be married to your father."

"Did Mr. Mihail die during the war?" I ask, ignoring her words.

Mama bristles at the mention of her first husband's name as if he were here in the room with us. "Yes," she says, and adds quickly, "Mr. Mihail died during the war."

"That explains it!" I'm relieved.

"Explains *what?*"

"How he died," I answer, but Mama just shrugs.

My MOTHER'S comings and goings are as mysterious as her past. No one ever asks her where she is going and when she will return. No one in the family ever mentions that she was married before, though they must know. One day Tata comes home early, and immediately after supper he puts on a jacket and tie.

"Where are you off to?" I ask.

"I'm going to your mother's ballet recital," he says, searching the room for his tobacco pouch.

"Mama is dancing?" I am mystified.

"Of course not. Her students are performing your mother's choreographed piece."

"Can I come?"

"No. It's past your bedtime. You must be very tired. Didn't you go to play in the park today?"

"No, I didn't. And I'm not too tired. Why can't I go with you? I want to see the recital."

"It's out of the question," Tata replies. "You should have gone out to the park. You spend too much time at home. That's why you have all this energy."

"No, I don't. I just want to see Mama's students dance."

Tata finally finds his tobacco pouch under the open book he's left lying on the bed. He slides it into his pants pocket along with his pipe. "Believe me, you won't miss much," he says with an amused smile that fades quickly. "I'd trade places with you if I could get out of it. It's going to be tough to keep my eyes open at this thing, and if anyone notices me snoring in my chair your mother will evict me from my own bed. A fate worse than death." Tata smirks as he offers me his cheek for a good-night kiss.

"But, Tata, I promise *I* won't fall asleep!" I plead as I plant a kiss on his newly shaved face and get a whiff of his French cologne.

"I'll ask your mother if there is a matinee next week," he says, slipping on his leather jacket. "Maybe you can go then."

After Tata leaves, I have trouble falling asleep.

A FEW DAYS LATER, Mama takes me to an afternoon dress rehearsal. The school auditorium is drafty. Each whisper resonates in the empty place as if it were directly spoken into your ear. Mama is holding court from the back of the auditorium. Ten adoring ballet students are squinting into the empty seats past the stage lights, all searching for her face. I slide down in my seat, hoping that the dancers are too intent on my mother to spot me. I feel very small, almost invisible, but I am safe because I don't have to dance for my mother. The accompanist's head is turned toward my mother, waiting for his cue.

"Places, people. Places. A one. A two. A three!" Mama's voice is silenced by the music.

The dancers move in a wave of color. Some of the ballerinas' tutus are light lavender, others are pink, and the rest are white. Mama taps her long stick on the back of an empty seat. The music stops abruptly, and all the faces onstage are now at attention.

"Carla, turn your head as you bend. Your arms are stiff. Curve them and tuck your thumbs into the palms of your hands." Carla does as she is told.

"That's better," my mother says. "Now turn your head to the audience and smile." Mama taps the back of the seat with her stick. "Don't grimace! The audience doesn't care if it hurts. Your job is to look as beautiful as a floating dandelion seed." Carla soars through the air gracefully on the silent stage.

"Good," Mama says. "Again. Places, people!" The ballet dancers scurry to their spots. "A one, a two, a three." The music begins again.

OF EARACHES AND LUCK—DECEMBER 1958

IT'S SNOWING OUTSIDE. I cannot bear even to look at the silent snowflakes as they hit the ground because I have an earache. My head is throbbing and my cheeks feel hot. There are gurgling sounds in my head like water running through pipes. I can make my ear pop by opening and closing my mouth rapidly several times.

They're so worried about me, they've kept me home from school. Grandpa Yosef went to the market in search of lemons. He says I need vitamin C. Grandma Iulia brought me a cup of tea on a tray and then left our room as quickly as she came in. Mama says she will take me to the doctor as soon as she gets home from work. Tata's not home, and Uncle Max is at work as well. Aunt Puica is probably reading in bed and smoking, as usual. The house is so quiet, I wouldn't mind talking to her. I tiptoe to her room and scratch on her door. She opens it without a sound. She is still in her underwear with a cigarette hanging between her lips. She slides back into bed under her pink satin quilted down comforter and continues to read while I curl up in Uncle Max's chair. The room is thick with cigarette smoke. I start to choke and cough. Aunt Puica looks up from her book.

"You look like you have a fever," she says. "Come over here and let me feel your forehead." I stagger from the armchair to her bed. She places her fingers on my forehead.

"You're burning." She grabs a skirt from her armoire, zips it up, and runs to the bathroom. She comes back with a wet, cold towel that she wraps around my head, turban style.

"Lie down," she commands. "I'm going to get you some aspirin," she says, leaving the room.

I gaze up at the ceiling through the cigarette smoke that moves slowly toward the bare bulb dangling on a string. A knife-like pain starts in the back of my head and radiates beyond my right ear to my cheek. Tears well up in my eyes, but I'm not really crying. I try to muffle the pain by placing Aunt Puica's pillow on top of my head.

I wish Mama were home from work. My head throbs so much, I'm not even afraid to go see the doctor. Aunt Puica returns with a glass of cool water and an aspirin cut in two.

"Swallow both halves," she says, handing me the aspirin. I gulp the water and taste the bitterness of the pill pieces as they slide down. "Open your mouth and let me see if you've got a sore throat," she tells me. "Wider. Stick your tongue out and say *Aaaah*," she says, peering deep into my throat. "Good. You can close your mouth now."

"Is it red, Aunt Puica?"

"No. Your throat's fine. But the roof of your mouth is black like a nasty dog's, just as I suspected," she says, laughing.

I've heard this one before. I know it isn't true because the first time she cracked that joke, I checked it out for myself in the bathroom mirror. When I told Aunt Puica that the roof of my mouth was pink and not black, she laughed so hard the whole room shook. But now she looks really worried, and she's just repeating the joke out of habit.

I MUST HAVE FALLEN ASLEEP, because the next thing I know, my mother and Aunt Puica are pulling my pants on and putting a sweater over my T-shirt. Each of them is rolling socks on my sweaty feet, two layers. Then Mama gets me to sit up on the bed, and everything begins to swirl.

"Do you want me to come with you?" Aunt Puica asks.

"That would be good." Mama's voice sounds far away.

They bundle me in my overcoat. I'm wearing boots and a dark blue wool hat with a huge pom-pom that my mother knit for me. Aunt Puica wraps an orange muffler around my face, allowing only my eyes to show. Mama puts mittens on my sweaty hands, and I curl my fingers into little fists inside them.

Out in the courtyard, Mama and Aunt Puica each grab of one of my hands. "It's a real blizzard." I can barely hear Mama's voice. The three of us walk in silence through the white. The wind is howling almost as loudly as the throb in my head.

At the doctor's office everything is white as well. Mama and Aunt Puica peel off my layers of clothes until I'm standing in my undershirt and underpants, feeling the cold floor tiles through my socks. I'm shivering even though I'm very hot. I can't stop my teeth from chattering as a nurse drapes a white sheet around my shoulders and pushes me gently into a metal chair. We wait for the doctor.

The door squeaks open, and a man wearing a white coat appears. He has a band wrapped around his head with a silvery headlight in the middle of his forehead, right between his eyebrows.

"Hello, Eva," he greets me. I wonder how he knows my name.

"I'm going to examine your ears," the doctor says, sitting down on his swivel stool. He pulls on my right earlobe, and I wince as he sticks a cold steel instrument into my ear canal. It hurts so much, everything that was white suddenly turns red.

"It's almost over," I barely hear him say. "I'm not going to hurt you any more," he murmurs as he takes out the cold steel instrument and then turns to my mother. I feel my breath seeping back into my chest.

"She's got severe otitis, and it has spread to her mastoid bone, right here." He touches a spot behind my ear, and I pull away. "We have to do surgery immediately to keep the infection from going to her brain. She will need antibiotics, but we barely have any for our hospital patients. There's a waiting list for drugs imported from the Soviet Union, but this is urgent." The doctor says this in a calm, thin voice while looking at Mother's feet. "Do you have any connections abroad? Anyone who could send you penicillin?"

Neither Mama nor Aunt Puica answers him immediately. Instead they exchange glances. Finally Mama murmurs, "We have a cousin in Paris, but it will take weeks before her package arrives."

"I'm afraid we don't have that long," the doctor says. "Your daughter needs surgery immediately."

"What does it entail?" Mama asks.

"We will drill the bone here at the back of her head." I can feel the doctor's smooth fingers running through my hair. "Then we'll open up her skull and drain the infection. It's not pleasant, but it's necessary. We will have to rely on whatever antibiotics we can get our hands on. There's no time to waste because there's already an infection, and it could quickly spread further to her brain. It's very dangerous."

"So she needs brain surgery?" Mama swallows hard.

"No. We will open up her cranium by the mastoid bone and close it as soon as we drain the infection. We're not operating on her brain, just exposing it briefly."

"Doctor, my daughter doesn't have a zipper located behind her ear!"

Aunt Puica smirks at Mama's comment, but the doctor is silent.

"I understand you're upset," he tells Mama. "But believe me, you don't have a choice."

"Puica, what do you think?" Mama asks.

"I think I would avoid major surgery at all costs," Aunt Puica tells my mother and then addresses the doctor. "I was a surgical nurse during the war, and I'm concerned about doing this without antibiotics. I hope you don't mind, but I think we need a second opinion."

"Suit yourselves," the doctor snaps. "But you haven't got much time. I wouldn't want this child's life on my conscience."

"Thank you, Doctor," Aunt Puica says while getting my clothes on. "We'll let you know just as soon as we make a decision." Then we're back on the street, trudging through drifts of deep snow. Everything is white again.

HOURS LATER, Mama is shaking me out of a dreamless sleep. I am very groggy. "Dr. Meyers is here to see you. Sit up, darling." Mama helps me up and puts a glass of water to my lips. Aunt Puica appears with Dr. Meyers, who is wearing a gray overcoat. There are melting snowflakes on his shoulders. Mama takes his coat and goes out to hang it in the foyer.

"Hello, Eva." Dr. Meyers takes my hand in his and pats it.

"Hello," I answer. I hear my bad ear crackling as I swallow, but I'm relieved to see Dr. Meyers, whom I've known since I was born.

"Your mother tells me that your right ear hurts. May I look inside?" Dr. Meyers asks.

I nod, trying not to wince.

"I won't hurt you," he assures me. "I know it's very painful."

I nod again as he brushes my hair away to look into my ear. "I'm going to place this instrument into your ear so that I can see what your eardrum looks like. You will feel a slight pinch, okay?"

It's not okay but I tell him, "Okay," and brace myself for the pain; surprisingly, though, there is none, just a cold sensation from the metal instrument.

"Thank you. That's all for now," Dr. Meyers says.

Aunt Puica talks first. "Does she have to have a mastoidectomy?"

"That would be my last resort," Dr. Meyers tells her. "It's major surgery, and we have no antibiotics. The risk's too high."

"That's what I thought," Aunt Puica says while Mama listens. "So what do you suggest?"

"I think we should drain her eardrum. That will relieve the pressure in her head and also a lot of the pain. If we're lucky, we can treat the infection and avoid surgery. I have a few vials of penicillin, but we will need more."

"Will we have to take her to the hospital?" Mama asks.

"In this weather that's very risky," Dr. Meyers answers. "There are no cars on the roads, and the trams are not running. You'll be waiting until spring for an ambulance."

"We can do it right here," Aunt Puica suggests. "I don't think we should take the child out into the cold again just to get her to your office. I can assist you. We can use our dining room table. It's large enough."

"That's good, thank you. I heard you were a very skilled surgical nurse during the war," Dr. Meyers tells Aunt Puica.

"Thank you, Doctor," Aunt Puica says. "Now tell me, what do you need from me?"

Dr. Meyers has gone back to his office to bring ether. Aunt Puica's in the dining room giving instructions to Sabina in a hushed tone. Grandpa Yosef and Grandma Iulia are in the kitchen cooking, and I can smell the aroma of chicken soup. How did they ever manage to buy another chicken without me? Maybe Grandpa told Ion that I'm sick. I don't know where Tata, Uncle Max, and Uncle Natan have gone, but it doesn't matter. They can't help me now. I'm scared.

"Mama?"

"Yes, sweetheart."

"What's Dr. Meyers going to do?" My voice is weak.

"He's going to drain your ear so that your pain will go away." Mama tries to reassure me, but her voice is full of dread. "Don't worry, I'm going to be right here, holding your hand, and you'll be fast asleep. You won't feel a thing." Mama sounds better now.

Dr. Meyers is back, and Mama brings me to the dining room in my pajamas. It doesn't look like our dining room at all. The table is covered with a white sheet, all the lights are on, and they've put Aunt Puica's floor lamp at the head of the table. There's a pillow placed right under the light.

Grandma and Grandpa have shut themselves in their bedroom, and Sabina has disappeared upstairs to her room.

"Okay, sweetie," Mama says, "climb up on this chair and lie on the table with your head on the pillow."

I can feel the thick wool of Grandma's needlepoint tablecloth beneath the white sheet they've laid on the table. Aunt Puica covers me with a white top sheet and then wraps me in a blanket, tucking me in so tightly I can't move my arms. She is standing directly behind my head next to the floor lamp, the palms of her hands cradling my cheeks.

"Did you boil the instruments?" Dr. Meyers asks.

"Yes, of course, Doctor." Aunt Puica's voice is different now, as if it doesn't belong to her. She sounds as official as a news announcer on the radio.

"I want you to place the ether over her nose and hold it down firmly," Dr. Meyers tells Aunt Puica.

"This is going to smell very strong," Aunt Puica tells me, "but before you know it, you'll be asleep and you won't feel a thing. I promise. Now count backward with me." She places the washcloth with ether on my face. I'm engulfed by a sweet, dizzying smell that makes my eyelids feel heavy.

"Ten, nine, eight, seven . . ." The last thing I feel is Mama's hand sliding under the sheet looking for mine. My hand is clammy, but Mama's is warm and dry.

SNOW. The tiny flakes are coming down lightly and melt as they hit my face. I'm gliding through white on a red sleigh that Grandpa Yosef is pulling. We're on our way to the market to pick out our Christmas tree. Grandpa's wearing his Santa Claus outfit, the one with the big black belt under his tummy and a fake beard made of cotton balls that look just like clouds. Grandpa pretends that he's Santa and that he's come all the way from the North Pole, but I know who he *really* is, because his eyes give him away as he winks at me.

"I'm going to puncture her eardrum very quickly, and I want you to turn her head sideways to drain it immediately on this towel," a voice says.

I am cold. Grandpa covers my sleigh with a blanket and says, "You're shivering. This will keep you warm." I can hear my teeth chatter in my head, but Grandpa's voice is gone now. The snow smells sweet, like hyacinths in the spring. I want to bury my face in the melting snow and fall asleep surrounded by the smell of spring. I sleep without dreaming for a long time.

When I wake, I'm in Aunt Puica's bed, tucked beneath her giant duvet with two huge pillows under my head. Uncle Max is sitting in his armchair, reading the paper.

"The Child's awake," he announces, looking at me over his newspaper.

"Good," Aunt Puica answers, "now I can give her her shot. You'd better get out of the room, Max."

Aunt Puica has a small rectangular silver box in her hands. She takes out a syringe and screws a long, thin needle into its head. She moves the plunger in, slowly releasing some of the liquid.

"This will feel as light as a mosquito bite," she reassures me. "Trust me. I'm better at this than any doctor. What are you staring at me for? Pull down your pajama pants and lie flat on your tummy."

I'm scared, but I do as she tells me. "Your mother may have given birth to you, but I'm the one who's saving your butt. Don't move!" she says firmly as she pulls the needle out.

• • •

WHEN I FEEL BETTER, Grandma Iulia serves the chicken soup she's made just for me. There are carrots and rice in the broth, and Mama feeds me, blowing on each spoonful. Tata has come home from filming on location and brought me a new book by Mark Twain that's been translated into Romanian from English. It's called *The Adventures of Huckleberry Finn*.

"I read this book in English when I was your age," Tata tells me. "You'll love it, even in this lousy translation."

I start reading the book and can't put it down. When I finish, I reread it several times. Huck Finn astounds me! I have never met a black person, much less thought about a friendship between a white boy and a black slave. This book instantly becomes my favorite, because despite how others view their differences, Huck and Jim are great friends who love each other.

Uncle Max brought me colorful pick-up sticks, and Grandpa Yosef has given me three hard candies. I've never gotten so many presents before, not even for my birthday!

"You are a lucky girl," Mama tells me. "You were lucky even before you were born."

"How could I be lucky *before* I was born?"

"The doctor didn't believe that I could get pregnant, and when I did, I had hepatitis and so did you," Mama explains. "That's why you looked jaundiced at birth. Then, when you were just an infant, you got sick with dysentery and we almost lost you. Dr. Meyers came over and fed you carrot juice and herb tea with pureed rice. We all took turns feeding you lots of liquids so you wouldn't be dehydrated, and here you are."

"What else happened?" I want to hear more now.

"Isn't that enough?" Mama laughs. "Actually, when you were nine months old, I was locking the front door when your carriage rolled down the steps and you landed upside down at the bottom with a big thud. I started to scream because I thought I had killed you, but you cried even louder than I did, so I knew you were still alive. You landed on top of all those baby blankets. You were frightened, but there wasn't a single scratch on you."

"What else makes me so lucky, Mama?"

"Well, you're lucky because you're not a genius," she teases.

"What's a genius?"

"A genius is a person with above-average intelligence, someone who's very, very smart. But trust me, you don't want to be a genius."

"Why not?"

"Because geniuses are generally unhappy people who don't fit in, that's why," she continues. "Don't worry, you're not a genius."

"I'm not?" I'm a little disappointed but don't want to show it.

"Nope. You've just got a wild imagination. Dr. Meyers had you tested when your kindergarten teacher called to tell us that you said a witch had put a spell on you so that a pencil would start to write stories in your guts. You insisted that it was a *good witch*."

"I remember that," I tell her.

"Of course you do. What a scare! Your kindergarten teacher said that you are either a genius or disturbed. Or *both*!"

"So which am I?" I swallow hard, but my ear isn't crackling anymore.

"Neither, of course." Mama laughs.

"Dr. Meyers had a talk with you and reassured me that everything is just as it ought to be. You're one lucky girl. So many people love you as if you were their own, even Dr. Meyers, who's

never had children. We're *all* lucky to have you. You're *my* miracle, Eva. What would any of us ever have done without you?"
Mama asks, smiling.

What *would* they have done? I have no idea, so I keep my
mouth shut.

A QUICK MARRIAGE AND A QUICK DIVORCE

UNCLE NATAN is getting married. That means he won't be sleeping on the cot in the dining room anymore and hiding behind his newspaper with those thick glasses of his that make his eyes look three times bigger than they really are. I asked Grandma Iulia how come Uncle Natan's getting married, and she snapped, "Your uncle Natan's got his needs, you know, just like all men."

I have no idea what she's talking about, but I can tell that she's not happy with the situation and doesn't really want to discuss it. Uncle Natan brought Rosa, his bride-to-be, home yesterday to introduce her to the family. Everyone was polite, especially Rosa. She wore a yellow dress with silk stockings, black pumps, and a blue silk scarf tied around her neck in a giant knot. Rosa would almost be pretty if she weren't so stiff. Grandpa Yosef didn't say much to her, and Grandma Iulia said even less and just kept looking her up and down.

Sabina served Turkish coffee in our white porcelain cups and pieces of *rahat*, a sugar-powdered, fruit-flavored, jellylike treat. I was surprised that Grandma Iulia didn't bake her famous *cozonac*, which she always serves to company, but maybe Uncle Natan didn't give her enough advance notice. Uncle Natan sat upright in a chair, holding Rosa's hand tightly the whole time. They didn't stay long, and after they left, Grandma Iulia started speaking in Yiddish, which is what she always does when she doesn't want me to understand what she is saying. Her words tumbled out, and Grandpa Yosef sat on their bed looking miserable and nodding. When she finally spoke Romanian again, it was a lament. "It had to be a *shikse* for my only son, Yosef? The war wasn't enough to teach him to stick to his own kind?" Grandpa didn't answer.

I'm HAPPY that Uncle Natan's moving out because now I can do my homework at the dining room table without feeling like I'm intruding on him. I love working here, where my notebook can rest on the hard surface of the table. It's so much better than writing in our room on the bed.

No one in the house seems to mind that Uncle Natan's getting married, except Grandma Iulia. It's been less than a week since he moved out, and she's been walking around with a long face, like the time she swallowed a fish bone at dinner and almost choked. Grandpa Yosef hasn't said a word about the marriage, but I notice that he's smoking more. Maybe he's worried about Grandma. Sabina hasn't commented about Uncle Natan leaving us, but I guess she must be happy, since she's got one less bed to make.

It's BEEN ALMOST three months since Uncle Natan left with Rosa. The house feels different. Grandma Iulia is still moping around with a face full of salt and vinegar, but I don't care. I'm happy because Andrei and I have become close friends. I have to be careful about this, though, because I don't want anyone to think that he's my boyfriend. Aunt Puica and Uncle Max have already made a few snide remarks. That's why I'm glad when Claudia, one of my classmates who lives three houses down the block, asks if it's okay for her to walk home with us from school. Now no one can tease me about Andrei since there are three of us walking home to-gether. Claudia is a tall, thin girl with spindly legs and bony arms. She wears starched dresses that rustle under her pinafore, and her hair is always tied with a giant white bow right on top of her head. She has huge birdlike eyes and a high-pitched voice, and she's an only child just like I am. Andrei is also an only child, so it's fun that the three of us are becoming friends.

Claudia's mother works nights and Sundays in a hospital emer-gency room. Her father used to be a teacher, but now he stays home because he's blind. He wears dark sunglasses even in the house. I had a peek at his eyes through the side of his glasses, and they look strangely caved in. It gave me goose bumps, knowing that his eyeballs might be missing. No wonder he covers them with sun-glasses.

Claudia invites Andrei and me to do our homework at her house. Everything is going just fine until her father gets involved. We are doing math when he appears in the dining room with his cane knocking against the furniture in front of him. Then he pulls out a chair, feels its edge with the backs of his legs, and sits down next to us.

"There's a much easier way to solve this problem." He speaks into the air. Evidently, he's been listening to every word we are saying.

"But, Tata," Claudia argues, "we have to solve the problem by the method that Comrade Popescu has taught us."

"Nonsense, Claudia. A problem should always be solved in the quickest, easiest, and most elegant manner." Her father's words spray a little spit into the air. "I don't know why your Comrade Popescu chose this method, but I can tell you that there is a far quicker, more efficient solution."

Andrei and I exchange glances and wait to see what Claudia will do. Andrei looks uncomfortable and mumbles something about having to go home to do his chores. He excuses himself and leaves quickly. I linger because I don't know what else to say and I feel sorry for Claudia, who looks like she is going to burst into tears.

"Tata, can't I just solve it the way Comrade Popescu showed us and I'll do it your way at home?"

"Absolutely not. The very basis of learning and teaching is to question your thinking, and you'll find out that there's more than one way of arriving at the same solution. I'm certain Comrade Popescu would approve of you exercising your gray matter. Do you know what gray matter is, Eva?" Her father blows this question like a big bubble into the dining room.

Before I have a chance to open my mouth, Claudia sighs and rolls her eyes. "No, Tata, she doesn't. What is it?"

"It's your brain, honey. It's what really matters!" Claudia's father laughs at his joke. Claudia looks upset, so I motion for her to come to the bathroom with me.

"Eva's got to go to the bathroom," she announces into the air. "I'm going to show her where it is and we'll be right back." Claudia walks backward without taking her eyes off her father, who continues to sit motionless at the head of the table with his hands folded on top of his cane handle. He nods at Claudia and looks up into the air from behind his dark glasses. When Claudia and I are finally in the bathroom with the door shut, I whisper, "Why don't you tell him that you'll do it *his* way and then just write it in the way Comrade Popescu wants us to do it? He can't *see* what you write in your notebook, and you won't get in trouble at school."

Claudia considers this for a moment and then whispers, "I can't do that. That would be lying to my father, and he can see right through that. Then I'll *really* get in trouble."

"What are you going to do?"

"I don't know." She shrugs. "I suppose I'll have to tell Comrade Popescu the truth and hope she doesn't get angry."

WHEN I GET HOME, Uncle Natan is lying on his cot in the dining room as if he has never left. I am really annoyed because I have to take my books back to our room and finish my homework on the bed. In the evening, Uncle Natan shows up at the supper table as well and no one says a word about it.

The next morning I notice that his cot has been slept in, so before taking off for school I stick my head into the kitchen and ask Grandma Iulia what's going on.

"He's getting a divorce," she says.

"Why? He's only been married three months!"

"You can't expect a man to stay married to a woman who encourages stealing." Grandma shakes a wooden spoon over a hot pot. "Aren't you late for school?"

"Mama," I ask as I'm getting into my pajamas that night, "why is Uncle Natan getting a divorce?"

"He and his wife, Rosa, had a big disagreement," Mama answers, "and when a couple doesn't get along, they stop living together and they get a divorce. That frees them up to go on with their lives."

"But, Mama, Uncle Natan's not going anywhere. He's back on his cot as if he's never left. How did he know so quickly that he can't get along with Rosa?"

"That's a good question, but I don't know the answer. All I can tell you is when people don't get along, there are little disagreements and there are big disagreements. My guess is that they had a very big disagreement."

"Grandma Iulia said that Rosa expected Uncle Natan *to steal*."

"Did she say that? It's possible, but you know, sweetheart, no one can really get between a husband and a wife. You'll never know the truth, because the truth is different depending on who's looking at it."

"Mama, isn't the truth the truth no matter what?"

"No. Most of the time the truth changes."

"I wish I knew what *really* happened," I say, and look up to see Mama's reaction.

"Then you'll just have to ask Uncle Natan. But all you're going to get is *his* side of the story, not Rosa's. And even if you were to ask her, you'd find that she disagrees with Uncle Natan, so you'll have to decide what the truth is for yourself."

"How can I decide what the truth is?" I ask.

"It isn't their truth that matters. It's *your* truth. And only you can decide that. Time for bed, darling." Mama tucks me in.

"Mama, are you and Tata going to get divorced?"

Mama's smile fades. "Of course not."

"But you don't always agree with Tata, do you?"

"Right. But we love each other far more than we disagree. You should never be afraid to disagree with anyone, Eva. It's just part of life. It takes a very big disagreement for two people to get a divorce."

"Please promise me that you won't get divorced, Mama, even if you have a big disagreement. Aunt Puica's said some awful things about Tata, and she thinks that you ought to divorce him."

"That's none of her business," Mama snaps. "Puica's got no right to talk about us. Don't you worry, we're not getting divorced."

"That's good, Mama, because I don't want you to, even though I'm not sure that Tata loves me."

"Oh my God, Eva, why would you ever say such a thing? Of course your father loves you! He loves you very, very much." Mama peers into my eyes as if I were hiding the truth there. I can tell that she believes Tata loves me, but I'm not sure that this is Tata's truth. If it is, then how come he never tells me he loves me?

THE HIDDEN TORAH

GRANDMA IULIA is sick in bed, her body propped up against her monogrammed, down-filled pillows. She is leaning against the headboard, her glasses perched on the tip of her nose, and her novel is turned facedown on her crisp, embroidered linens. Her feet are raised on three stacked pillows, her unpolished toenails are yellowing. There are dark brown, almost black leeches placed all over her legs. The shiny worms swell up as they suck the blood out of Grandma Iulia's thin veins. I am so disgusted, I want to run out and scream until all the walls of our house shake the worms off of Grandma's legs, but she isn't frightened. Instead, she smiles and takes my hand. Her hand is so soft and thin you can see the blue of her veins beneath her skin.

"Don't worry, the leeches are doing a fine job," she says, adjusting one of my braids.

"Do they hurt?" I ask her.

"No, not really," she says serenely. "The leeches are helping thin the blood in my legs to prevent a clot." She motions for me to sit next to her. "Last night I had my first phlebitis attack since the war,"

Grandma explains. "Dr. Khan is coming to check on me and re-move the leeches soon." I can't take my eyes off the slick leeches as they grow fat with her blood like inflated black balloons. Two min-utes later, Grandpa comes in to announce Dr. Khan's arrival.

Lunch is waiting for me in the dining room. Sabina has prepared my favorite sandwich, Sibiu salami sliced paper-thin and served with butter on crusty black bread. I usually love having lunch alone at our dining room table, but today I don't feel much like eating. I can't stop thinking about the leeches that are attached to Grandma Iulia's swollen legs, and I wonder how Dr. Khan will ever make those bloodsuckers let go of her. I am sipping my tea with lemon with a sugar cube tucked in behind my teeth when Grandpa comes in and sits across from me. He is hiding something in his right fist as he waits for me to finish eating.

"I'm not hungry, Grandpa," I tell him, sliding the plate away.

"That's all right," he says. He watches me intently as I sip my tea. His dark brown eyes are moist, and there are deep wrinkles etched beneath them, just above his cheekbones.

"I have a present for you, my little Leah." I wonder why he's using my middle name, but before I have a chance to ask, Grandpa opens his hand, revealing a small metal container nes-tled in his palm. I stare at it from across the table. Grandpa rises abruptly and comes over to my side. He places his present in my right hand and closes my fingers around it, his hand cupping mine.

"What is it?" I feel the cool, smooth metal in my hand.

"It's better than magic," Grandpa whispers.

I open my palm and look curiously at a metal cylinder. I know the name of the shape because we have just started to learn geometry in school.

"What's inside?"

"The truth," he answers. "If you hold on to this truth, always, your innermost and highest wishes will unfold. Open it up," he says. I pull off the cap and peer inside the small tube, where I can barely see the edges of a scroll rolled up tightly. Grandpa takes the cylinder out of my hand and taps it lightly onto the table until the top of the scroll emerges. He slides it out, unfolds the thin parchment with great care, and lays it flat on the table. The entire scroll is smaller than the palm of my hand. The text is in ink, but it isn't Romanian. The tiny black letters stand out against the cream of the parchment, and they are very beautiful.

"What does it mean?" I ask.

"I told you, the truth," he says, without taking his eyes off my face. "And when you learn to read it, study it, and believe it, what is in your highest interest comes true. Always." Grandpa cups his hand over mine and curls my fingers around the metal container. "Not to be taken lightly, but to be held in your heart at all times." He takes both my hands and taps them on my chest.

"How can I hold this in my heart, Grandpa, when I don't even understand what's written on it? Tell me what it means."

"I have trouble reading the text myself, but you will have to take my word for it, on faith. If you wish, you will study and understand the meaning of this writing in good time," he answers, and leaves the dining room as quietly as he entered.

I examine the scroll. It feels powerful, even though it is so small. I roll up the thin parchment and slide it back into the metal tube. I decide then and there not to tell anyone about this; not Mama or Grandma Iulia, not Uncle Max, certainly not Tata—not even Andrei. I kiss the cylinder and decide to put the magic powers of its contents to an immediate test.

I tiptoe to Aunt Puica's room and scratch lightly on her door, expecting her to bark back her usual "What do you want? Go away. Can't you see that I want to be left alone?" But instead, a calm voice I barely recognize answers.

"Come in," Aunt Puica says.

I enter her bedroom, where the black curtains are drawn as usual and my eyes have to adjust to the dark and blink against the sting of her cigarette smoke.

"What is it, sweetheart?" Aunt Puica looks up from her thick novel, her hand picking away at an ingrown toenail.

"Nothing," I answer, walking backward toward the door. "I just wanted to see how you are doing." Aunt Puica smiles at me as I depart, still clutching the hidden metal tube in my hand. It works! Grandpa's right. Even the most unlikely wishes, like Aunt Puica behaving kindly, come true when you believe they're possible. This *is* better than magic. This truth works.

I decide I must learn the meaning of the words written on the hidden parchment. I kiss the cylinder again, and this time I wish for Grandma Iulia to recover from phlebitis. I hide the metal tube along with all of my treasures in my new turquoise toiletry box that Renée gave me. It is always within reach on my nightstand. Sometimes I take it out and place it under my pillow, my hand warming the smooth metal before I drift off to sleep.

THE MOLE

A FEW DAYS LATER we have a visitor. Silviu, Uncle Max's closest friend and co-worker at the Ministry of Construction, is sunk into the most comfortable armchair in Aunt Puica's bedroom. Aunt Puica is at the dressmaker's, the only place she ever goes without Uncle Max. I am sprawled on the Oriental carpet with my drawing pad and colored pencils nearby. Neither Uncle Max nor his visitor takes any notice of me, and that's just fine by me.

Silviu is a quiet man with big hands and giant feet. He doesn't look as tall as he really is because he slouches. His knees are bent uncomfortably in the low chair with his hands resting on the arms. A cigarette dangles from his yellowed fingertips, and the rest of his hands are curved tightly around the chair fabric. He has a dark complexion and hair that's slicked back. His eyelids are so heavy, he looks half asleep, but his voice does not match his face. His lips are thin and curved at the corners into a fixed smile as his words shoot out.

"There are rumors, Max. There's going to be a crackdown at the office. It's time you cooled it with the Party jokes."

"Yeah, right," Uncle Max answers, dragging on his cigarette. "You are such an alarmist, Silviu. Do me a favor and mind your own business."

"It's time to keep your big mouth shut, Max. I'm telling you this for your own good."

"Are you threatening me, Silviu? I'm not even a Party member. *That* privilege is yours. What are they going to do, expel me from the Party I *don't* belong to?"

"Cut the sarcasm, Max, and listen. I'm risking my neck to keep you out of trouble." Silviu's Adam's apple moves up and down as he speaks, but his body does not flinch. "Max! You're not listening."

"Who asked you to risk anything?" Uncle Max snaps. "Perhaps you have delusions of grandeur and think that you're in charge at the office." Uncle Max pauses for a moment to inhale the smoke from his cigarette, his eyes riveted on his friend. "It was Comrade Manciulescu, wasn't it, who started this idiotic rumor?"

"The consequences, Max, are *severe and serious*," Silviu hisses back, blowing smoke in Uncle Max's direction. "A joke is only funny once, and yours are getting tired. Your job is at risk."

"Your mother, and your Communist Party!" Uncle Max shouts, smoke billowing out of his mouth. "Don't *ever* threaten me, Mr. 'Severe and Serious,' and don't play the mysterious informer with me!" he says, waving his cigarette.

"For God's sake, Max, this is not a threat. It's fair warning." Silviu leans forward in his chair. "I *happen to know* that the Securitate has recruited a mole within the department. That's a fact—not a rumor, Max." Silviu's face is flushed. "Manciulescu doesn't have a clue about any of this." Silviu falls back into the armchair and waits for the news to register.

"And *you* do? That's interesting, Silviu. Moles infiltrating *our* office?" Uncle Max's tone is nasal.

I open my mouth to ask what a mole is, but Uncle Max seems completely unaware of my presence. I thought moles were furry animals that burrowed underground. I pick up my pencil and start to draw a mole running through a tunnel. I color the earth brown, but above the ground, I add flowers and a house with people in it who are holding their hands over their ears.

Uncle Max scrutinizes his friend's face. "Do you expect me to believe any of this, Silviu?"

"Don't say I didn't warn you," Silviu snaps. "What do I have to do for you to believe me, Max, prove it?"

"Yes."

"You are so goddamn predictable, Max. I knew it would come to this." Silviu takes off his jacket. He rolls up his left shirtsleeve, revealing a wire connected to his wristwatch and leading to a hidden tape recorder in his shirt pocket. He presses the button. Uncle Max's voice cuts through the heavy smoke and echoes in the room. *"Severe and serious."*

"Turn it off." Uncle Max's voice sounds as if it belonged to someone else.

"I warned you—" Silviu starts to speak.

"Turn it off. And get out of here," Uncle Max interrupts.

"Don't worry, Max, I'm not going to turn you in," Silviu pleads, rewinding the tape. "Here, we'll erase this crap together. Don't freak out. I promise you, this conversation never existed. I'm your *friend*, you idiot! Do you think I'm the only mole? There are thousands of people planted in every ministry. Every office is covered. I just happen to be assigned to ours. If I wanted to turn you in, I wouldn't stick my neck out and expose myself to you. Promise me, Max, you'll watch what you say. Okay?"

Uncle Max has stopped listening. He looks up at his friend and sighs. "How much are they paying you for this, Silviu?"

Silviu glares at Uncle Max, his face hard, his thin lips still curled into the same fixed smile.

"Better yet," Max continues, "what the hell did they have on *you* to make you do such a thing? Did someone tell the Securitate that you're half a Yid and you can't be trusted with Party secrets?"

"Shut up!" Silviu yells, stubbing his cigarette out in the ashtray. "You're one lucky idiot because I still consider you a friend." Silviu puts on his jacket and leaves.

Uncle Max remains sitting and smoking in his white T-shirt and boxer shorts for a long while, his hairy legs swaying heavily over the edge of the bed.

"Hey, kid." He turns to me, becoming aware of my presence. "Hand me my pants and slippers from the armoire."

I open the armoire door with a squeak and watch him slip his legs into his pants. "Don't breathe a word about this to your aunt Puica, or anyone, okay?" He winks and slides his belt through his pants loops. His face is the color of cigarette ashes. I nod to let him know that I know how to keep a secret.

"I love you, Uncle Max."

"I love you too, kid."

OUT OF THE DARK

SOON AFTER SILVIU'S VISIT things begin to change. The other adults still go about their business as usual. But Uncle Max stops whistling on his way home from work. Instead, his heavy footsteps in the yard are followed by the sound of the front door latch. I run to the foyer to greet him, but Uncle Max stands for a moment in front of his bedroom in silence, hangs his hat on the doorknob, and takes off his shoes. Sometimes he rumbles under his breath a few curse words that end with "that imbecile mole," and when he catches me snickering, he asks, "So you think *moles* are funny too, huh?" I shake my head until my hair is in my eyes, but Uncle Max is already knocking lightly on his bedroom door and enters before an answer comes from within. He no longer asks me for his slippers, and I don't offer to fetch them. Aunt Puica and he remain in their room until suppertime.

At the dining table, the meal is eaten in relative silence, except for the occasional "Would you please pass the salt, the butter, or the bread?" Gone are the squabbles between my mother and Aunt Puica, as well as any political gossip exchanged by the men.

Something has shifted. There is a disturbing feeling of politeness in the air, the kind usually reserved for strangers.

On the few occasions when the grownups talk politics or anything that may compromise us, all the windows in the house are shut *hermetically* (Tata's word, not mine), and I am given the chore of covering the telephone with a giant down pillow as an added precaution. "Just in case the phone is tapped and the Securitate is listening in," Grandma Iulia says. Even then, the conversations are whispered.

THE NIGHT IS MOONLESS without any reflection from the terrace. Even the back of the bookcase that separates my bed from my parents' side of the room is invisible in the darkness, but I know it's there. The room is so quiet, it feels empty. I realize that Tata's even snores are missing. I call for my mother, but no one answers. I crawl out of my bed and into theirs, hoping to find the reassuring comfort of their bodies. The discovery that my parents are gone spreads through me from the pit of my stomach down to my toes and back up my spine all the way to where I feel my hair connect to my scalp.

I have been alone in our room before, but never at night. I listen for unusual sounds, but all I hear is my own shallow breath. I dart out from under the covers and run straight into Grandma Iulia and Grandpa Yosef's bedroom without knocking. I am met with the same stony silence, the same thick darkness. The dining room is empty as well. I can barely make out the outline of the dining table. Uncle Natan's cot is illuminated by the cinema's blinking blue light coming in through the window overlooking the back alley. His bedcovers are thrown back as if he has just gotten up. I choke back tears, wiping my face with my pajama sleeve, tasting salt. My heart is pounding. I scratch on Aunt Puica's door as softly as a mouse.

"Come in," a voice answers. I am relieved to hear Aunt Puica but wonder why Uncle Max is not in bed next to her. She is propped up against her giant pillows, the light from her cigarette barely illuminating her profile. "What do you want?" she asks.

"No one's home," I tell her.

"I know," she says, blowing the cigarette smoke out through her nostrils.

"Where is everybody?"

"Out. Standing in line at City Hall, waiting to file passport applications so that we can finally leave this hole. Thank God, Max can apply for both of us. I hate standing in line in the cold for anything."

"Leave?" I swallow. "Where are we going?"

"To Israel, of course, where all Jews belong."

"*Jews?*"

"Yes, of course, Jews, stupid. Do you think the Communists are dumb enough to let the goyim go too? No one would be left in this godforsaken country if they opened the borders to everyone."

I remain standing by her bed. I want to sink into the comfort of her armchair or, even better, I'd like to slide under the covers next to her and go back to sleep. But instead, I ask the obvious:

"*We are Jews?*"

"What the hell do you think we are, Nazis?"

"We are Jews," I repeat.

"Of course. Stop gaping at me and get back to bed," she says, waving me out with her cigarette.

• • •

BACK IN BED I pull my covers around me and wait to warm up. In the dark, I reach for the surface of my nightstand and find my turquoise box. I open it and feel for the small cylindrical container that Grandpa Yosef gave me just a few days ago. Even with my eyes closed, I can see the black letters written on the cream parchment that's hidden inside. I clutch the cool metal tube in my hand until it gets warm, and finally I fall asleep.

DURING SABINA'S VACATION

IN THE MORNING my parents' bed is still empty. Instead of Grandpa Yosef, it is Sabina who wakes me with a knock on the door, bringing a tray with a small pot of hot chocolate and pouring me a frothy cup. I breathe in the steaming aroma before I take a sip. The anticipation of my first taste is more delicious than the entire cup. I love the thick chocolate mingled with fresh cream, love dipping my upper lip into the froth to create a mustache I can lick off. Sabina has cut a crusty baguette into even, buttered slices and arranged them on the plate in a flower pattern, adding a touch of color in the middle with a dollop of strawberry jam. Rather than retire to the kitchen, she sits on the edge of my bed and watches as I eat.

"Master Yosef and your grandma Iulia went out last night with the rest of them," Sabina finally says, tucking a stray strand of hair into her turban. "I told Doamna Iulia that it's not a good idea for her to be standing in line all night in the cold, especially after her bout with phlebitis, but she wouldn't listen. She's bound to catch pneumonia and her legs will swell up again. Then she'll have to contend with those ugly leeches all over, and Dr. Khan will be angry, but she's a stubborn one, your grandma."

"Sabina, did you know that we're Jewish?"

Sabina stares at me blankly. "So? What's that got to do with anything?"

"Nothing," I lie, trying to act as casual as possible. "I was just wondering if we'll get in trouble with the Party."

"Don't you be worrying about the Party, Miss Eva. The Communists have only been around since the end of the war. Jews are nothing new around here."

"Why does everyone hate Jews?"

"How should I know? I'm not a Jew, thank God." Sabina crosses herself. "Maybe it's because Jews don't believe in Jesus," she says, smiling and showing off her gold front tooth. "But then," she adds with a huge grin, "neither do the members of the Communist Party, do they? So who are *they* to talk?"

"Do you believe in Jesus, Sabina?"

"Of course," she answers indignantly. "What a question!"

"Who was Jesus?" I ask, guessing that Jesus must be the same Lord whom Andrei is always talking about with such reverence.

Sabina looks at me funny and crosses herself again. "Jesus Christ, how can you *not* know who Jesus is, even if you *are* Jewish? What a shame! Jesus is our Lord, our savior, and the son of God." She puts her palms together as if in prayer and raises her eyes up past the cracks in our ceiling. "Even the poorest of the poor and the dumbest of the dumb from Bucovina, people who can't read and write, know that."

I don't comment, knowing that Sabina herself can barely read and write. She rolls on. "Why aren't those Bolsheviks down on their knees in church where they belong? If they're so high and mighty, why is everyone so miserable since they've come to power? I'll tell you why—because there's only one High and Mighty, and that's God. And Jesus Christ our Lord is His son, and this entire country has lost sight of that. That's why we are being punished with this Communist scourge. It's a damn shame when children like you don't even know who Jesus is. They ought to teach you about Jesus in school." I have never heard Sabina express an opinion so passionately about anything before.

"They don't teach us religion in school, Sabina," I try to explain, but she interrupts.

"I'll tell you who Jesus was. Jesus gave his life for you and me. He preached peace, and instead, his own people, the Jews, betrayed him."

"Jesus was Jewish?" I ask, stunned.

"Yes," Sabina answers.

"Then how come people hate Jews?"

Sabina doesn't seem to hear my question. "The Romans crucified Jesus and placed a crown of thorns on his head," she continues. "He died on Good Friday for all of our sins, and he rose again on Easter Sunday." She crosses herself again.

"They took him off the cross after he died?"

"Yes. But he was resurrected."

"What's resurrected?" I ask.

"It means he came back from the dead."

"Is that possible?"

"Only if you are Jesus."

"Are you sure about that?"

"Absolutely. Do you know anyone else who was resurrected?"

"No," I have to admit, but I think that maybe there are other people who might have been resurrected and we just didn't know about them since they're not as famous as Jesus. I wonder why Jews don't believe in Jesus and why a Jew would betray another Jew. I save these questions for Grandpa Yosef. But I still don't understand why most people hate Jews, especially if Jesus was Jewish.

I wonder if Andrei will stop being my friend once he finds out that I'm Jewish. And I'm worried about how I can explain to him that Jews are just like everyone else when I don't even know the difference between a Jew and a Christian. All I know is that yesterday I wasn't Jewish and today I am. I am still the same person, yet everything has changed overnight.

"Sabina, do you hate me because I'm Jewish?" I ask, looking up at her turban.

Sabina crosses herself again before answering. "Hate you? Why would you ever think such a thing, Miss Eva? I *love* you," she says, giving me a huge hug. "You didn't kill Jesus, even if your kind did."

"Is *that* why people hate Jews?"

"I don't know why anyone hates anybody. I guess many people hate the Jews for killing Jesus, but I think they're wrong. We may as well hate the Italians, who are Catholic, just for being descendants of the Romans, because they were in power at the time and ordered Jesus' crucifixion. But that would be just as wrong as hating Jews. If you ask me, hating anyone is against what Jesus preached." Sabina shakes her head, her turban slipping and settling a little crooked right above her forehead.

"Jesus said, 'Thou shalt love thy neighbor as thyself.' When you believe that, there's no room for hate in your heart." Sabina tears a piece of baguette and chews loudly, the few teeth left in her mouth having a hard time with the crust.

"Speaking of Jesus," she continues in between bites, "I'm going home on Friday for my nephew's christening, so I'm counting on you to set the table while I'm gone. Agreed?"

"Are you coming back?"

"Of course. I'll be back in a week. Are you going to miss me?"

I wrap my arms around Sabina and give her a big hug, and as she hugs me back I feel her belly shaking up and down with laughter under the folds of her peasant skirts.

MAMA AND TATA are home from work on a Monday, but we're not going on vacation. Uncle Max shows up early for lunch, and even Uncle Natan is resting on his cot, hiding as usual behind his newspaper. Aunt Puica hasn't emerged from her bedroom, and Grandma Iulia has disappeared into the kitchen. Grandpa Yosef is taking a nap. The house feels just like it did the night they were all standing in line at City Hall, waiting to fill out passport applications so we can leave the country. Except now the house isn't empty. Everyone is home and the mood is somber.

Since Sabina is away at her nephew's christening, Grandma Iulia has brought in Margareta, a temporary housekeeper from Transylvania, to help with the laundry. Margareta takes a big knife and starts hacking away at a huge bar of brown soap. She places the soap slices in a glass bowl, eyeing me.

"What are you staring at, Miss Eva? Doesn't your Sabina slice soap for the washing machine?" Margareta asks.

"Nope. She grates it like Parmesan cheese," I whisper.

"Is that so?" Margareta smirks. "Let Sabina work harder, if she's got nothing better to do. Soap dissolves just as quickly when it's sliced in chunks as when it's grated. Too much work."

I notice that Margareta is younger that Sabina, and she doesn't wear a turban or peasant skirts. She's wearing a khaki army skirt and matching shirt with buttoned lapels at the shoulders. A small golden pin with sheaves of wheat, Romania's Communist crest, is pinned onto her shirt collar. Her two thick braids meet in a crown that's neatly pinned at the top of her head.

"Eva," Grandma Iulia's voice calls from the kitchen, "please set the table."

I leave Margareta with her bowl of soap slices by the washing machine and run into the dining room. Everyone except Grandma Iulia is already seated at the table, but eating seems to be the last thing on their minds. They don't notice me as I lay out the table-cloth and place the silverware and plates in front of them. After I set out the water glasses and napkins, I sit at my place, but still no one mentions food.

Mother is sitting across from Grandpa Yosef, with her hands folded on the table. "I don't know what else to tell you, Papa," she says. "It happened so quickly. Maria, the principal's secretary, came into the ballet studio and apologized for interrupting my class. She told me to report to Comrade Nicolai's office right away. When I got there, Comrade Nicolai just handed me a letter she had received early this morning from the Ministry of Education. The letter states that any citizen who has recently filed for a passport to emigrate to Israel is to be dismissed from work immediately." Grandpa is speechless, waiting for my mother to continue. "Comrade Nicolai started crying as she hugged me goodbye," Mama says. "That's all there is to it, Papa. I don't have a job anymore."

"That makes two of us," my father whispers as his fingers press some loose tobacco into the bowl of his pipe.

"Make that three," Uncle Natan chimes in, making a snorting sound from behind his paper.

"Stop that!" Aunt Puica snaps. "It's so disgusting."

"I can't help it," Uncle Natan says, embarrassed. "I've got allergies."

"And I thought I had it bad." Uncle Max sighs. "They told me that due to my indispensable function as an expert housepainter, I get to keep my job at half pay at the Ministry of Construction."

"This isn't funny, Max. What are we going to do?" Aunt Puica's voice is filled with panic.

"Survive," Grandpa Yosef answers.

"How?" Aunt Puica's voice is shrill. "Do you propose that all seven of us, plus the Child, live on Max's half salary? What about Sabina?"

"I don't know yet *how* we will survive," Grandpa says, "but we will. Iulia and I still have our pension. We didn't receive any notices."

"Your pension will buy us just enough food to impale on a toothpick," Aunt Puica says with a smirk.

"And we all have some savings," Grandpa continues.

"How long do you think our savings will last?" Aunt Puica asks. "A week? A month, if we all go on a diet? What about the rent and the phone? Or maybe you think we should give up the phone and live in the dark ages all over again?"

My parents reach for each other's hands. Uncle Max finally speaks, choosing his words carefully. His mustache twitches with each word. "With all due respect, Papa, we are not living in the old days, when you could replace a job with another job. Today there's only one employer, the Communist Party." His words hang in the air.

"I am well aware of that," Grandpa Yosef answers. "We're just going to have to be creative."

"Creative? Papa, have you lost your mind?" Aunt Puica raises her voice. "Do you want us to get so creative that we all land in jail for working illegally?"

"Sweetheart," Grandpa Yosef says to her, "why get upset? It's not going to help the situation. Let's eat. I'm hungry. We'll all feel better with a little bit of food in our stomachs. Eva, go into the kitchen and help your grandmother bring out the food."

IN THE MORNING, my parents are in bed, since they have nowhere else to go. It feels like a holiday, but I am late for school. I wash quickly and run into the kitchen for my hot chocolate. Still tasting the sweetness in my mouth, I slide my schoolbag straps over my shoulders and race down the stairs, jumping the last two stairs into our yard, where I nearly knock Margareta over.

"Watch yourself," she mumbles indignantly as she struggles with a huge valise.

"I'm sorry, I'm late!" I answer breathlessly and run off wondering why Margareta is leaving before Sabina has returned.

AT SCHOOL no one mentions anything about their parents losing their jobs, so I assume that my parents must be the only ones. I am so relieved I never told any of my friends that I'm Jewish.

When I come home, I find Tata sitting on the terrace floor with a bunch of newspapers laid out in front of him. He is holding the vase that usually stands on top of our Biedermeier chest of drawers, the vase that once belonged to his mother, which curiously still smells of lilac branches and roses. The vase is broken into many pieces; the only part intact is the base. Tata is so intent on gluing the pieces back together that he doesn't even look up when I step onto the terrace.

"What happened?" I ask.

"I found it broken on top of the bureau," Tata says without looking up. "I was going to ask you if you knew anything about how this happened."

"No," I stammer. "I didn't see it broken, but I was late for school and I ran out."

"Well, it was broken when your mother and I got up this morning."

"I didn't do it, Tata, I swear."

"I hope not," Tata says as he holds a sharp shard of porcelain with a pair of tweezers and tries to fit it together with another broken piece. I notice that his face is flushed, but Tata's hands are as steady as if he were doing surgery on a person. "Who would do such a thing without owning up?" he asks, never lifting his eyes from his work to look at me.

"I don't know," I tell him, and let out a long breath. "But I saw Margareta leave this morning with a big valise."

"She left this morning?" Tata asks.

"I bumped into her in the yard on my way to school."

"I thought she wasn't due to leave until Sabina comes back, not for at least another week or so. Go ask Grandma. Hurry!"

Grandma Iulia is napping with her mouth half open. The book she was reading is resting on top of her duvet. My entrance startles her even though I tiptoe in.

"I'm sorry I woke you," I say.

"That's all right, sweetheart. It's not good for me to nap during the day. Now I'll be up all night again."

"Grandma, Tata's upset because he found his mother's vase broken in pieces on top of our bureau, and Margareta is gone."

Grandma sits up at once. "What do you mean *she's gone?*"

"I saw her leave this morning with a big valise."

"Oh no," Grandma groans, reaching for her robe. She opens the armoire door and slides her hand under the stacked linens. Not finding what she is looking for, she takes everything out, placing all the crisp sheets and pillowcases on her bed and sifting through each one. "I was afraid of this," she murmurs.

"What's wrong, Grandma?"

"That little witch did a lot more damage than break your father's vase," she whispers through pursed lips. "She stole the only piece of jewelry I had left."

"What jewelry?"

"After the war I sold everything. I'm not one for baubles, and with the Communist takeover, it was too dangerous to keep any gold and stones anyway. But I saved a gold chain with a Magen David pendant for you."

"What's a Magen David, Grandma?"

"It's the Star of David, darling, the Jewish star. But it's gone now. I am so sorry," she says. Her eyes are full of tears.

"That's okay, Grandma. I wouldn't be able to wear it in school anyway."

"I know, but I wanted you to have it. I was hoping you could wear it someday."

"It's not your fault, Grandma," I tell her, trying to make her feel better, but she is as upset as Tata. Except she can't glue the pieces back together.

CINE ŞTIE CÂŞTIGĂ—
THOSE IN THE KNOW ARE IN THE DOUGH

UNCLE NATAN shows up in the dining room with a bunch of books and plops them down next to mine. I'm doing my homework. He sits across from me, opens his notebook, and starts writing on the lined pages with a squeaky pen. Every now and then he takes off his thick, greasy glasses and wipes them with his T-shirt. When he does this, he always makes a snorting sound as if he's about to sneeze. His nostrils flare and I can see the black hairs sticking out of his nose, but his sneeze never happens.

"Uncle Natan?" I ask softly, not wanting to disturb him.

"What?" he answers, without looking up from his notebook.

"What are you studying?"

"I'm reading up on Charlie Chaplin," he says, sliding one of the books across the table so I can see it. The book has a black-and-white photograph on its cover of a little man with a mustache. The guy is wearing a round hat, and his pants and shoes are too large for him.

"Who's Charlie Chaplin?" I ask.

"Charlie Chaplin is the greatest comedian in the world," Uncle Natan declares, his frog eyes looking up over his glasses. "Your grandpa used to show his films all the time, when we owned the movie house. Before the war, I saw every Charlie Chaplin movie that was ever made, at least three times."

"Is he funny?"

"Hilarious."

"I wish I could see him," I answer. "What made him so funny?"

"Everything. You see the outfit he's wearing?" Uncle Natan asks, pointing to Chaplin's baggy pants. "He created this character called 'the Tramp,' who always gets into trouble."

"What's so funny about the Tramp getting into trouble?"

"People like to laugh at other people's misfortunes. It's called 'comic relief.'"

I can tell Uncle Natan is getting impatient with me, but I'm too curious to stop. "Why are you studying him if you've already seen all of his movies?" I ask.

Uncle Natan shuts his Charlie Chaplin book with a thud and answers me in a solemn voice. "I've been invited to be a contestant on a new game show on the radio, *Those in the Know Are in the Dough*. I could win a lot of money if I do well."

"You're going to be on the radio?" I ask, astounded.

"I am." Uncle Natan taps the end of a cigarette against the table and lights his match with a single flick of his wrist. His nostrils push out two long tunnels of smoke as he continues. "You're going to have to be a good girl and allow me to study so that I can win for all of us. We need the money now."

"You mean because no one has a job anymore, except for Uncle Max?"

Uncle Natan ignores my question. Instead he announces, "If I do well, I'll buy you any present you want."

"You will?" I'm so excited I pinch myself right above my knee-highs under the table.

"Yes, I'm going to buy everyone a present. Grandma Iulia and Grandpa Yosef, your mother and father, Aunt Puica and Uncle Max, even Sabina."

"How does the game show work? Are you sure you can win?" I ask.

"I hope so. They give every contestant a choice of category, such as geography, history, economics, Romanian literature, theater, and so on. I chose film, of course."

"Of course," I add quickly. "But what made you choose Charlie Chaplin?"

"Why not?" Uncle Natan asks. "They gave me a choice between comedy and horror. No contest there, but I still have to study."

"How much money can you make?" I wonder out loud.

"Enough to buy you two presents instead of one. What would you like?"

"I don't know," I answer quickly, hoping he won't change his mind. "I definitely want a blue velvet dress with a white lace collar and also a toy or a game, but I'm not sure what yet."

"Done. The blue velvet dress will be yours," Uncle Natan says, smiling. "You let me know what toy you want and I'll add that to my list. But now you'll have to run along so I can study, okay?"

I don't mind giving up the dining room table for a while, not if I can get my blue velvet dress and a toy out of it. On my way out I bump into Uncle Max, who's just arrived from work. Uncle Max already knows all about Uncle Natan's upcoming appearance on *Those in the Know Are in the Dough.*

"Natan's going to win," he reassures me, picking me up in his arms and giving me an itchy kiss with his mustache.

"How do you know, Uncle Max?"

"Because Natan's smarter than all of us put together." Uncle Max laughs. "That boy's got a photographic memory. If *I* had his brains, I would be a doctor living the good life in South Africa, which is exactly where he could have been today if he weren't scared of his own shadow. You can thank your grandmamma for that. She's coddled him as if he were still in diapers." Uncle Max takes me into his room and sinks into his armchair with a sigh. He loosens his shoelaces and takes off his shoes. "What is this, Eva? I can't count on you for my slippers anymore?"

"They're under the armchair," I tell him, sliding his slippers under his feet. "Uncle Max, do you really think Uncle Natan's got a chance at winning on *Those in the Know Are in the Dough?*"

"Absolutely. Unless he blows it all on the last question."

"What do you mean?"

"They give you an all-or-nothing choice at the end. If you answer the ninth question correctly, then you have a chance to double your earnings. If you blow it, then you've just forfeited all of your previous winnings and go home with nothing. What do you think, that Communists are stupid? No one likes to give away money. That's why they always save the most difficult question for last. Of course, Uncle Natan can pass on answering the ninth question, in which case he gets to keep all his earnings without doubling them. That's up to him."

"Wow. Do you think he'll want to answer the ninth question?"

"I have no idea. It all depends on how he does up to that point. If he gets eight questions right, then chances are he'll have the correct answer to the ninth as well."

"I want him to *win big*, Uncle Max." The thought of losing my beautiful blue velvet dress even before I get it is dreadful.

I'M DYING TO FIGURE OUT what kind of game I can get, but I don't know where to look. I've never been to a toy store. I'm not even sure that they exist in Bucharest. Where do toys come from, anyway? Certainly not from the farmers' market where I got my chicken with Grandpa Yosef.

"What are you daydreaming about?" Uncle Max asks.

"I still haven't figured out what kind of toy I should ask Uncle Natan to buy me when he wins on *Those in the Know Are in the Dough*."

Uncle Max looks at me with a big grin on his face. "How about I take you out to the toy show that just arrived in town? Then you can have something to dream about."

"There's a toy show in town?"

"There is. There are marvelous toys on display from abroad. What do you say? Want to go?"

"Can we go right now?"

"Now? I just got home and haven't even eaten. Your aunt Puica will get mad if I skip a meal."

"Can't you eat when we get back, Uncle Max?"

"Go grab your coat," he says.

I'm in the hall closet in a flash, tugging my coat to loosen it from the hanger that's too high for me to reach. The coat lands on the floor in a pile of dust, and I push my arms through the armholes so quickly that my sweater bunches up. Uncle Max grabs his hat and shouts in the direction of the kitchen, "Puica, I'm going out with the Child. We'll be back in a couple of hours and we'll eat then."

Uncle Max lets the front door slam behind us before hearing a reply. I take his hand and pull him down the stairs and through the front yard before anyone has a chance to call us back.

THE TOY SHOW is in a huge, crowded tent in one of Bucharest's central squares. Parents and kids are fighting for space around the display tables to see the latest toy imports. Most toys come from other Communist bloc countries, like Hungary, Bulgaria, Poland, and the USSR, but there are a few tables featuring dolls from France and board games from Italy. Those tables draw the largest crowds. I let go of Uncle Max's hand and crawl on all fours, maneuvering between the spectators' legs and feet until I reach a table. I pull myself up with both hands anchored to the edge of the table and take a good look.

"Eva, *where are you?*" Uncle Max's voice floats above a sea of drab winter kerchiefs and fur hats that smell of cigarette smoke.

"I'm here," I answer, but I don't care if he's heard me. I only have eyes for what's on that table. The track before me is a whirlwind of speeding color. Ribbons of red, blue, and yellow toy cars are racing one another as voices from around the table cheer them on.

"Red, red, revolution red! Goooooo, red!" a boy with a red ski cap is hollering while waving his fists in the air. "True blue. Go blue. Blue is true!" chant a father and son in unison. "Yellow, yellow, yellow brings good luck," an old man with gnarly hands is muttering under his breath while shaking his finger at his favorite car as if he could magically make it win the race.

I am so hypnotized by the speeding cars that I cannot blink. I imagine myself in the driver's seat of the red car with the air rushing past my ears. My eyes are glued to the road. My mind wills the wheels to respond to my commands. "Go steady on the right and gain on yellow." The car swerves right, following my thoughts. The finish line is in the distance, but a blue car is gaining on me to the left. I press on the accelerator and change lanes. There are blinking lights and flags waving as my car races past the gate. "We have a winner here! Red is the winner!" a voice booms as the blood rushes to my ears. I step on the brakes, and the car rolls to a halt.

A shrill whistle blows directly above my head. I look up and see Uncle Max standing in front of the table with the race cars, with two fingers stuck in his mouth, signaling everyone to come to attention.

"Ladies and gentlemen, comrades and esteemed members of the Communist Party . . . has anyone ever seen anything as exciting as this recent import from our lowlife capitalist neighbors? Imagine, comrades, if we work our butts off and pool all of the cash from around this table, perhaps we can buy a real car for all of us to *cooperatively* share by the end of the century. Excuse me, I meant by the end of our next five-year cooperative economic plan. But it really doesn't matter, since we don't have far to drive. We can drive around the block in Bucharest, or around this game board, because God knows, we can't drive out of this country, not even if we're Jewish. Forgive me, comrades, how stupid of me to mention God. No, we must be firm believers in Mother Russia and our savior, the Communist Party." Uncle Max is surveying the tent with a straight face, but I can see the hint of a smile breaking under his mustache.

I lower myself onto my hands and knees and slide under the table again. Doesn't Uncle Max remember Silviu's warning? "Comrades, *this* is the closest any of us will ever come to sitting our asses down in the driver's seat of one of these vehicles." An uncomfortable silence descends. I get up and grab Uncle Max's hand and tug at him to go. Everyone around us is smiling sheepishly.

A man behind the table wearing an official-looking name tag eyes Uncle Max carefully and breaks into a polite smile. "Sir, are you interested in purchasing this game?" he asks.

"I am." Uncle Max takes his glasses out of his shirt pocket and wipes them with his handkerchief.

I am so worried that Uncle Max will get into trouble with his big mouth that I don't even care about the game anymore. He'll definitely catch hell from Aunt Puica for buying it, especially since his money now pays everyone's bills. She's always reminding me, "You must allow Max his rest, Eva. He doesn't have the energy to play with you like he used to. We can't afford for him to get sick."

"Let's go!" I whisper and pull him away. But Uncle Max is walking confidently out the door with the race-car game in a shopping bag.

Back home, I'm relieved that Uncle Max doesn't allow me to play with my new game. "This must be put away until Natan wins on *Those in the Know Are in the Dough*," Uncle Max tells me as he slides the brown box tied with red string onto a high shelf in his armoire. "We'll have a big celebration and unveil the game then. Don't tell anyone that I bought it. It will be a great surprise," he reassures me with a loud kiss on my cheek. "Natan better win, because I spent three months' rent on your game."

• • •

THE COUNTDOWN BEGINS. Every day after school I run into the dining room to check on Uncle Natan's progress, but he just says a curt hello and ignores me. He is intent on reading up to the last minute about Charlie Chaplin. His notes have filled an entire notebook.

On the day of the contest Uncle Natan is decked out in a gray suit, white shirt, and navy silk tie. His hair is slicked back with brilliantine, and his thick glasses are grease-free. The corner of a folded white handkerchief peeks out of his jacket pocket. His black shoes have been polished to a mirror shine. On his way out, Grandma Iulia spits three times into the palm of her right hand and pats him on his head — "to ward off the evil Communist eyes," she says, giving him a hug. An hour later, Grandpa Yosef brings his Grundig radio from their bedroom into the dining room, where we are all gathered to listen to *Those in the Know Are in the Dough*.

The music swells and fades as the show's announcer comes on. "Good evening, comrades." His voice sounds as if he's holding his nose. "Tonight we are proud to bring you two contestants ready to prove once again that *those in the know are in the dough*! Comrade Roxana Grigore has chosen geography as her category, and her topic will be the Great Rivers of Europe. Please welcome Comrade Grigore." The music swells again as everyone at our dining room table waits intently for the announcer to introduce Uncle Natan. "Our second contestant is Comrade Natan Natanson, who has chosen film as his category and the great comedian Charles Chaplin as his topic." Everyone at our table bursts into nervous laughter and starts to applaud. Grandpa is still clapping long after the music has stopped.

"Shhh, they're starting," Aunt Puica says, and we all fall silent. The rules of the game are spelled out by the announcer, and he begins by asking, "Comrade Grigore, are you ready to play *Those in the Know Are in the Dough?*" The audience roars, *"Yes!!!"*

I am too anxious for Uncle Natan's turn to listen to Comrade Grigore's answers about the great rivers of Europe. Besides, who cares about a bunch of rivers we're never going to see? Tata once told me that, before the Communists came to power, you could travel throughout Europe, and anywhere else in the world. All you needed was a passport and money. But now the Communist Party issues passports only to officials on diplomatic business abroad and once in a while to performers or artists who are on tour. That's how my cousin Mimi got to see the Great Wall of China.

Comrade Grigore blows the eighth question, so she doesn't get a chance to double her winnings.

"Congratulations, Comrade Grigore! What are you going to do now that you are seven thousand lei richer?"

"I'm going to take my husband and little boy on a beach vacation to Constanţa and perhaps on a day cruise on the Danube."

"What a great idea. Let's all give a hand to Comrade Grigore, a true lover of rivers!"

Grandma Iulia darts to the kitchen door and sticks her head in. "Come on, Sabina, Natan's on now." Sabina emerges from the kitchen and tucks the folds of her turban behind her ears so she can hear better. Grandpa Yosef pulls out a chair and motions for her to join us. Mama and Tata are holding hands under the table in a tight fist. Aunt Puica and Uncle Max both have forgotten the cigarettes hanging between their lips. The smoke is rising toward the ceiling, and the ashes are accumulating. Grandpa is hunched by the radio, his ear right up against the speaker. And Grandma sits in her chair, her hands clasped in her lap.

For the first eight questions, Uncle Natan gets every answer right. Everyone around the table breaks into nervous laughter and applauds after each of his answers.

"Comrade Natan Natanson," the announcer's nasal twang resumes over the airwaves. "We now pose the most difficult question of all. Do you want to try your luck with question number nine for a chance to double your winnings? Take your time . . . You've got exactly thirty seconds to make up your mind. Comrades, let's see what's it going to be . . . Double . . . or nothing?" The theme from the game show is playing.

"Don't be a fool, Natan, go for it!" Uncle Max shouts at the radio.

Aunt Puica starts to giggle. Sabina's mouth is gaping open, her turban slightly askew. Tata whispers in Mama's ear loud enough for me to hear, "He's not going to take it." Grandpa's ear is still glued to the radio, while Grandma shakes her head and mutters, "A bird in the hand is a bird in the hand."

Nine thousand lei or eighteen thousand lei—that's a lot of money for the grownups to buy food and pay bills for a few months. Who cares? I can see myself already dancing in my new blue velvet dress at our big family celebration. All of my younger cousins will be green with envy.

"Your time is up, Comrade Natanson. Which is it going to be? Will you take the money or take your chance?"

"I'll take the money," Uncle Natan answers flatly.

"Good boy," Grandma Iulia says, nodding her head.

"You *idiot*!" Uncle Max shouts and leaves the room.

"Max, come back here!" Aunt Puica yells after him in a panic. "They're about to ask him the ninth question, to see if he would have gotten it right."

"Who cares?" Uncle Max hollers back.

"Of course he would have gotten it right," my father says with a disgusted smile.

"Who asked you?" Aunt Puica quips.

Mama turns to Tata. "Ignore her rotten mouth."

The announcer's voice continues. "Comrade Natanson, just to satisfy our curious listeners and our studio audience, who have all been rooting for you, please answer the ninth question, which comes to you in two parts. What is Charlie Chaplin's wife's maiden name, and who was her famous father?"

Uncle Natan answers without hesitation. "Charlie Chaplin's wife's name is Oona O'Neill, and her father was the American playwright Eugene O'Neill."

"You are so right, Comrade Natanson. Unfortunately, we cannot count your answer since you declined our double or nothing offer. Congratulations! You still get to go home with nine thousand more lei in your pocket. I almost forgot to ask, what are you going to do with the money?"

"I'm going to share it with my family. My niece has asked for a blue velvet dress and a toy, which she will surely get now."

"You are a generous man, Comrade Natanson. Good luck, and don't forget . . . *Those in the know are in the dough!*"

MY DREAM COMES TRUE. We have a huge family get-together, for which Grandma Iulia cooks for an entire week. I don't know how much the money helps with the household bills, but it surely puts everyone in a better mood. Sabina sweeps every corner of the house, gets up on a ladder to dust away the cobwebs, and applies a thick coat of wax to all the furniture. Grandpa Yosef goes to the market several times that week and brings back every goody he can get his hands on: a hard Hungarian salami from Sibiu, beef bones for vegetable soup, new potatoes and tiny green peas for Grandma's Viennese potato salad, feta cheese and black Kalamata olives for Aunt Puica's "Oriental" salad, and chopped meat from which Mama makes *mititei*—herb-spiced Romanian hamburgers in the shape of little sausages—and Greek-style grape leaves stuffed with rice. Aunt Puica is in charge of the hors d'oeuvres, the salad, and the drinks. My mother also bakes a chocolate cake using a stash of chocolate bars that had been saved for just such an occasion, and Grandma bakes her famous *cozonac*.

The entire house smells like a birthday party. I take in the aromas wafting from the kitchen and dance from room to room in anticipation of our guests' arrival. All of Grandma's siblings are expected along with their families. Grandpa's sisters will also come with their own spouses and children. Uncle Lazăr, Grandpa's older brother, is invited as well, which is a huge concession on Grandma Iulia's part since she has never forgiven him for his hand in our being detained behind the iron curtain to live like cattle in this godforsaken, Communist, cockroach-infested country where we are all bound to rot—unless, God willing, God will intervene.

TRUE TO HIS WORD, Uncle Natan gives my mother money to buy my blue velvet dress, which magically appears laid out on my bed before the party, complete with white lace collar and mother-of-pearl buttons. The dress is a perfect fit. The blue velvet is as deep and as soft as the view of the dusk sky from our terrace in early summer. How did Mama know the exact color I had been dreaming about? How did she figure my size without my trying on the dress? When things go this well, I learn not to ask questions and just be happy. I put the dress on and linger in front of the armoire mirror. Nothing feels tight. Everything flows in the right places. I so wish I could wear this dress to school every single day. Then perhaps I could lift up the hem of my stiff uniform and show Andrei the color of my dress.

GRANDMA'S SISTERS AND BROTHERS arrive with their children, who are not children at all; they are close to my parents' age, and they bring *their* children, my second cousins, whom I rarely see, except at birthday parties. But this is no ordinary birthday party, it is a big family celebration, and all of us kids run around, playing hide-and-seek behind the furniture, scaring each other with *boos* and horror tales, filling the entire house with new energy.

The food keeps coming out of the kitchen as steadily as the flow of gossip and the noise escalates. Political rumors, however, are uttered in whispers. "Have you heard that they might open up immigration to Israel?" my cousin Carol asks Uncle Max, who nods knowingly. "I heard Mrs. Mandelbaum is expecting a shipment of silk stockings from Hungary," Aunt Fanny confides to Mama.

The men retire to the dining room, where the table is draped with a heavy needlepoint rug, one of Grandma's prized possessions from before the war that appears out of hiding. Bets are made and cigarettes are chain-smoked as the men play backgammon, chess, and cards.

The women move from bedroom to bedroom in small groups and talk fashion. Aunt Puica brings out two dog-eared French magazines from under her bed. Every seam on every dress featured in those magazines is carefully analyzed, the fabric's weight, texture, and color are discussed in detail, the necklines scrutinized, the proportions of the hemlines in relation to the shoes assessed. Oh, the shoes! The shoes are the biggest heartache, because they cannot be made by hand by a clever Romanian seamstress with a good eye who can copy anything she is shown in a French magazine. The shoes have to be smuggled in from Italy at great cost, and you have to have money tucked away for just such a rare occasion, because you never know when a shipment might arrive. Good timing, in fashion as in life, is everything.

My cousins eye my new velvet dress, but none of them comment on it until I bring it up. They all ask where I got the dress. I tell them that Uncle Natan bought it with money from his radio show winnings, but I don't know where my mother found it. We all run to find Mama and ask her. She says that it was custom-made by the same seamstress who makes the costumes for the national ballet corps. "I gave her your white cotton dress for size and told her to make it just a bit larger," Mama says. "She did a great job, don't you agree?"

I am thrilled that my dress is so special you can't buy it in a cooperative store, and all my girl cousins touch the fabric with great longing and get in line to try it on when Mama intervenes. "You can feel the fabric as long as your hands are clean, but you may not try it on because I don't want the fabric to stretch or rip. This is Eva's dress, and only she is allowed to wear it."

I am relieved, because I don't want to get undressed in our drafty bedroom and stand in my white underwear while my cousins gawk at me.

It isn't as easy with the race-car game. Mama mentions it to make my cousins feel better, and they start to screech — "*We want to race! We want to race! We want to race!*"—until Uncle Max brings the game to the dining room.

Once the race-car game is set up on the dining room table, everything in the house stops. It's as if the game contains some kind of a magnet or silent siren that brings everyone together. Uncle Natan shuts his backgammon case while the men put out their cigarettes and gather around the table. The women drift in, their voices quieting to murmurs. Grandma and Grandpa emerge from the kitchen, with Sabina following close behind them. Even Andrei, who hasn't been invited because Mama told him the party is *only for family*, appears from upstairs.

Uncle Max sets up the game in silence. The motor under the track starts to whir as the cars pick up speed. We move our heads from side to side, following the bands of color looping around the track in a hypnotic trance. It is clear that the race-car game no longer belongs to me. We are all dreaming about what could be, yet the outcome of the dream is different for each of us.

TATA BUILDS HIS DARKROOM

NOW THAT UNCLE MAX is our sole "provider," everyone treats him with exaggerated politeness. Mama has stopped squabbling with Aunt Puica about favoring Uncle Max at dinnertime with a larger portion on his plate. And Aunt Puica is careful not to overdo it because she knows she'll get in trouble with Grandma Iulia.

On the same day that my parents lost their jobs, all the other Jews in the city who had filed for passport applications got fired as well. Virtually overnight, the entire Jewish population in Bucharest became unemployed. The few exceptions were those who hadn't yet filed—Jews without family who did not wish to leave the country, or those who held high-paying jobs in key positions within the Communist Party and who were content to stay. There were some who were too old or too sick to emigrate.

"Bucharest will have no cultural life once all the Jews have gone," Tata jokes with Mama between drags on his pipe. "The Gentiles want to leave just as bad, but they don't have an excuse like we do—to be *repatriated* in their homeland. Look who's leaving: Jewish teachers and other artists like us, whom undoubtedly no other country wants, except Israel. Also economists, lawyers, engineers, scientists, doctors, nurses, and architects—maybe other countries want them. Who knows? Maybe we've got a few loud-mouth big shots sprinkled in, since we Jews certainly don't have a shortage of those. For now, whether we've been big shots or clerks—we're *all* unemployed and unemployable. Our glorious Party has made certain that unemployment is the *great leveler.*" Tata's voice is bouncing off our bedroom walls while Mama listens. "Just as death was the *great leveler* during the war. Did you know, Stefica, that in America they have such a thing as *unemployment benefits?* Can you believe that there could ever be a benefit to being unemployed?"

Mama sits on the bed, listening in silence and knitting the sleeve of a sweater. Seeing that she has nothing to add, Tata concludes, "Of course, some of us are just too important and therefore indispensable to the Party, like Max. He gets to keep his job, at half pay. After all, the great proletariat needs a housepainter who can paint the Party's gathering halls spanking white for their committee meetings."

"That's enough, Gyuri." Mama sighs, looking up from her knitting. "I won't have you speaking ill of Max. He's putting bread on the table for all of us. We're lucky he's working." Tata looks at Mama in amusement but adds nothing more.

Mama and Tata have these talks often. She remains calm and steadfastly optimistic, never doubting that we are going to get out, that this suspended state of unemployment and life cannot last forever. She insists that the Communists will eventually come to their senses and issue us our passports. "We just have to be patient and wait our turn," she says. "Why would the Romanian government give us permission to apply for passports if they never intended to allow us to leave?"

"Good question, Stefica," Tata retorts, pressing the tobacco tightly into his pipe bowl with his thumb. "You are so naïve, but I love the fact that at least one person in Bucharest is still employing some form of logic."

ON SUNDAY MORNING Mama asks me to go and help clear out her things at the ballet school.

"How are you going to get in?" I ask.

"Easy," Mama answers. "Esther, the principal, gave me this. See?" She dangles the key to the school in front of me. "Esther still trusts me, but she wants me to do it on a Sunday, when the place is empty, so that my presence won't upset the students and the rest of the staff."

At the school Mama cleans out her locker and her desk in less than ten minutes. We are on our way out when she stops in front of the auditorium door. "Do you remember my students' ballet recitals, Eva?" she asks.

"Yes, Mama, the dancing was so beautiful," I tell her, knowing this will make her feel better.

"Come on." She grabs my hand and pulls me into the dark theater. Somehow Mama's feet know exactly where to go, and we find ourselves backstage. She flips on a switch, and the stage is suddenly flooded with light. "Go on," she says, giving me a push. I am standing on the empty stage with the orchestra pit below and a sea of empty seats staring back at me from the darkness. "Dance," Mama whispers. "Get up on your toes and keep your head high. Lift your arms, that's right," she says. "Can you hear music, Eva? Hear the music in your head and keep dancing." Her voice is only a whisper, yet it resonates in the empty theater. I can't hear any music in my head, but I don't want to disappoint Mama, so I fake it. I twirl and twirl until I get dizzy. I leap across the stage with my legs and arms spread wide open like an eagle or a plane, and to my surprise, I land safely. I squint, trying to make out Mama's outline in the wings as I elevate myself onto my toes again and try to do a pirouette the way I had seen her advanced ballet students do it. When my own two feet stumble upon each other, I gasp for breath and run off into the wings, straight into Mama's arms. She catches me. "That was great!" she says. "Isn't it wonderful to dance, Eva? Even without music, it's marvelous to dance."

"But, Mama, I have no idea how to *really* dance. I've never had any lessons!" I tell her.

"I will teach you."

TATA IS HOLED UP in the bathroom when we return home. He is hanging a black curtain on the window and installing shelves for trays and chemicals in the bathtub.

Mama takes off her coat and throws it on the bed. "Get out of the bathroom, Gyuri, I need to pee," she says. "What are you doing in there?" she asks.

"What does it look like? I'm setting up a mobile darkroom," Tata answers.

"You're what?"

"I told you, Stefica, I'm building a darkroom that I can easily assemble and disassemble so that I can print photographs. Victor was here earlier to offer his condolences about my losing my job. He also offered help. He came armed with optimism and a list of artists who need portraits right away—starting with most of the actresses and actors from the film studio. I'm setting up a darkroom so I can process the film and print the photos right here."

"Have you lost your mind, Gyuri? You can't do that! This is a shared bathroom for the whole family. There are seven of us, plus Eva, Gyuri—"

"I can count, Stefica, and I'm well aware of the drawbacks," Tata interrupts while fitting a rubber tube onto the bathtub spout.

"Gyuri, *it's illegal.* All private enterprise, *including freelancing,* is illegal, you know that! You'll get arrested if you get caught, and I can't live like that."

Tata keeps working, but his body turns toward Mama. "Can you live without food, Stefi? Can you live beholden to your darling little sister's husband? Is that okay with you?"

Mama looks blankly at him and finally says, "Have you at least asked their permission?"

"Whose permission? If you mean have I asked your parents' permission, then the answer is *no.* It's not their business. And if you mean have I asked your darling little sister's permission, then that's a *definite no.* And, Stefica, please don't even dream of telling me to ask Max for anything, because then surely we will have a war in this house. I'm not going to ask anybody's opinion or permission about what I should or shouldn't do in order to support my family. They're all just going to have to knock whenever they need to use the loo."

"That's not fair," Mama mutters.

"Don't talk to me about fair," Tata snaps.

TATA BUILDS HIS mobile darkroom in our common bathroom, and miraculously no one raises an objection. His loyal friends begin

showing up right away for photo portraits. Most are well-known actors and actresses. They sit for him either in our bedroom, where
Tata sets up lights and his camera on a tripod, or, on sunny days,
on the terrace.

Tata processes the film in the bathroom, and a few days later he
meets with his "clients" in our bedroom over Turkish coffee to
show them contact prints and proof prints of the best shots. If his
clients visit in the afternoon when I'm home from school, I listen
to the conversation while pretending to do my homework. Everyone raves about Tata's work and pays him in cash. Tata sometimes
sheepishly refuses payment, but invariably each one of his models
insists, "I am lucky to have such a great artist shoot my portrait.
Please accept this as a small token of my appreciation." The folded
money is pressed gently into Tata's hand, and then he graciously
accepts it as he puffs on his pipe and smiles.

When things are slow because people are on vacation, Victor
gets on the phone and drums up new clients. I don't know how he
does it, since he's risking his hide because this is all illegal, but
Victor gets results without getting caught. Friends and friends of
friends ask for family portraits and photographs to mark birthday cel-
ebrations, weddings, and anniversaries. Victor acts as Tata's agent—
never taking a penny for his services. Though not an artist himself,
Victor is in awe of art and the people who produce it. Despite all he
has endured in the *lagers*, and the fact that he lost his entire family
during the war, Victor remains one of those human beings who sees
good in everyone.

EVENTUALLY, Mama stops talking about how Tata could be arrested for carrying on an illegal freelance business, but I'm sure

that the thought is lurking in the back of her mind, as it is always gnawing at me. We both know that a single phone call from an unfriendly or anti-Semitic acquaintance could land Tata in jail indefinitely. Whenever Mama alludes to being fearful, Tata reminds her that we simply have no choice but to trust our friends. One winter evening when the sun has set early, Grandpa comments over a bowl of vegetable broth at suppertime that we have to trust God. Tata makes no comment and continues to sip his soup.

I long for the days when both my parents went to work. Tata still gets up at the crack of dawn. He showers and gets dressed as if he had somewhere to go. Grandpa Yosef, who is used to being the first one up, has a hard time adjusting to Tata's presence in the kitchen.

"I'll make coffee," Grandpa says, gently shooing him out. But Tata doesn't want to hear of it. "Thanks, Papa, but I prefer to make my own coffee." Grandpa Yosef is hurt and mentions the incident to Mama, who in turn confronts Tata.

"Stefica darling," Tata argues, "you simply don't understand. The way I was raised is that one doesn't expect an elderly gentleman such as your father to cater to me. I am fully capable of brewing my own coffee. Besides, I do a better job of it." Tata smirks and draws on his pipe.

"You just hurt Papa's feelings, Gyuri," Mama pleads.

"I did no such thing," Tata insists. "Your father chose to feel hurt."

Mama rolls her eyes and sighs.

It's been six months since my parents lost their jobs, but it feels much longer. Our bedroom is even smaller since Tata camps out in it all day. He sits on the bed and fills his pipe with tobacco, never finishing the bowl before tapping the half-smoldering ashes out. Between smokes he cleans his pipe meticulously, pulling a thin brush through the narrow pipe stem, then refilling the still warm bowl. He does this with his nose stuck in a book, ignoring anyone who enters the room. In the afternoons, he occasionally takes long walks, with his camera always strapped around his neck. He never takes Mama or me along, but sometimes he meets friends from the Studio for coffee. On those days, his mood lifts, and when he returns home he is more like his old self.

I TURN EIGHT in the spring, and I am close to completing second grade in June. My friends know nothing about my parents being unemployed. In school, I become more indoctrinated in Communist ideology, while at home I'm a Jewish girl in hiding, waiting to leave the country for Israel, a place I know nothing about. I try to imagine what Israel looks like, but I have no pictures of the land or books about it. Even though no one in my family has ever been there, Israel is now the center of our dreams and hopes. Sometimes I shut my eyes tight and wait for a glimpse of the place to come to me, but all I ever see is a glow of gold light that makes me feel warm and safe. Israel is more a feeling than a place.

The thought of leaving home makes me terribly uneasy, yet it doesn't matter. What choice do I have? The adults are going to leave with or without my permission, and they are going to take me with them. None of them, not even Grandpa, asked my opinion about whether they should stand in line all night for passport applications. None of them ever thought they would be unemployed because of it either. I'm tired of their lack of work and their long faces, and I'm tired of their tiptoeing around the house as if nothing's happened. Even more, I'm tired of being afraid of being discovered as a Jew by the other kids in school. How can I defend myself if I don't even know what I've done wrong? It's not my fault that I was born Jewish. What is a Jew anyway? More than anything, I wish the world would stop hating Jews because I'm still the same person I was before I knew I was Jewish.

"IF ALL JEWS WERE LIKE YOU"

GRANDMA IULIA AND GRANDPA YOSEF are in their bedroom. The door is closed and they're speaking Yiddish. It's easy to figure out that they're talking about me, since I understand enough to get the gist of what they're saying. Several times they go back and forth between Yiddish and Romanian, totally forgetting that I'm right here in the room with them.

"Have you lost your mind, Yosef?" The more upset Grandma Iulia is, the higher her voice gets. "You want she should go to a rabbi? What on earth for? She's a *girl*!" When Grandpa doesn't respond to this clear evidence, Grandma starts filling in the blanks, then reverts to her own point of view. "I was so happy, Yosef, when she was born a girl. *Baruch HaShem!* No need for a bris to tear us all apart. Remember how Gyuri vowed not to have the baby circumcised if it was a boy? And how you promised me to take the baby to a mohel without the father's permission? We would have had World War Three in this house, Yosef, and your own daughter would never have forgiven you. But God was merciful, because *she is a girl*. Now what do you want to do, Yosef?"

Seeing that Grandpa still doesn't answer, Grandma catches her breath and continues. "You want to look for trouble! We're lucky we don't have to send her to study for a Bar Mitzvah, lucky we don't have to hide her studies from the Communist scum. We should be grateful that this child has brought some peace to our home. Don't *you* spoil it, Yosef."

Grandpa is as still as a rock, so Grandma rolls on in Romanian now, apparently oblivious to my presence. "You've forgotten that we're surrounded by goyim who hate us, and what do you do? You promise this girl she can study with a rabbi no less. Only a *meshugeneh kopf* like yours would think of such a scheme. Yosef! You're not listening!" Seeing that Grandpa doesn't flinch, Grandma proclaims in a definitive voice, "You must explain to the child that this is not a good idea, Yosef. That's all there is to it."

"Are you finished ranting, Iulia?"

"*How come no one ever told me that I'm Jewish?*" I shout. Both my grandparents stare at me as if I've suddenly appeared in the room.

"*I* never hid anything from you," Grandma Iulia finally answers. "We've been speaking Yiddish in front of you ever since you were born."

"But I didn't know that Yiddish was Jewish talk! You never told me."

"That's true." Grandpa Yosef smiles. "Let's just call this a sin of omission."

"What does that mean?" I ask.

"It means Grandma Iulia and I left out some vital information." He adds quickly, "Out of respect for your father, and for your mother's sake as well."

"I don't understand!" I cry.

"Your father went through hell during the war because he is Jewish, and he didn't want you to suffer the way he had."

"How could he avoid my suffering just by not telling me that I'm Jewish?"

Grandpa shrugs. "He can't, but he clearly doesn't see that."

"I don't care! I just want to understand about being Jewish."

"What's there to understand?" Grandma Iulia asks. "We're Jews, and that's all there is to it."

"Look, Iulia, I promised," Grandpa says. "The child wants to know about being Jewish, so she needs to study with a rabbi. That's not such a bad idea. What do you expect me to tell her, that her grandmother's afraid?"

"Yes. Tell her you've made a mistake. Tell her being Jewish is *dangerous*. Yosef, tell her what we went through during the war!" Grandma Iulia is now red in the face.

"Now who's *meshugeneh*?" Grandpa asks.

"And putting her in harm's way is *not*?"

"You're getting paranoid, Iulia. I will make sure that Eva is safe."

"How can you say I'm paranoid, Yosef, when we barely survived the slaughterhouse?"

"That's in the past, Iulia. I'm grateful that we are alive."

"I suppose you think that it can't happen again, since the Communists love us so much. You better tell the child *the truth*, Yosef."

"What truth?"

"That being a Jew isn't easy, and it isn't only about Torah."

"Iulia, being a Jew *is about Torah*. Your parents knew it and so do you."

"Leave my parents out of this, you fool. What happened to us during the war, I suppose that was in the Torah too?"

"If I were a rabbi, I would say yes, it is somewhere in the Torah—but I don't know. This child has a right to question and to learn."

"Learn that people hate us, Yosef? She already knows it. Where is it written that girls have to study Torah?"

"*You show me* where it's written that girls *don't* have a right to study."

"I'm sure the rabbi will agree with me," Grandma Iulia says indignantly.

"I hope not." Grandpa Yosef puts on his cardigan. "I'm going for a walk, Iulia. You want to come?"

"Get out of here, you crazy old fool."

THE ROOM IS as still as twilight. I have never witnessed such a serious argument between my grandparents, and it is all on my account. I feel so bad I wish I could disappear, but instead I can't help asking:

"Grandma?"

"Yes?"

"Why don't you want me to learn about being Jewish?"

Grandma doesn't answer. The room gets darker, and her duvet covers take on ominous proportions. Eventually I get up and start toward the door, but her voice stops me.

"Before the war, before the lousy Communist scums took power and *nationalized* all our property, including the skin on our back, there was a king in Romania," she begins. "His name was King Carol II. The only redeeming feature about King Carol, as far as I'm concerned, is that he had a Jewish mistress who influenced him not to murder Jews. During his reign, King Carol allowed us to live in relative peace. We were free to own businesses and have our own homes. And as long as we didn't publicize it, we could practice our religion. We owned several businesses, and we were free to travel abroad. I dragged your grandfather to France, where he was more interested in eating oysters than in sightseeing in Paris. He squeezed lemon over those *treif*—unkosher—oysters and slurped them with gusto, declaring them *'magnifique!'* After Paris, he sent me to a Swiss spa, where every part of my body was rubbed with the most exquisite potions on earth. I went on a diet so that I would be even more attractive in his eyes. Those were good times." Grandma sighs.

I hate it when Grandma goes off in a different direction. "What happened with King Carol *during* the war?" I ask, trying to steer her back on track.

"The rat ran away as soon as things got rough with the Germans," she says, pulling the duvet around her waist. The room is so dark now that Grandma Iulia is just a shadow sitting up in her bed. "In Germany, Hitler and his Nazi gangs came to power. But in Romania we had our own brand of fascists, the Iron Guard. They were called the Legion of the Archangel Michael, and they wore green shirts and spewed venom. Of course, Jews were at the top of their enemies list. The Legionnaires incited the goyim to rise up against the monarchy and against Jews, with empty promises of a better life."

"What does *goyim* mean, Grandma?"

"Don't interrupt me. *Goyim* just means 'non-Jews.' Where was I?"

"You were saying that the Legionnaires were evil."

"Yes, they were a bunch of lunatics. They performed Romanian Orthodox religious rites, and the Romanians, who love drama, ate it all up and hated the Jews even more. The Legionnaire leader was Corneliu Zelea Codreanu—he was not a man but the devil himself. When King Carol saw that the Legionnaires were a threat to his monarchy, he ordered his men to kill Codreanu and fourteen Legionnaires. The king's men stripped the Legionnaires naked and strangled them. Then they doused the bodies with acid, so they would be unrecognizable, and buried all fifteen, including Codreanu, in a mass grave. This murder incited the Romanian population of Bucharest into a fanatic religious frenzy. The Jews had no hand in the murder, but we were blamed." Grandma stops abruptly. "My mouth is very dry. Be a good girl and fetch me a glass of water."

I bound out of the dark bedroom, hoping that Grandma Iulia won't change her mind about telling me the rest of the story. In the kitchen I find Sabina looking quite exhausted, slumped on a stool with her mouth half open and her head propped against the windowsill. I let the water run until it is cold and fill up a glass. Sabina snores softly through it all. Then I tiptoe back to Grandma Iulia's bedroom and hand her the glass.

"You're an angel," she says between gulps, finishing the entire glass. "Where was I?"

"You were talking about the Legionnaires."

"Ah yes, the war came. Eventually Romania joined the Axis powers, the Nazis. There were a lot of German army personnel swarming all over Bucharest. The Jewish population was forced under peril of death to treat the Germans as honored guests.

There was a terrible shortage of food and housing. Jews were ordered to wear armbands with yellow Stars of David, and we had to obey a night curfew. Our children were assigned to do forced labor for the Nazis. Your mother had to draft maps of key local roads and bridges, and your aunt Puica became a surgical nurse at a clinic that cared for injured German soldiers. Uncle Natan was part of the team of Jews who had to cart off the bodies to the morgue after the Allied bombardments of Bucharest. I never knew if my children would come home alive at the end of the day, and whenever Natan did appear, he smelled of death. I was too scared to ask him where he had been."

"I don't understand why you had to wear armbands with yellow Stars of David, Grandma," I say.

"How else were they going to know who is Jewish and who isn't?" she answers. "It was an easy way for them to identify us."

"But why did they need to identify Jews if we look just like everyone else?"

"This isn't about our looks, it's about *who* we are," Grandma explains. "When the sirens started to blast announcing an air raid, Jews were the last ones allowed into the bomb shelters, so we suffered the highest casualties. Your uncle Natan had to cart off several of his school friends after air raids. Our nightly curfew was also set much earlier than the rest of the population's, and our ration cards were even more meager than theirs."

"Couldn't you just refuse to wear the Star of David armband?" I wonder out loud.

"We had no choice," Grandma goes on. "We were lucky that we weren't deported to concentration camps, like your father.

We had heard horror stories about so many other Jews from Transylvania, from Hungary, Germany, Austria, Poland, and the rest of Europe. What is hard labor when you compare it to a death camp?"

"But, Grandma," I argue, still trying to understand, "how would anyone know that you were Jewish unless you told them?"

"They would know, believe me. Our identity wasn't a secret before the war. You can never hide who you really are, Eva."

"I didn't know that I'm Jewish until now, so you *can* hide who you are!"

"Shhh, let me finish my story," Grandma continues. "In the midst of all this, your grandpa Yosef and I were forced to take in two Nazi SS officers, Lieutenant Schmidt and Lieutenant Bundt."

"Did they know you were Jewish?"

"Of course. Not only did they know but they showed up for three kosher meals a day, meager as our food supply was. They expected me to set out my finest china and silver and join them in German conversation while they ate at our table. They loved hearing their mother tongue uttered from Jewish lips." In my mind I could see Grandma smile despite the total darkness that surrounded us.

"Were they mean?"

"No. They were extremely polite and neat. They made their beds every morning. Their uniforms were spotless, and their shirts were always pressed and starched. They never brought women to the house, and most important, they didn't touch my daughters or make lewd remarks. I was so grateful, because I had heard such horror tales from many friends who had to house other Nazis . . ." Grandma's voice trails off.

After a while, I ask, "So what happened?"

"On January 22, 1941, Lieutenant Schmidt and Lieutenant Bundt showed up early for dinner, toting guns. The Legionnaires were already in power, and I was terrified. I had no idea why they were home so early. The two men barked orders at us as if we were members of their platoon or, worse, their prisoners—which is precisely what we were.

"'Close your window shutters and nail them shut,' they said as they ran around the house making sure that all our windows and doors were locked. Then, after bolting everything, they barricaded the doors with furniture. They spoke to us in German but offered no explanation. When they had secured the house, they stationed themselves inside by our front door, shotguns in hand, and waited.

"I made strong Turkish coffee and placed their cups on a chair by the door. Just after five P.M., there was a loud knock, and I felt my heart leap into my mouth but I couldn't utter a sound. I started toward the door, but Lieutenant Schmidt and Lieutenant Bundt had already opened it a crack with the tips of their guns. The afternoon light leaked in, revealing two silhouettes. It was the girls, Stefica and her best friend, Rachel Goldman, coming home late from ballet practice. Lieutenant Schmidt quickly pulled them inside. Rachel pleaded with him, saying that she was expected home for supper, but he wouldn't let her go. I was grateful that my daughter was home safe, but not knowing what was about to happen, I was terrified. I wondered if the girls would have been better off at the ballet studio or at Rachel's house. But at this point, we had no choice. All that mattered was that we were together, even though we were prisoners in our own home."

"Grandma," I whisper, "do you think that Mama remembers this?"

"Of course she does, she was right there with us when it happened. How could she forget such a thing?"

I nod in the dark, not fully comprehending, since Mama has never told me anything like this about the war. "Go on, Grandma," I tell her.

"Darkness fell early. It was frigid. The air felt as if it would freeze in our throats. Natan was ill with the flu, and he huddled in his cot under five blankets. The only sound you could hear in the house was his breathing. Your aunt Puica hid in our pantry closet and chain-smoked. She knew how much I hate cigarettes, but I made believe I didn't see or smell anything. Yosef sat at the dining room table, playing solitaire, turning each card softly in order not to make any noise. I took off my shoes and paced from room to room, checking on everyone. I had to make sure that each and every member of my family was really here and safe.

"When I first heard the singing, I thought that one of my children had turned on the radio. I rushed to turn it off but realized it was coming from outside. The sound of Romanian Orthodox hymns grew louder until it reached fever pitch. Then I heard truck tires screeching to a halt. Fists pounded on our door with frozen knuckles.

" 'Who's there?' Lieutenant Schmidt asked in German.

" 'Open this door or I'll break it!' a voice barked back in Romanian.

"The two men remained stationed at our door. That moment's silence was heavier than anything I had ever felt. When it broke, there was pounding everywhere and the sound of shattered glass. 'We know that there are Jews in this house,' the voice hissed from the other side of the door. 'Open up and let the kikes out and you will be unharmed.'

"Lieutenant Schmidt slowly unbolted the door, sliding the barrel of his shotgun out first. He then popped his helmeted head out and carefully addressed the man in front of him.

"'I told you to go away. No one enters this house, by order of the Führer,' he said.

"'Show me your orders on paper,' the voice demanded.

"'These are my orders,' Lieutenant Schmidt snapped, rattling his shotgun against the doorframe.

"'Nicu! Nicu, get back over here!' Shouts in Romanian came from the truck outside. 'Let's not waste time. There are plenty more kikes where these came from.' I was standing in the dark, close enough to the door to see the glare of headlights illuminating the top of Lieutenant Schmidt's helmet. Then I heard the crackling of boots against pebbles followed by the sound of the truck taking off.

"I don't have any recollection of the rest of that night. The next day Lieutenant Schmidt and Lieutenant Bundt remained in our house guarding us. I cooked them a meal that consisted of our entire week's rations and told my family to tighten their belts. We were nearly out of food, but we were alive. When the Germans determined that it was safe for us to venture out, they gave us strict orders to return as soon as we had foraged for food."

"WHAT I LEARNED at the marketplace was far worse than the terror we had experienced the night before. The Legionnaires had gone on a killing spree. The truck in front of our house was part of a convoy that had carted off hundreds of Jewish men, women, and children from their homes to Bucharest's slaughterhouse. There, in the red-brick building of the slaughterhouse near the icy black waters of the Dîmbovița River, the legionnaires ordered the Jews to strip naked and kneel on the ice-cold floor next to the lifeless cattle that hung from hooks. Our people were made to crawl on their hands and knees onto the conveyor belt. No one was spared. Not even the babies. Jews were slaughtered like cattle, torn limb from limb, our blood gushing everywhere.

"Everywhere an endless river of tears. I heard that there was so much blood, the Legionnaires had trouble finding a spot to mark the flesh with a stamp that read 'Kosher meat, fit for human consumption' before hanging each lifeless body on a hook alongside lambs and other meat. The parents of Rachel Goldman, your mother's friend who had come to our home that night, were among the victims. Rachel was the only one in her family who survived.

"Later I found out that many more people were killed. Over thirteen hundred Jews were tormented or killed during three days of anti-Semitic riots throughout Bucharest. Some were burned alive in their homes after being robbed. Others were taken to the forest and shot into open pits that became mass graves. Women were raped in view of their children and then murdered. Eva, that is how the Legionnaires took revenge on us Jews for what King Carol's men had done to their leader.

"When I got home, I didn't allow myself a moment to think about what I had heard at the market. I didn't even tell your grandfather until much later. I had a responsibility toward Lieutenant Schmidt and Lieutenant Bundt, who had saved our lives. I had to cook and be a good hostess. After dinner, I asked the kids to each personally thank our SS men. 'No problem,' Lieutenant Bundt said, toasting all of us with one of my crystal glasses filled to the rim with red wine. 'If all Jews were like you, anti-Semitism would not exist in the world.'"

THE GRAY DOOR

GRANDPA YOSEF pokes his head into our bedroom and motions for me to join him.

"Let's go for a walk. It's beautiful outside."

"I'm reading, Grandpa," I tell him, stretching my arms and yawning.

"You can read later. We're going out."

I slide off my bed and slip on my shoes, wondering what's going on. Grandpa is usually so easygoing, but not today. He takes my hand as we walk past the yard gate and turn left.

"Where are we going?" I ask.

"You'll see," he answers. "Look how sunny it is. I told you it's a gorgeous day. The walk will do you good."

We turn the corner, and Grandpa stops to light a cigarette. "I want you to keep your eyes open and remember exactly where we are going, because the next time you go you will have to do it alone," he says, his voice soft but firm.

"What are you talking about, Grandpa?"

"Don't ask so many questions. Just keep your eyes open and remember the way we're walking."

We walk for about three blocks, and then Grandpa stops again, throws his cigarette on the sidewalk, stubs it out with his shoe, and nods toward a house to his right.

"See that building?" he says without looking at the building or at me. "That's the place you want to remember." He searches his pocket for his cigarette pack again, gets another one out, and lights it. I see a gray building with no windows. There is a gray wooden door with a peephole. No number. No nameplate. Nothing anyone would ever remember. "Why do I want to remember this building?" I ask, pointing to it.

"Don't point," Grandpa says, pushing my hand down. "This is where you will meet the rabbi and start your Jewish studies. But next week you will have to come here by yourself. Do you think you can do that?"

I look around. We are just three blocks from home on a street I've passed every day on my way to and from school. There are trees and lampposts on this street, and most of the houses have wrought-iron gates guarding their front yards. I note again that the gray building to our right has no yard, no gate, and no windows— just a gray wooden door with a peephole. That's the only thing that makes it different. No yard. No gate. I can remember that. I grab Grandpa's hand. "Let's go!" I tell him, pulling him back toward home.

WHEN WE ARRIVE HOME, Grandpa makes me a tall glass of homemade raspberry syrup with seltzer, my favorite Romanian soda. He pours the thick syrup, and I watch its red ribbon trail to the bottom of the glass. Grandpa shakes the blue seltzer bottle, and with a single move of his wrist he swishes the seltzer into the glass, then stirs it with a long spoon. The bubbles rise to the surface. I gulp the delicious drink down as soon as he hands it to me.

"Why can't you take me to meet the rabbi?"

"It's not a good idea for me to take you there and drop you off on a regular basis. The rabbi thinks it might attract attention, and we've got enough problems right now. The last thing we need is more trouble because some Communist anti-Semite gets wind that you are getting a Jewish education. Your grandmother gave me hell about your safety, and I promised her that not even a hair on your body would be harmed. You understand?"

"Is it dangerous, Grandpa?"

"I'm not taking any chances."

"What could happen?" I draw up the last of my syrup and bite the straw.

"Nothing. Nothing bad is going to happen to you. It's not illegal to be a Jew, and it isn't illegal or wrong to study any religion, including ours. It's just that the Communists think all religion is superstition and they're anti-Semitic. So they might try to make our life a little more difficult than it already is." Grandpa pauses. "But we're not going to allow them to do that, are we?" he asks, looking at me.

I shake my head in agreement, but I am terrified.

"Good. Your first lesson will begin next Friday after you get home from school, so we've got all week for you to practice getting there and back."

THE EMBROIDERY LESSON

"**WHAT ARE YOU DOING?**" I ask Mama one afternoon later that week.

"I'm embroidering a flower, see?" Mama points to a red petal against the crisp whiteness of the tablecloth.

"Who taught you how to do that?"

"My grandmother Eliza. She taught me how to sew and how to knit." Mama smiles, looking up from her work.

"Is it difficult?"

"Not if you practice. You want to try?" Mama places the needle between my fingers, cups her hand around mine, and pulls the thread.

"Mama," I ask cautiously, "do you remember the war?"

"Of course," she says, still guiding my hand.

"What do you remember the most? What was the scariest thing?"

Mama places her embroidery in her lap and looks up. "What do I remember? I remember too much. I remember being hungry, so hungry that I would have eaten anything. One night I came home from a ballet class and Mother prepared a dish that she said was rabbit, but it looked like cat. I was too hungry to ask, but it surely didn't look like rabbit or chicken to me."

"Grandma Iulia cooked a cat?"

"I don't know. I never asked, and I'm certain she wouldn't have told me anyway. But we were all so hungry, we didn't care. We ate it, whatever it was."

"I would have thrown up," I assure her.

"Perhaps." Mama smiles.

"What else do you remember?"

"Let's see, I remember walking in pitch darkness after the curfew with my cousin Mimi and being terrified that we would get caught. I stumbled and fell into a construction hole, and poor Mimi had to pull me out. That was terrifying."

"Did you hurt yourself?"

"I sprained my ankle, but I was lucky not to have broken anything."

"Did you tell Grandma?"

"Of course not. She had enough to worry about."

"Mama, do you remember the Nazis who lived with you?" I try broaching the subject that has been haunting my dreams.

Mama arches her left eyebrow. "Of course I remember Lieutenant Schmidt and Lieutenant Bundt. What about them?"

"Grandma told me that they saved your life."

"They did." Mama seems surprised that I know the story, but from the look on her face it is clear she does not want to revisit the topic.

"What was the scariest part of the war, Mama?"

"Everything. Everything was scary and terrible," she says.

"Yes, but what was the very worst of it?" I press.

Mama eventually looks up from her embroidery. "I suppose the worst of it was when Father cheered on the American airplanes to bomb us."

"Grandpa wanted you to get bombed?"

"Of course not, silly," Mama says. "But he wanted the Allies to win so bad, every time the sirens went off before an air raid, your grandpa was the last person to get into the shelter. Instead, he would cup his hands like binoculars and look up at the sky, waiting for the planes to arrive and drop their bombs. As they approached, he would start cheering them on. 'Yes! Yes! Yes!' His fists flew through the air in victory until the bombs could be seen dropping from the sky and Mother would lunge out of the shelter, grab him by both his arms, and pull him down into safety. 'Yosef, you crazy bastard,' she'd shout, 'you're going to get us all killed!' "

"Why did Grandpa do that?"

"I don't know." Mama shrugs. "He couldn't help himself. He wanted the war to end."

I concentrate on Mama's embroidery. She has finished the red petals of the flower and is now working on its stem and leaves.

"Don't you want to know what my best memory of the war is?" she asks.

I wait for her to tell me.

"The best day of the war took place when I thought an air raid had hit us but it was something else entirely. I was taking a ballet class when I heard a terrible rumble and the light fixtures started to shake and then the walls in the studio fell one by one, all around us.

I started to run, but everywhere I ran there was rubble to climb over, and people were screaming. I saw a hand moving just above the ground, its fingers stretched up as if reaching to grasp the sky, but the body attached to that hand was buried alive. None of the buses were running, and the tram had stopped as well, so even though I was very far from home, I kept running. And the closer I got to home, the more dead bodies I encountered. I stumbled over people who were injured. Many more were dead or dying, and the smell of burned rubber was in my nostrils, in my hair, and on my clothes. I thought, *This is what death smells like.*

"There were sirens blaring, and rescue crews were beginning to pull people from beneath collapsed buildings. The shouts for help were everywhere. Somewhere at the back of my head I thought, *Maybe I'll run into Natan*, whose job was to cart off the dead after the air raids, but this was no air raid. It was the worst earthquake that had ever hit Bucharest. I kept running, and the earth at one point opened up right in front of me, so I ran in the opposite direction. I closed my eyes and kept running, blinded, but all the while, though my eyes were closed, I could see my mother, who was home in bed with phlebitis. I ran and I prayed and I ran and I prayed, 'Dear God, please, please, please make sure that Mother is safe. Please. I'll do anything, God. Anything you want me to do. Whether you are there, God, or not. Please. Anything. Please. Only keep her alive. Please.' Out of nowhere, a man with a horse and buggy appeared, and the horse reared up on his hind legs as the man shouted, 'Hey, beautiful, you need a ride?' I got in and begged him to take me home even though I had no money to give him. He took pity on me because I must have been crying. 'Don't worry, beautiful,' he told me. 'If God wants you to die, you will die, but if He wants you to live, you could be in the eye of the storm where it's calm, or in the middle of the raging ocean, or in this cab with me during this earthquake and you will survive.' And as he said that we turned the corner onto our street."

Mama pauses and smiles. "I will never forget the image of my mother waving her white handkerchief as she sat perched on the ledge of a wall that had been part of her bedroom. Beneath her dangling feet hung a framed needlepoint depicting a couple having a picnic in a pastoral setting. The man was playing the lute, and the woman was gazing lovingly at him. That giant gilded frame was still on the hook, though completely crooked. It had hung right above Mother's bed. Mother was all black from soot, but she was alive. I climbed through the rubble and helped her down, and I couldn't stop crying because she had been spared, and my prayers had been answered. We were so lucky. My father, Puica, and Natan—every one of us had been in a different part of the city, and we all survived the earthquake. That miracle was the best day of the war for me."

"And the house?" I ask.

"Gone. It collapsed like a house of cards. Later we all went back and rummaged through what was left. Most of our stuff had been destroyed. But still, we found so many things intact. We salvaged several paintings. Some clothing. Pots and pans. Dishes. Forks, knives, spoons. I even found a dozen eggs in the icebox. They were completely unbroken. We made an omelet for supper that evening at Cousin Mimi's house. What a feast that was."

"Where did you live after that?"

"My father searched long and hard for a new home, but there was no point in buying another house, because at any moment we could have been bombed. When he found this place as a rental, he grabbed it, and we've been here ever since."

Mama puts her embroidery down. I try to take it all in.

TOURIST BOXES

THE DINING ROOM TABLE is covered with sheets of newspaper. Tubes of oil paints, a can of turpentine, and a jar filled with paintbrushes and a rag are lying on top of the newspapers. Mama has lined up several carved wooden boxes in front of her, in soldierlike fashion.

"If *I* were a tourist from the West, I would buy one of these gift boxes as a souvenir. Wouldn't you, Eva?" she asks, holding a carved wooden box close up and painting the stem of a flower on its lid.

"I guess so."

"Come help me out," she says. "It's fun."

I sit down next to her, and she shows me how to use the end of the brush handle to create a pattern of perfect dots on the box.

"This will turn out to be the center of the flower," she says, dipping the tip of the brush into yellow paint. "If you do a good job, I will show you how to paint petals next."

"How come tourists can visit Bucharest but we can't go anywhere?"

Mama smiles. "Have you ever met a tourist, Eva?"

"No. Wait a minute, isn't Renée, Beard's girlfriend who gave me my turquoise toiletry kit, a tourist?"

"Yes, I suppose she is," Mama answers without looking up from her work, "but she came here as a puppeteer. Tourists go places just for fun."

"Why can't *we* have fun?"

"We *are* having fun, darling. We're painting boxes with pretty flowers."

"I'd like to be able to travel to other countries, Mama."

"So would I, but you will have to be patient until the Party lets us out."

We sit together and paint these gift boxes with Romanian motifs until my hands are covered with specks of oil paint and my fingers are numb. I have no idea how Mama got this job or who is paying her, but she says that it's a great way for her to continue to contribute to the household income now that she no longer teaches ballet. When we are done, we allow the boxes to dry overnight. On the following afternoon Mama wraps the boxes in old newspapers and packs them in a shopping bag.

"Let's go deliver these," she says.

Outside, it's beginning to drizzle, and we don't have an umbrella with us. Mama walks faster, and I keep up with her—until she stops abruptly and turns around as if she's forgotten something.

"What's wrong?" I ask, tugging at her arm.

"Nothing," she mutters under her breath. "I saw Mrs. Antoniu walking down the street and I didn't want to bump into her."

"Why not, Mama?"

"Because every time I see that woman, her whiny voice drives me crazy. She always ends the conversation by asking, 'Do you have enough to eat?' But she never offers help and she doesn't stop talking long enough to listen. I have no use for people like her, Eva. I'm down enough without having her bring me any lower."

We turn back when Mrs. Antoniu has gone and deliver the boxes to an apartment in a large building. A maid wearing a white apron opens the door and takes Mama's shopping bag. We wait in the foyer until the maid reappears a few minutes later with an envelope. Mama opens it and counts the cash. The maid hands my mother another bag.

"There are twenty-five boxes in this order. The boss says to stick to the floral motifs and the geometric patterns."

"Fine. I'll keep that in mind. See you next week," Mama tells her.

"*La revedere*—until we see each other again," the maid answers, and then the door latches behind us.

When we're back on the street, Mama squeezes my hand. "Not a word about this to anyone, right, Eva?" she asks.

"Right," I reassure her.

As soon as we arrive home, I grab my jump rope and get out of the stuffy house. The yard is empty, and I'm eager to exercise.

"Can I jump too?" I hear Andrei's voice when I'm in midair.

"*Unu, doi, trei, patru, cinci* . . ." I count as my feet fly over the rope. I am on a roll, so I keep going without answering him, way past one hundred, at which point I lose count.

"Sure," I finally tell him and hand him the rope. I am completely out of breath. Andrei jumps for a while, until beads of sweat break above his upper lip and his cheeks are flushed. Then he sits next to me against the yard wall, his legs stretched out, his socks crumpled around his ankles.

"Andrei"—the question pops out of my mouth—"what would you say if I told you that I'm Jewish?"

"You're joking, right?" he asks, looking up. "No kidding," he murmurs, whistling softly and crossing himself.

"No kidding," I tell him as Andrei runs his hands through my hair, feeling for my scalp.

"What are you doing?" I cry, brushing his hands away. Andrei has never touched me before.

"I'm looking for your horns. My father says all Jews have horns."

"I don't have any," I whisper, trying to push back my tears.

"Then you can't be Jewish," he says, relieved.

"But I am."

"You can't be. Your hair feels just like corn silk to me."

ALEPH

GRANDPA YOSEF makes good on his promise. We practice the route to the rabbi's house every day when I get home from school for the rest of that week. When we find ourselves in front of the gray house with the wooden door with the peephole, Grandpa Yosef lights a cigarette and says, "Don't do it now, but on Friday you will knock on this door three times like this"—his knuckles tap my head gently—"followed by just a single knock. Then the rabbi will know it's you and he'll open the door. But you must go in very quickly. You understand?"

"Yes." I nod. "Grandpa, what is the rabbi's name?"

"It's *Rabbi*." Grandpa smiles. "Just call him Rabbi and he'll be happy."

ON FRIDAY when I get home from school, Sabina has my lunch ready in the dining room, but I'm not hungry.

"Eat. You're going to be hungry later," Grandpa Yosef tells me, looking at my untouched Swiss cheese sandwich. "It's going to be a long afternoon."

I take the slice of cheese out of the sandwich and nibble on it. Grandpa sits down next to me.

"You'll need something to carry the book that Rabbi will give you. Also a notebook and pencil," he says.

"What about my schoolbag?" I suggest.

"Not a good idea. That would look odd since you won't be going during school hours," Grandpa murmurs, deep in thought.

"I could pretend I'm going to Claudia's house to do homework."

Grandpa shakes his head. "Better not to involve anyone else."

"I know!" I tell him, running to my room and returning with the turquoise plastic toiletry box that I got from Renée. It looks just like a lunch box, only prettier. It's big enough for a book and a notebook, and is easy to carry by its two sturdy handles. Best of all, it has a little metal latch that snaps tightly shut.

Grandpa Yosef checks it out carefully. "Perfect," he declares.

Finally, at 3:15, Grandpa stops sipping his tea and says that it's time to go. I take a quick look at myself in the mirror. The nine-year-old girl with pigtails who stares back at me is very determined. I try smiling at her, but she doesn't return my smile, so I stop. I am ready to begin my Jewish studies.

GRANDPA WALKS ME to the yard gate. This time he isn't going with me to the gray house. I kiss him goodbye.

"Make sure you come straight home," he tells me, looking at his watch. "You'd better not be a minute later than seven tonight or I'll have to send your mother and father after you."

I wave at him without turning my head; my other hand is swinging my toiletry box. I know that if I look back I won't be able to keep walking. My first impulse is to run. I know my feet can fly to the gray house in less than three minutes flat. But Grandpa cautioned me against running.

Don't run. Walk, I tell myself. My breathing is shallow. I think about Andrei, and my heart starts to pound just as hard as if I were skipping rope. What would Andrei say if he knew that I'm on my way to study with a rabbi?

I try to push these thoughts away and concentrate on the streets. This is the same route I take every single day to and from school. But this time it's different because I am doing it as a Jew, and being Jewish is dangerous. My feet speed up. My right hand is holding the handles of my turquoise toiletry box so tightly, my wrist hurts. My palms are clammy. Everything around me is blurry, except for my racing thoughts.

If Grandpa Yosef had enough courage to cheer the Allied planes on to drop their bombs on Bucharest, I can walk to the rabbi's house. If Mama could come home after an earthquake to find her house had been destroyed, I can walk to the rabbi's house. If Tata could survive the *lagers* and the Russian gulag, I can walk to the rabbi's house, even if Tata doesn't believe in God.

The words of the horse-and-buggy driver in my mother's story echo in my mind. "If God wants you to die, you will die, but if He wants you to live, you could be in the eye of the storm or in the middle of the raging ocean and you will survive." But my father's parents hadn't survived. Did God want them to die? What had *they* done?

I start to run. I run past the rabbi's house and don't even notice. I run straight into a woman walking her dog. She yells, *"Hey, watch where you're going!"* I stop. Where am I? I look around and backtrack. This time I walk very slowly, counting every step in my head so that I won't break into a run. I am relieved that Grandpa isn't here to see me screw up so badly. I knock on the door of the gray house three times, rapidly. I wait. Then I knock again, just once. Someone looks through the peephole, and the door opens. A hand grabs my arm and pulls me in. My eyes have to adjust to the dark.

"You must be Eva," Rabbi says.

I nod my head. He brings me a glass of water. "Sit down and catch your breath," he tells me.

The cold water is delicious. "So your grandfather tells me you want to study Hebrew." Rabbi's voice is kind.

I had never said that I wanted to study Hebrew, but I'm not about to argue with him. All I ever asked was "What does it mean to be Jewish?" I wait for Rabbi to continue, but he just sits quietly and surveys me. I start to fidget. I want to take stock of him as well, to take a really good look at his face, but I am too uncomfortable to do it. He has a beard, just like Tata's friend Beard. *How does Rabbi get away with that?* I wonder.

Rabbi takes a book from the shelf behind me and places it on the table between us. "This is a Tanach," he says. "What do you have in that box?"

I snap the box open, and my notebook and pencil fly out. The magic metal cylinder Grandpa has given me rolls onto the table.

"Oh, a *mezuzah*," Rabbi says, picking it up and examining it.

"What?" I ask.

"I see you have a mezuzah," Rabbi says, sliding the hidden parchment from its cylinder. "Good. This will be our first lesson." He unrolls the parchment and lays it flat on the table.

He thumbs rapidly through the thin pages of the Tanach book. "Take a look," he says, pointing to the beautiful black letters in the book and then back to the little scroll he has just unfurled. The same black letters are in Rabbi's book as on the scroll that Grandpa Yosef has given me!

"This is Hebrew," Rabbi explains. "If you want to study Torah, you'll have to learn Hebrew first, so today we will start with the *Aleph Beit*, the Hebrew alphabet. You know what an alphabet is, don't you?"

I nod and finally get enough courage to look up. The skin around his deep-set eyes is thin. His eyebrows are bushy and meet in the middle. He has long, white fingers. He wears a small round hat even though we are indoors. When he catches me staring at him, he smiles. "Come with me," he says, getting up and leading me back to the door of the apartment. Affixed to the inside of the doorframe is a metal cylinder identical to mine. "A mezuzah is supposed to be placed on the outside of your doorpost," he tells me, "but these are uncertain times, so God will forgive us for placing it indoors." He points to my metal cylinder. "I see that you carry your mezuzah with you."

"I didn't know that it's called a 'mezuzah,'" I confess, and add quickly, "but I know that it's magic."

"Magic?" he asks, both his heavy eyebrows going up at the same time. I think about Mama and how her left eyebrow always seems to have a mind of its own. But his are different; they remind me of a giant black paintbrush.

"Yes. Magic. Because it works," I try to explain.

"Hmm," Rabbi says. "I never heard of a magic mezuzah before, but I suppose anything's possible. Tell me, how do you figure that your mezuzah is magic?"

"Grandpa says that it contains the Truth," I answer him.

"He's right about that." Rabbi smiles. "Let me read it to you." He unfurls the small parchment and holds it open with two fingers on the table. But he doesn't read it; Rabbi starts to chant: *"Sh'ma Yisra'el, Adonai Ehloheinu, Adonai Echad! V'ahavta et Adonai Ehlohehcha b'chol l'vav'cha uv'chol nafsh'cha uv'chol m'odehcha. V'hayu . . ."*

As his voice rises, his eyes are half closed and his body starts to roll back and forth almost as if he were rocking himself to sleep. His voice is deep and full of feeling, and as the sound resonates through the book-lined walls all the way down to the carpet under my feet and back up toward the ceiling, it seems to stop just above the light fixture and lingers there long enough for me to notice that the glass on the light fixture is trembling. I wonder if the neighbors can hear him and if they will call the Securitate and complain that a bunch of crazy Jews are disturbing the peace. Surely we are about to get into big trouble.

Rabbi's voice stops abruptly with three loud knocks at the door. He gets up and stands by the door in silence. I hold my breath. There is one more single knock, after which Rabbi opens the door quickly and shuts it just as quickly. Three people appear in the foyer. A man with a gray cap, a woman wearing a blue silk kerchief tied around her head, and a young boy, who pulls off his wool cap and shuffles his feet nervously.

"Good Shabbos, Rabbi," the man says, taking off his cap.

"Good Shabbos," Rabbi answers, helping the woman with her coat.

"I baked a challah," the woman tells the rabbi, placing a white string shopping bag just like Grandpa's on the table. "It's still warm."

She unwraps a blue-and-white checkered kitchen towel from the braided loaf of bread. It smells delicious.

"David"—Rabbi turns to the young boy—"say hello to Eva. She's going to be a guest at your Bar Mitzvah." David is silent. He nods and looks nervously around the room, avoiding my gaze. Eventually he walks through the archway into the other room, where he sits on a folding chair.

"Make yourselves at home," Rabbi tells David's parents. "I'm only going to be a minute with Eva." He turns to me and opens a thin notebook in front of me. "This is the Aleph Beit, the Hebrew alphabet. You are going to study the letter Aleph at home with your grandfather, and when you come back, we will practice pronouncing it again together. I will teach you how to write and say each letter of the alphabet one at a time, and then we'll put them together to form words, sentences, paragraphs, and eventually stories."

I open the notebook. Each letter is inscribed in black ink on thin, slanted-lined paper. "In Hebrew, we write from right to left," Rabbi says. "It's not backward, it's just a different way of looking at the world. Now repeat after me. Aleph." His mouth opens wide as he holds up his index finger.

"Aleph," I repeat.

"Good. That's very good. You have a good accent. Aleph is the first letter of the Hebrew alphabet, the very beginning, and sometimes we also think of it as the number one. Again," Rabbi says, smiling at me.

"Aleph," I repeat, looking at his bushy eyebrows.

"Good. That's enough for the first day. Now come with me," he says, taking my hand and leading me into the other room. "Let's hear David chant his Torah portion for his Bar Mitzvah."

The room is almost bare with the exception of some shelves filled with books and a few folding chairs. David stands behind a wooden pedestal, his back as straight as if he had swallowed my mother's ballet stick.

Rabbi reaches behind one of the books on the bookshelves and retrieves a box of candles. He takes out three white candles and melts their bases with a match. On the pedestal are two tall silver candlesticks. He places two of the candles in their wells and hands the third to David's mother. She lights them, covering her eyes and waving her hands above the flames with a whispered blessing, *"Baruch atah Adonai, Ehloheinu melech haolam, asher kid'shanu b'mitzvotav, v'tzivanu l'hadlik ner shel Shabbat."* She then secures the third candle on a saucer. Rabbi holds out a glass filled with red wine. He chants another blessing over the wine. Everyone says *"L'Chaim!"* except for me.

Then Rabbi passes the wineglass around. I wrinkle my nose and take a sip. The wine is very sweet. I don't think Mama would approve of me sharing a cup with anyone because of germs, but I won't tell. Rabbi blesses the bread that David's mother has baked, breaking off a piece and passing it around. It's delicious. David's father wraps a white shawl with black stripes and fringes around David's shoulders. The room grows dark, but the candles are bright enough so that I can see. Rabbi goes over to the bookshelves again and takes out more books. Hidden behind the books is a door in the wall, which he opens carefully. He pulls out a large object wrapped in red velvet with two wooden rollers sticking out, one at each end. He holds it in his arms as if it were a newborn baby. Two lions standing on their hind legs and holding up a set of tablets with Hebrew letters are embroidered on the front of the red velvet cover.

Rabbi slides the cover off, revealing a giant scroll. He places the scroll on the stand in front of David and unfurls it by its wooden rollers. Rabbi winks at me. "This is the Torah," he whispers, pointing to the Hebrew text. I rise up on my toes to get a better look. The writing on the scroll looks like a bigger version of my mezuzah.

David's father stands next to his son, rocking back and forth with his eyes half open, just as Rabbi did earlier. He chants a blessing in Hebrew very quickly and the room grows quiet. David's voice crackles, breaking the silence. His face is intent on chanting each word written on the scroll correctly. Every time he opens his mouth to form a word, I imagine a beautiful Hebrew letter flying off the Torah scroll and up toward the ceiling until all the letters are gathered in a crown of dancing words above us. The light from the candles flickers, casting moving shadows on David's face. The air feels thinner as his chant grows stronger. David's parents are standing behind him, the fingers of their hands intertwined like the braids of the challah. His mother's eyes close as she listens to her son. David struggles with the wails and whispers that emerge from his chest until his voice breaks into song.

TATA'S SECRET

IT IS TATA, not Grandpa Yosef, who greets me at the door that evening after my first lesson with Rabbi.

"Where's Grandpa?" I ask.

"He went to the movies with your grandma. How was your first lesson?"

Tata's acknowledgment that I am studying with Rabbi takes me by surprise. I realize that Grandpa must have told him something after all.

"It was all right," I answer as casually as I can, placing my turquoise toiletry box on my bed. I don't unpack it since I don't want Tata to see my mezuzah and start asking questions. I'm exhausted, and all I want to do is to crawl into bed and snuggle under the covers. I don't want to think about anything—not about what it means to be Jewish, not about Rabbi or even about David's Bar Mitzvah.

"What did the rabbi teach you?" My father's voice wakes me from my reverie.

"I learned the letter Aleph."

"Aha," Tata says. "That's all?" A mocking smile emerges on his lips.

"Yes, that's all," I tell him. My father is in deep thought as he contemplates my answer. Eventually he turns to me, his brown eyes looking as serious and as sad as ever. "Eva, if you want to know what it means to be a Jew, all you need to grasp is the essence of the *Shema*." My father's mocking smile disappears. I have no idea what he's talking about. I thought Tata didn't *like* being Jewish. "The *Shema*?" I ask.

"*Sh'ma Yisra'el Adonai Ehloheinu, Adonai Echad!*" Tata pronounces each word clearly and translates, "Hear, O Israel, the Lord is our God, our God is One."

I recognize the Hebrew words from Rabbi's chanting earlier this afternoon, but I had no idea what they meant since Rabbi didn't translate. How does Tata know this?

"Yes. *Sh'ma Yisra'el Adonai Ehloheinu, Adonai Echad!*" I say to him in reply.

"Yes, indeed," Tata continues. "It sounds simple, doesn't it? Yet entire books have been written on the subject."

"How do you know?"

"I studied for my Bar Mitzvah before I turned thirteen."

"You had a Bar Mitzvah?" I try not to sound too surprised since I don't want to offend Tata.

"Of course," he says. "My mother insisted on it."

"What is a Bar Mitzvah?" I ask casually.

"It's a rite of passage for Jewish boys when they turn thirteen. They officially become members of the Jewish community. But there's a lot of study involved prior to the ceremony, because without being able to chant Torah, you can't become a Bar Mitzvah."

"Did *you* chant Torah?"

"Yes, of course, and I was very relieved when it was all over and done with, so I could go back to my tennis lessons."

"Can I do that?"

"Play tennis? Of course, I'll teach you if you like."

"No! Chant Torah."

"What on earth for? Girls aren't obligated to chant anything."

"What if I want to?"

"Suit yourself," Tata says, shrugging and falling silent. After a while, he lifts my hands and examines my palms.

"They're clean," I assure him.

"I know they're clean," Tata answers impatiently. "Can you do this with them?" He lifts both his hands above my head and separates his pinkies and ring fingers from the rest. Both of his hands now form Vs. Tata seems pleased as I mirror the position of his hands.

"That's how a *Kohane* blesses. We are *Kohanim*, Eva."

"What does that mean?"

"It means we are descendants from the ancient priestly clan, the *Kohanim*."

"How do you know?"

"My father told me, just like I'm telling you."

"What was he like?" I ask.

"What was *who* like?"

"Your father."

Tata stands in silent thought. Suddenly he looks at me as if he had not been aware of my presence until this moment and says, "He was a lot of fun!"

I can't imagine my father having any fun, much less being a little boy who played with his father, so I wait for him to continue.

"We used to bowl with eggs," Tata says, smiling at the recollection. "One time, the two of us stole a dozen eggs from the icebox, propped them up with wet sand, and competed to see who would crack the most eggs with a small bowling ball."

"Who won?"

"Nobody. My mother caught us and gave us hell. *'Emile, what are you teaching your son?'* she yelled, just as my father hit three eggs with a big splat. I was in stitches, but my mother was furious. She gathered all the rest of the eggs into her apron before I had a chance to crack any more. 'I'm making an omelet with these for brunch,' she said.

" 'We already made an omelet,' my father shouted after her.

" 'Good,' she said, 'in that case, you won't need brunch.' "

TATA DOESN'T BRING UP my Jewish studies again. He knows I am going to the rabbi's house once a week, but from that evening on, he says nothing more about it. I continue to knock on the gray door every Friday afternoon, and before long, I start to read Hebrew.

"You've got a terrific accent," Rabbi encourages me, but I'm not happy. I'm not learning what I came here for. I want to know everything about being Jewish, and all I'm learning is how to pronounce a bunch of Hebrew words I don't understand. I have no idea what I am saying, and Rabbi doesn't seem concerned about explaining the meaning of the text. I don't know if this is because I am a girl. My sense is that the boys who come when I'm there don't know what they are studying either. I never ask Rabbi to translate and explain the text.

After several months, my walk to Rabbi's house on Fridays ceases to frighten me. On my way out, I grab an apple from the kitchen and bound down the stairs, sinking my teeth into the fruit and letting its delicious juice fill my mouth. I skip across the hopscotch grid in the yard, half-bitten apple in one hand and my turquoise toiletry box swinging from the other. Once there, however, I often feel restless and get bored. I never see another girl come in. There are only boys, each studying for his Bar Mitzvah, struggling to pronounce every word. I never talk to any of them, and no one asks me why I'm there, the only person with pigtails among them. Rabbi walks from one of us to the other, making us each repeat the Aleph Beit, then specific words, and eventually full sentences. Sometimes he comments on my pronunciation or my handwriting, but for the most part, he just keeps increasing my workload. When I get home, no one inquires about where I have been, not even Grandpa Yosef. Seeing that we didn't get into trouble with the Securitate, Grandma Iulia stops nagging Grandpa about my studying Hebrew, although I feel that she somehow manages to block the thought out of her mind.

During school, I too block the thought of my visits to Rabbi's house out of my head, and anything to do with being Jewish—especially the fact that Mama and Tata are no longer working. At home, the number one topic of conversation is how are we ever going to get out of this *godforsaken country* and join the ranks of the lucky few who have gotten their papers and left for Israel. Uncle Max brings home a popular joke from the office.

"The way the authorities are deciding who will be issued a passport next is totally scientific." He delivers this tidbit with a straight face while everyone at our dining room table listens. "It depends on the clerk's height." A faint smile starts to appear on his lips, but he suppresses it as he continues the joke. "If the clerk is tall, he pulls out a folder from the top shelf and works on it for the next three years or more, and if the clerk is short, he pulls out a folder from the bottom shelf and also works on it for the next three years or more, until eventually you'll get your passport and get out. But if your folder happens to be filed somewhere in the middle, you're out of luck." A few chuckles are exchanged as Uncle Max continues. "These bureaucratic imbeciles make believe that they are working, and the Party makes believe that they are paying them."

"Well," my father says, taking his pipe out of its pouch, "at least they are making believe that they're getting paid. I've forgotten what that's like altogether."

I get up without excusing myself and go out to the terrace for some air. Listening to them is useless. I can hear their thoughts even when they are silent.

MY PIONEER OATH—JUNE 1959

"**YOU WILL WEAR** your Pioneer scarf with great pride," Comrade Popescu tells us as she demonstrates how to make a square knot out of the triangular silk fabric. "Class, what does the color red of your scarf symbolize?" she asks. We answer in unison, "The red flag of the USSR!"

"Right." She nods. "And if you ever come to school with stains from last night's dinner on your new Pioneer scarf, you will have to deal with me—and so will your parents," she adds. "Understood?"

"*Understood!*" we shout back.

Becoming a Pioneer isn't easy, and it's compulsory. We study the history of the Party. We have to swear to uphold all of its Communist values and act accordingly. "Only then will you be indoctrinated in a special ceremony to which your parents will be invited," Comrade Popescu announces.

After weeks of more studying she tells us, "Next Tuesday at ten a.m. sharp you will all become Red Pioneers. Tell your parents not to bother coming if they're going to be late. At the end of the ceremony, you will each receive a special gold pin with the Romanian crest. Once awarded, this pin *must* be worn at the correct angle on your school uniform at all times. Should you lose the pin, you are to inform me, Comrade Popescu, immediately, and your parents will have to pay for its replacement, plus be fined a loser's fee. Who wants to be a loser?" Comrade Popescu asks.

The silence in our classroom is unanimous.

THE PHONE IS RINGING as I run up the stairs and unload my backpack onto the foyer floor.

"*Allo?*" I answer into the mouthpiece.

"Eva, is that you?" It is my cousin Mimi.

"Yes, hello, Mimi."

"You sound out of breath," Mimi says.

"I just got home from school. I am going to become a Pioneer next Tuesday!"

"That's wonderful!" Mimi shouts back. "Am I invited to the ceremony?"

"Uh . . . I don't know. My teacher says we have to invite our parents. I haven't had a chance to tell Mother and Father yet."

"Well, tell them I'm coming. I am so proud of you," she says, and hangs up. I wonder why Cousin Mimi called in the first place.

THE NEXT THREE DAYS are spent in anticipation of Tuesday morning's Pioneer ceremony. Somehow, Cousin Mimi has wormed her way into attending.

"She can have my place," I overhear Tata tell Mama in a disgusted tone of voice. "The last thing I want to do is attend my daughter's indoctrination into the Party machine."

"Don't be selfish," Mama tells him. "It means the world to your daughter."

"Don't be so sure," my father retorts. "*Your* daughter is studying Hebrew."

"I don't see why these two things are mutually exclusive, Gyuri."

"You must be joking, Stefica," Tata says, looking up from his book.

Mama's knitting needles stop in midair. "I'm joking. Of course," she answers, throwing her unfinished sweater and the knitting needles onto the bed. The door slams behind her. Tata shakes his head and continues to read.

The truth is, I *am* proud of becoming a Pioneer, because if I didn't I would be singled out as a student who has failed or who is not worthy of being Romanian. What any of this has to do with my studying Hebrew I have no idea, but I'm not about to interrupt Tata's reading to ask. I do wish he would change his mind and come to the ceremony.

PIONEER DAY is filled with tension. Cousin Mimi shows up early in the morning. Tata hands Mama his camera and shows her how to take some snapshots of me since, despite Mama's begging, he isn't coming after all. Cousin Mimi wears a navy blue beret with a pearl hatpin. Her bright red lipstick has smudged one of her front teeth, and when she smiles it looks like her mouth is bleeding. I cringe every time she beams at me.

I stand in the second row, grateful to hide behind Claudia, whose giant white bow on the top of her head bobs up and down every time she opens her mouth to sing. Andrei stands next to me and smells of fresh soap and starch. His cowlick is slicked back with brilliantine, his blue eyes are fixed on the flags on the podium. We pledge allegiance to the Communist Party in front of the tricolor Romanian flag and the red flag of the USSR, with its yellow hammer and sickle. Comrade Popescu hands out the pins enameled with the Romanian crest and urges each of us to wear ours with great pride. She then turns to face the audience and makes a long speech about how we are the hope and future of Communism in Romania. Cousin Mimi keeps smiling from the front row with her lipstick-bleeding tooth. I look down to avoid her gaze and notice that Comrade Popescu has a run in her stocking that crosses its black seam from left to right and disappears below the rim of her left pump.

Walking home, Cousin Mimi talks about how proud she is of me and how Communism may be a difficult path to follow but it is *the right* path nonetheless. To my surprise, Mama nods in noncommittal agreement. Neither of them looks up from their conversation as we pass Rabbi's house, with its weathered gray door. I feel like a foolish yet proud impostor.

COUSIN MIMI PAINTS MY PORTRAIT

"You should have seen how beautiful your daughter looked!" Cousin Mimi gushes to my father when we arrive home.

"Eva always looks beautiful," Tata mutters without looking up from his book. I stand speechless in astonishment since I have never, ever heard Tata pay me such a compliment.

"Of course she's gorgeous," Mimi retorts, "but now that she's a Pioneer there is something different about the way she holds herself." Mimi closes one of her eyes and surveys me as if I were a statue standing in the park. Tata closes his book, picks up his pipe, and goes out to the terrace to light up.

"What's the matter with him?" Mimi asks.

"Nothing." Mama sighs. "Gyuri's just tired of the Communist Party line. He can't wait until we get out of here."

"He ought to be ashamed of himself!" Cousin Mimi explodes. "It's because of the Communists that we are now free from the Nazis."

Mama sighs. "I don't believe that's quite how Gyuri sees it."

Mimi follows Tata onto the terrace while Mama settles on the bed and picks up her knitting. "How *do* you see it?" she asks him.

"See what?" Tata draws on his pipe and narrows his eyes. I sit on my bed and watch them through the open door.

"Communism," Mimi says.

"Let's not get into this," Tata says. "Then we can stay friends."

"Why *not*? If we artists can't discuss politics among ourselves, then who the hell will take a responsible stand?"

I start to change into my regular clothes while listening to their argument. Mama gets up and goes to the terrace.

"Give me a break, Mimi," Tata says. "You may be an artist, and a very fine one at that, but believe me, my dear, you know next to nothing about politics and even less about Communism."

"Don't patronize me, you traitor!" Mimi screams.

"I beg your pardon?"

"If you weren't married to my cousin and Eva's father, I would report you to the Securitate right now."

"Stop this! Both of you," Mama interrupts. "The Russian neighbors downstairs will hear you."

Tata ignores Mama and continues to rant at Mimi. "Go ahead. Maybe then the Securitate would put me away and feed me for free rather than keep me in this giant jail of a place without being able to work."

"That was your choice," Mimi hisses.

"Choice? I didn't *choose* to lose my job. I chose to leave this hellhole where all art has to pass the muster of the *Artistic Content Committee* and where I can't even take care of my family."

"I am an artist, and I express myself just fine," Mimi states solemnly.

"Yeah, right, since you swallow all the Communist crap hook, line, and sinker. Don't talk to me about how good the Party is, you who get chauffeured around in your husband's limo from one museum opening to another."

Mimi slaps my father's face hard, turns on her heel, and leaves. Mama runs back into the room and furiously resumes her knitting. Tata watches from the terrace as Mimi marches out of the yard and turns the corner. Two days later, Mimi telephones Mama and apologizes. Then she asks permission to paint my portrait in full Pioneer regalia.

I AM STANDING in Mimi's light-filled studio. It is Tuesday after school, and I am still wearing my red silk scarf around my neck, but not my white headband. Instead, my hair is held back with a bobby pin.

Mimi is standing at an easel with a stretched canvas in front of her, and she keeps looking from me to the canvas and back. She holds one very long, thin paintbrush between her front teeth, and another in her right hand. Her eyes narrow as she stares at me for long periods of time.

"Don't move and keep looking straight ahead," she says. "You can have a break in another fifteen minutes, and then we'll have some lunch."

I don't flinch, but I wiggle my toes, which are getting numb.

"Don't you have another pair of shoes besides these god-awful clunky ones?" Mimi asks.

"No," I answer.

"Well. We're just going to have to change that. I can't paint you wearing these horrendous shoes. They'll ruin the entire painting."

I eye the bowl that's resting on a table next to Mimi. It's full of oranges and bananas and other fruit I've never tasted.

"Ever have a banana, Eva?"

I shake my head no.

"If you're a good girl and have a bit more patience, you will. I promise you a banana for every sitting from now on. They're delicious, and they're good for you. Herman gets them for me through one of his foreign connections. How about an orange? Ever taste an orange, Eva? Don't answer that. Keep your mouth shut and be still."

I move my head up and down to convey "Yes, I've tasted an orange before." "I told you not to move," Mimi mutters, still holding the paintbrush between her teeth. Her head moves from side to side, surveying my face as her green eyes reflect the light from the window. Mimi has the most beautiful and intense face I have ever seen. Her jet-black hair is straight and cut short and blunt, with a stylishly unruly lock that keeps falling into her eyes. She runs her fingers through her hair, forgetting that she's got oil paint and turpentine on her hands.

Finally she says, "Let's take a break and eat," and she steps away from the canvas and wipes her hands on the back of her pants.

I walk toward the easel to take a look.

"No! Don't!" Mimi shouts, rushing to steer me away from the canvas. "I never show anyone my work until I'm completely done. Especially not my model." Seeing the disappointment in my face, she adds, "Don't worry, you'll see it when I'm finished. Let's eat."

Mimi's housekeeper serves us lunch in the studio. We have a wonderful white bean soup with grated Parmesan cheese. A sprig of parsley floats on top of each bowl. There is also a tomato salad with black olives and a baguette still warm from the oven.

"I want to see your face when you have your first bite of that banana," Mimi says, peeling the yellow fruit and handing it to me. I examine the banana carefully. It reminds me of an ice cream cone, so I start to lick it from its base.

Mimi bursts into laughter. "Don't lick it. Bite into it," she tells me as I take a giant bite and taste the strange new flavor. The banana is warm enough to soften in my mouth, and I finally swallow.

"Delicious, huh?" she says. I nod and take another bite.

Herman, Mimi's husband, sticks his head in the doorway. "Hello," he says, entering the room. "Look who's here."

He is a very tall man with large hands and gray hair. He looks as old as Grandpa Yosef. He extends his hand to shake mine and joins us at the table.

"So," he says, looking at Mimi, "how's it going?"

"Take a look," she answers with her mouth full. She waves her fork toward the canvas on the easel.

Herman gets up and stands in front of the painting. He bends his head to his right shoulder, then to his left, looking at the painting from different angles, but he doesn't make any comment.

"What do you think?" Mimi asks.

"It's good," he says, bowing to me and excusing himself. "See you next week."

Mimi looks relieved. "He's allowed to peek, because he was my art teacher when we met," she confides. "Tanti Iulia, your grandma, never thought that we would last because he's thirty years older than

I am. But here we are," she says, smiling. "Let's get back to work before I lose my light. It's good for another half hour."

Sitting for Mimi's painting every Tuesday afternoon has become my second after-school activity. Mimi insists that I wear nicer shoes for the portrait, so I bring my black patent leather shoes that Cousin Netty sent from France two years ago, even though I have outgrown them.

"Slide them on and see if you can take it," Mimi says. "If they hurt too much, maybe you can crush the backs down and stand on them. At least until I get a chance to sketch them in."

I try, but the shoes really hurt. My toes have grown and my feet have gotten wider. I keep them on for as long as I can, which isn't very long.

Mimi decides that she needs an interesting, colorful background behind my checkered uniform. "Let's go to my bedroom and see if we can find some fabric we can hang behind you." I follow her, barely resisting the urge to peek at my portrait.

Mimi and Herman's bedroom is like a far-off land I have never imagined exists except in books. Every centimeter of wall space is covered with paintings. Mimi's signature is in the bottom right-hand corner of many of the canvases. Herman's paintings have a lot of triangles and cubes. There are works by other artists too; my favorite is of sunflowers whose giant yellow- and brown-petaled wheels look like the moving gears of a clock. When I finally take my eyes off the walls to look at Mimi's bed, I wonder what it must be like to sleep there every night. There are tasseled silk pillows on a crimson bedspread, each a colorful jewel: red, gold, royal blue, purple, emerald green, and turquoise—I long to touch everything in sight, but I am too overwhelmed to do anything but take it all in.

Mimi is oblivious to me. Her head is in her closet, her round bottom sticking out. She is intent on finding just the right piece of fabric to hang behind me.

"Go sit at the dressing table, so I can hold these fabrics in the mirror and see what works," she orders. I sit while she flips through a lot of fabrics quickly, her face contorted in disapproval as she holds up each one. My eyes fall onto her dressing table and an open treasure chest overflowing with beaded necklaces. I reach out to touch a carved green bracelet.

"That's Chinese coral. I got it on my last trip to Peking," Mimi says. She looks at me in the mirror. "Want to try it on?"

I shake my head.

"Go ahead. You can try anything on," she tells me, sliding a purple bead necklace over my head. "This is amethyst from Czechoslovakia," she says, suddenly running to her bathroom and coming back with a striped bath towel that she holds behind me. "Finally! The perfect background for your portrait." She smiles at my image in the mirror. "Get up, we've got a lot of work to do this afternoon."

Mimi makes strange faces as she paints. It is as if she is in another world, where she can see what other people cannot, and her face reflects that. Standing still for her isn't any fun, but I start to look forward to my visits to her house, because each time I come, I discover something new. Her living room is filled with art books and even more beautiful treasures from her travels than her bedroom. There are African masks on the walls and a smooth white marble sculpture of a bird that looks like it is about to spread its wings. Mimi tells me that her tribal carpets come from Turkey.

"Look at these amazing patterns. Each is more beautiful than the next. This is as much art as any painting, Eva."

AT HOME I ask Grandma Iulia about Mimi. How come she gets to travel all over the world when no one else I know is even allowed to leave the country?

Grandma says that maybe Mimi got lucky being married to a big-shot Communist like Herman, who is the director of the National Museum in Bucharest, though he is old enough to be her father, and so what if Herman's daughter from his first marriage is two years older than Mimi? Mimi deserves all the riches in the world since she suffered so much as a six-year-old girl who lost her mother.

"I ought to know," Grandma continues, "since I took care of her after her mother, Nina, died, because my brother, Sandu, married a series of gold diggers so he could drown his grief in their bosoms. Except he forgot his responsibility to that poor motherless child. All of her stepmothers hated Mimi, because even as a young girl, she was far more beautiful than all of them combined, and a constant reminder to Sandu of the woman he had lost. Mimi's mother was one of the loveliest creatures ever put on this earth, and her daughter had to endure one rotten stepmother after another. So if you ask me, Mimi deserves a husband who worships her. So what if they're both big Communists? They're still Jews."

"Why did Mimi's mother die so young?" I ask. I hate it when Grandma gets sidetracked.

"Nina, God rest her soul, died of a burst appendix, and my brother didn't treat her right in the end. But Mimi doesn't know

any of this, and you'd better not breathe a word about it, or I'll kill
you," Grandma says.

"What did Sandu do to Nina that was so bad?"

"It's not *what he did*." Grandma stops to make her point. "It's
what he *didn't* do! He refused Nina's last wish. She asked him on
her deathbed to bring a Romanian Orthodox priest to give her last
rights, but Sandu wouldn't allow it."

"Why not?"

"Because Nina had converted to Judaism in order to marry
him, that's why. But you see, in her heart at the end, she was still
Christian."

"Then why did she convert?" I had never heard of anyone
wanting to be Jewish before.

"Because she was in love with my brother and he wouldn't have
married her unless she became a Jew. It was the only way to ensure
that their children would be Jewish."

"I don't understand, Grandma."

"A child is not Jewish unless the mother is Jewish. That's the
law."

"But if Mimi's mother wasn't really Jewish in her heart, how can
Mimi be Jewish? And how could a Jewish man not have enough
heart to allow his wife her last wish?"

"You're too young to understand the Halacha, Eva."

"What's the Halacha?"

"The Jewish code of law."

Grandma is right. I don't understand the Halacha yet.

FE∆THERS

THERE'S A BALLERINA in a pink tutu in our foyer. She is practicing lifting her leg up in the air, but I can tell that she's not very good because she's wobbly. She is wearing toe shoes, a sure sign that she hasn't yet been scrutinized by my mother. Mama would never allow a beginner to go up on pointe. I wonder where my mother is and why she's allowed a stranger to practice in our home without her. Since she lost her job, Mama has taken on a few select students who are applying to Bucharest's famous ballet school. She is training them to take the entrance exam. The referrals always come through a trusted friend from the school.

The ballerina's back is turned, and she doesn't see me standing behind her as she concentrates on walking straight across a length of string laid out on our foyer floor. Her back is muscular, as are her arms, and one of the thin satin straps has fallen off her shoulder. Her calves are thick and hairy, and when she lifts her arms, I notice her unshaved armpits. I wonder if Mama is so desperate for money that she'll take anyone on for private lessons, even the clearly untalented and cloddy. Quietly, I tiptoe toward the dining room, homework in hand, but the ballerina becomes aware of my presence.

"My dear young lady, would you mind standing on the end of this rope to hold it down? I'm afraid I may lose my balance." Uncle Max's voice resonates out of thin air. I stop in my tracks as the ballerina whirls around and bursts into laughter. "Aha! Fooled you, didn't I?" Uncle Max booms, but I'm still confused. I take another look at the ballerina's face and recognize the laughter in his eyes, but something's very different. Then I see it—Uncle Max has shaved his mustache and he's wearing a blond wig!

"Uncle Max, what are you doing?"

"I'm having a dress rehearsal for next week's Purimspiel. How do you like my outfit?" He adjusts the fallen satin strap on his shoulder and tucks in a few cotton balls that have flown out of his brassiere. "I had to bribe your mother to borrow this from the ballet school," he tells me. "If I've fooled you, I'm sure to fool everyone at the Purim party. Do you think your mother will approve of my ballet performance? I thought it would be a good idea to add a little suspense by walking a tightrope, even if it is on solid ground." Uncle Max spreads his arms and demonstrates his walk across the floor. I'm hooting so loudly that Aunt Puica appears from the bedroom with curlers in her hair and Sabina rushes out of the kitchen.

"Max, you crazy fool!" Aunt Puica yells between coughing fits and laughter. "You forgot to shave under your arms!"

"I'm sure you're looking forward to helping me with that, darling," Uncle Max says, then plants a kiss on her cheek. "You know, I'd just as soon wait until Purim to shave so I won't have to do it again. I dread getting a rash under my delicate armpits," he says, pinching Aunt Puica's rear end. Sabina goes back into the kitchen, her turban lopsided from laughter.

"Can I go with you to the Purim party?" I ask.

"As long as your mother gives you permission," Uncle Max says.

"You can't take the Child, Max. *I'm* not even going," Puica says, as if her presence must determine anyone else's attendance.

"And why not take the Child?"

"Because." Aunt Puica glares at Uncle Max.

"Because *why*?" he asks.

"You know very well why she can't go," Puica pleads.

"Why the hell *not*?"

"Because there are going to be a bunch of Jews gathered in one place, and if the Securitate gets wind of it, they're not going to like it," she answers.

"So? Aren't we already a bunch of Jews gathered in one place right in this house? Do you think the Securitate *likes that*?"

But Aunt Puica's not buying it. "Let's not involve the Child, Max. If you get into trouble, that's your business, but the little girl is another matter." Aunt Puica retreats into their bedroom. "You know what I mean."

"No. I don't," he answers, making a clumsy rat-tat-tat sound with his toe shoes as he follows her.

"No one else is bringing children. It's an *adult* Purimspiel." My aunt's voice can be heard through their closed door.

"So *what*?" Uncle Max has never had the last word before.

I HAVE NO IDEA what *Purimspiel* means. All I care about is going to the party. I wonder if I could wear a costume too. That would be so much fun! Still, when Uncle Max emerges from his bedroom dressed once again as himself, I ask him what this dress-up party is all about.

"Aha! Just as I thought," he says. "No one's bothered to tell you the most important thing—the Purim story."

"No."

"Purim is great because you can laugh, get drunk, and make a total fool of yourself. Show me a Jew who can't laugh at himself and I'll show you a Jew in trouble."

Uncle Max begins his story. "Once upon a time there was a man by the name of Mordechai, who lived in Persia. He was one of many Jews who lived in exile more than a thousand years ago."

"Uncle Max," I interrupt, "what does *exile* mean?"

"Oy." Uncle Max's forehead is a river of creases. He finally answers with a heavy sigh. "Exile. *Exile* means 'not at home, not living in your own country.' Exile. Like the way we are living now, Eva, waiting and praying to get back to Israel."

"But, Uncle Max," I argue, "I was born here. I'm not living in exile!"

"You are, Eva. A Jew can be born anywhere, but unless you're living in Israel, you are in some fashion living in exile, even if you are doing well and you're rich, as was the case with my family when we lived in Spain."

"You come from Spain, Uncle Max?"

"I was born here just like you, but my family was from Spain. They were Sephardic Jews who were expelled from Spain during the Inquisition."

"Uncle Max, I don't understand."

"Jews have been living in exile all over the world for more than two thousand years. Some of us have been feeling so at home in foreign lands that we forget where we came from. But sooner or later, a Haman or a Hitler tries to wipe us off the face of the earth. Purim is about laughter because, despite all of our hardships and the pogroms, and even after what happened during the war, God has never abandoned Jews and Jews have never abandoned God. Or maybe it's the other way around. In any case, being alive is certainly something for us to celebrate. Even here."

I am uncomfortable with what he's telling me, since I've always thought of Bucharest as my home. "I see what you mean by 'oy,' Uncle Max."

Uncle Max cracks up. "Not just 'oy,' kid, but 'oy, vey, zmir'!"

We start to laugh and make faces at each other. "So what happened with Mordechai?" I ask, giggling.

"Mordechai had no children of his own," Uncle Max continues, "but he took care of his beautiful orphaned cousin, whose name was Esther." He pauses and looks at me. "Anyway, there was a very rich king in Persia who got tired of his wife, Queen Vashti, so he asked his courtiers to find him a new, younger, and more beautiful wife."

"And Esther got chosen?" I guess.

"You got it. Except there's one problem." Uncle Max's index finger goes up in the air. "Esther is Jewish, and King Ahasuerus is not."

"Why is that a problem?"

Uncle Max rolls his eyes. "Eva, do they like Jews around here?" I shrug.

"All right then, what makes you think that it was any different back then?" Uncle Max continues: "So Mordechai tells Esther to do the only sensible thing—he tells her to *hide the fact that she is Jewish.*" Uncle Max pauses.

"Just like you guys hid it from me?"

"What are you talking about, Eva?"

"Uncle Max, I didn't know that I'm Jewish until everyone lost their job," I tell him, and then I add quickly, "Except for you."

"Eva, there are times when hiding being a Jew is a good idea, as Queen Esther proves. In any case, the king marries Esther. Shortly after the wedding, Mordechai uncovers a plot to kill the king, reports it, and saves the king's life—but the king is completely unaware of this. Instead of rewarding Mordechai, the king appoints Haman, an evil man, to become his prime minister. Mordechai refuses to bow down to Haman, so Haman builds a gallows in order to hang Mordechai. Haman also plans to kill the entire Jewish community."

"Queen Esther knows this?" I ask.

"Of course! Mordechai asks for her help, and she risks her life by telling the king the truth about Haman's plans. She also divulges that she is Jewish."

"What does the king do?"

"He has Haman hung on the very gallows he's prepared for Mordechai. He also signs a decree that the Jews are allowed to defend themselves."

"Uncle Max?"

"Yes, sweetheart."

"That's a scary story, but I'm glad that it ends well."

"Yes, well enough for us to have a great party and get drunk!" Uncle Max laughs. "I'll see what I can do about having you join me."

• • •

UNCLE MAX convinces everyone that I can go to the party with him. Mama volunteers to make a costume, and when Cousin Mimi hears about it, she offers to help and invites Mama and Aunt Puica to her studio to research ideas. Having to produce a unique costume in just a few days gets the three of them focused. But they forget to ask *me* what I want to wear.

"Take a look at these beautiful tribal African women," Mimi says, opening up a giant book on her coffee table entitled *Native Costumes of the World.* "Don't these women look like magnificent sculptures?"

"They look like very tall, topless women to me," Aunt Puica comments.

"So what?" Mimi snaps. "There's no shame in going topless in many countries, including on some of the best beaches on the French Riviera."

"Bucharest is not the French Riviera or Africa, thank God," Aunt Puica says, rolling her eyes.

"Look, I've got a tribal skirt that I brought back from Africa and lots of beads and bracelets. I've even got a very curly black wig. Let's just try it and see how she looks." Mimi is not about to take no for an answer, so she rushes to her bedroom and reappears with armloads of stuff for my costume. Before I have a chance to protest, they pull off my clothes until I am standing in my underwear.

"Take off your undershirt," Mimi orders, "and let's get some makeup on your body to see what you look like with black skin." She dips her hands in a round jar of dark brown makeup. She examines my face as if it were one of her canvases, and in seconds my skin turns dark beneath her hands. I stand in front of the mirror and notice how the whites of my eyes suddenly seem to glow. I smile at myself and notice that my teeth also look whiter. Aunt Puica pins up my hair and pulls Mimi's wig onto my head, tucking in every stray wisp of blond hair. The wig fits snugly. The tribal skirt is way too big, so Mimi wraps it around my waist several times, and Mama secures it with a brooch. Mimi slips brightly colored necklaces over my head and gold and silver bangle bracelets on my arms. Mama paints my lips bright red and darkens my eyebrows to match the wig. The three of them look at their creation in the mirror. I stand motionless and watch as I am transformed into an African girl. I have never seen a black person before. She is beautiful but topless. Inside, I feel the same: beautiful but naked.

"You are absolutely gorgeous," Mimi gushes. Mama and Aunt Puica nod in agreement but I tell them, "*No.*" Three bewildered faces look back at me in the mirror. "What do you mean, 'No'?" Mimi asks.

"I'm not going anywhere naked like this," I answer.

"You're *not* naked!" Mimi shouts. "You're wearing a magnificent African tribal skirt and gorgeous jewelry. It's the way they dress in Africa."

I shrug. "I don't care," I tell her. "I won't go without my undershirt."

Mimi explodes. "Are you crazy, Eva? African girls don't wear ugly white undershirts. Take a look at how stunning you look," she says, pointing at my reflection in the mirror.

Aunt Puica smiles. "She *is* beautiful, but she's got a point. I wouldn't want to go to a masked ball topless either, even if I was as flat as she is."

"Flat or not," Mama says, turning to me, "if you're not comfortable, you don't have to do it."

Mimi glares at my mother. Aunt Puica smiles, waiting to see who will win out.

"I'm not going to the Purim party anymore," I cry, pulling off the wig.

"Don't be such a crybaby," Mimi says. "Of course you're going."

I shake my head and try to push back my tears.

"We'll just have to make you a new costume!" Mimi declares, pulling me into her living room with Mama and Aunt Puica trailing us.

"Show me which costume you'd like, Eva," Mimi says, opening the *Native Costumes of the World* book on her coffee table.

I am about to sit down when she yells, "Don't! You'll get makeup all over my white couch."

Mama takes me into Mimi's bathroom, where I shower and watch the colors run off my face and body. When I get back into my clothes, we rejoin Aunt Puica and Mimi, who are huddled over the costume book.

"Let's give Eva a chance to look at some costumes by herself," Mama suggests, to which they both quickly reply, "Of course."

There are costumes from the various regions of France, Romania, Russia, Germany, Italy, and many other countries, but they don't interest me. I keep looking for a Jewish one, but I can't find any listed. Then a picture of a man wearing a magnificent crown of feathers catches my eye. I point. "What's that?"

"That's an American Indian chief!" Mimi is thrilled. "See, it says here, 'Navajo chief headdress.'"

"I love that," I say.

"Where on earth are we going to find all those feathers for the headdress?" Aunt Puica asks.

Grandpa Yosef makes a special trip to the farmers' market at dawn and enlists Ion's help. "Anything for Miss Eva," Ion tells Grandpa, and shows up the next day with close to fifty turkey feathers from the farm. He even brings some duck feathers and one eagle feather. Mimi picks the best ones and dips several of their tips in red oil paint, leaving the bases either brown or white, but she does not touch the eagle feather. "I'm using that one for the center of the headdress," she says.

Mama makes leggings from a light beige felt that looks like suede, and Aunt Puica decorates them with fringe and beads. Mama then sews a light blue silk tunic and embroiders its collar with blue and white triangles. Aunt Puica finds several strings of tiny multicolored beads in Mimi's treasure chest and makes rosettes that she sews into the headdress and down my tunic arms for decoration. The three of them continue to consult Mimi's book for reference, but the costume is really their unique creation.

The day before Purim, we get together for a final fitting at Mimi's house. I stand in front of the mirror in full Native American regalia, with the three women oohing and aahing at their creation.

"Stop smiling for a second so that I can paint your face properly," Mama says, adding several bold strokes of color to my cheekbones. I stand still and watch the American Indian chief in the mirror make a face at me. He looks ready for anything, even a Jewish girl's first Purimspiel.

PURIMSPIEL—MARCH 1960

UNCLE MAX AND I are ready, but we cannot go out on the street in our Purim costumes. "Don't worry," Uncle Max, says adjusting his blond wig. "My sister Tirtza will be sending a car for us."

"I didn't know you had a sister, Uncle Max," I tell him, touching the pink tulle of his tutu.

"There are a lot of things about me that you don't know," he answers. "Tell me if my mascara is running." He bats his eyes at me, and I crack up. "Eva, you're laughing at me, and it's premature," Uncle Max says, taking my hand. "Save it for the Purimspiel."

MY HANDS ARE CLAMMY as we enter Tirtza's apartment. There's so much noise that I wonder if Aunt Puica was right about my staying home. I don't know anyone here, but they're all laughing and talking at the same time. The lights in the rooms are dim, silhouetting the guests against the dying sun from the terrace.

"Oh my God, look who's here," a woman screeches, flapping her ears in Uncle Max's face and planting a kiss that leaves lipstick marks on his cheek. She is dressed as a white bunny rabbit. "It's Max as a pink ballerina!"

Heads turn. Everyone approaches until we are surrounded by masked people. Seeing that he has an audience, Uncle Max opens his makeup bag with a flourish.

"Ladies and gentlemen, mademoiselles and messieurs, comrades and esteemed members of the Proletariat, you are about to witness an act of ingenuity that will demonstrate how our revered Party courageously strikes a delicate economic balance." The crowd quiets down. Uncle Max retrieves the ball of string from his bag as if he is pulling a rabbit out of a hat and holds it up for everyone to see.

"Voilà, my tightrope," he continues as people chuckle in anticipation. "Not since Houdini came to Bucharest has anyone witnessed a feat like this." He lays the string on the parquet floor, sits next to it, and slips on his toe shoes. Then he gracefully crisscrosses the pink satin laces up his thick calf muscles. "Madame," he asks Miss Bunny Rabbit, "would you be kind enough to give me a hand? I am a little unsteady on my toes." Everyone roars as he gets up and brushes off his tutu. Uncle Max tucks in his belly and turns to introduce me. "My lovely assistant here, Chief Eva of the American Bird Feathers, will stand on one end in order to ensure that I will not fall as I walk on the Party's budgetary tightrope."

I stand on the end of the string just as he asks, but Miss Bunny Rabbit won't let go of my arm. "Isn't Max hilarious?" she gushes. "And you look like a turkey has just spread its tail on top of your head. What a marvelous costume!"

"I am a Native American Navajo chief," I inform her politely.

"Oh." She laughs. "Are you an American turkey?" She pinches both of my cheeks. I pull my face away without losing my footing. "You're smudging my paint," I tell her.

"Max, your niece is adorable! I'm so glad you brought her." Miss Bunny Rabbit's breath reeks of *vişinată*—homemade Romanian cherry liqueur.

"Kiki, my little bunny rabbit," Uncle Max teases, "stop torturing the Child. You're breaking my concentration. Tirtza, let the music begin!" Uncle Max's sister hurries to a turntable and places the needle on the record. The voices of a Russian choir singing the Internationale fill the room as Uncle Max demurely puts one toe in front of the other and dances across the tightrope on the floor. As he makes his way past someone he recognizes, he stops to curtsy. When he reaches the other side of the room, he does a headstand to the crowd's thunderous applause. With his legs in the air and his tutu hanging upside down, he quickly lifts his right hand off the floor and scratches his rear end. I am so embarrassed, I wish I had stayed home. Everyone's applause is drowned out by laughter.

The rest of the night is a whirlwind of people laughing, talking, eating *mititei*, and drinking beer, *ţuică*, and *vişinată*. A man dressed as a clown reads the Megillah in Hebrew, which no one seems to understand. We are given glasses and spoons and told to make as much noise as possible every time he utters Haman's name. The chanter lets us know when to make noise by shaking his head and ringing the bells on his clown hat.

Uncle Max circulates through the apartment. I lose track of him but eventually find him in the bedroom engaged in heated conversation with a heavy man who is sprawled on Tirtza's bed.

"I heard that the Securitate is beginning to visit houses about two to three months before issuing exit visas," Uncle Max says. The man slides his mask on top of his bald, sweaty head.

"Yes, I heard that too." The man nods. "But why?"

"Why?" Uncle Max echoes.

"I can't figure it out," Mr. Sweathead answers.

"You can always speculate that they want something. The Securitate always wants something," Uncle Max tells him.

"Like what? The skin off our backs?"

"That too. But maybe they'll start with our homes," Uncle Max murmurs.

"Our homes?"

"Yeah, our homes. We can't sell them, and we can't transport them on our backs to the West."

Mr. Sweathead whistles softly. "You're a genius, Max. If what you're saying is true, they'll start with those of us who have the largest apartments so they can get their grubby hands on them."

Max nods in silence.

"And if you don't happen to have a two-bedroom apartment with a terrace—"

Uncle Max finishes the man's thought. "Let's just say you will enjoy Bucharest's ambience a little longer."

"*Ce porcărie*—what a disgusting mess!" Mr. Sweathead cries.

I tug at Uncle Max's tutu.

"What is it, sweetheart?"

"I want to go home."

"What? You're tired already? It's only eleven o'clock. I haven't even gotten drunk yet." Uncle Max smiles, looking naked without his mustache. "Why don't you lie down here on Tirtza's bed and have a nap? We'll go home soon enough. Come on, Puiu, let's go talk in the other room. The Child needs her rest."

I take off my headdress and place it on the bed next to me. I curl up with my nose touching the feathers. Uncle Max covers me with his overcoat, and the two men leave the room.

When I wake up, Tirtza's house feels as if it is swaddled in a blanket of hushed whispers. I put my headdress back on and tiptoe into the living room. It is empty. I walk toward a voice that comes from the dining room. It is Uncle Max's. "Jews should never spend Purim alone," he says. "I've had so much to drink that the liquor has kicked me in the butt. This coffee is good. Tirtza, please make me another cup, and make it strong."

Most of the guests are gone. The few remaining are seated at the table sipping Turkish coffee. Their masks are all off, with the exception of a tall man with the mask of comedy and tragedy, who is still wearing his. A green bottle of seltzer with a silver spout and lever is on the table next to Uncle Max. I tap Uncle Max's arm and point to the seltzer. He shakes it and fills my glass.

A lone voice starts to sing at the table. *"Kol'od balleivav pen-imah . . ."* Uncle Max grabs my hand and whispers in my ear "It's *Hatikvah*, 'The Hope,' Israel's national anthem." As the voice gains momentum, each person around the table stands up and starts to sing. Those of us who do not know the words sing the melody. We are all standing and singing, except for one person, the man who is still wearing his mask of comedy and tragedy. Uncle Max picks up the green bottle of seltzer, shakes it, and sprays him from head to toe.

"Get up on your feet, Jew!" Uncle Max tells him.

The man gets up and pulls his mask off. Uncle Max's friend Silviu, the mole, is grinning and dripping seltzer.

Moments later there is a knock on the door. Two Securitate men in gray coats and hats appear and ask if Silviu Florescu is here. Silviu gets up. His face is as white as a sheet as he identifies himself. The two men surround him, each putting an arm around him, and walk him out. Tirtza follows them out the door. I hear a car door slam and the car drive off. Tirtza comes back to the dining room and asks Max for a cigarette. Max hands his sister the pack even though Tirtza isn't a smoker.

"They took him," she says, shaking between drags. "The Securitate men said there was a raid on Silviu's house earlier this evening. They found a box filled with *cocoșei*—old Romanian gold coins called 'little roosters' that were minted before Communism—hidden behind an armoire."

"God help his wife and children," Uncle Max says.

One by one all of Tirtza's guests go home. The Purimspiel party is over. When we arrive home, I go straight to my room, take off my costume, and get into my pajamas. When I slide under the covers, I notice it. The portrait that Mimi has painted of me is hanging above the clock on the Biedermeier chest. I get out of bed to take a closer look. There I am, in full Pioneer uniform, standing straight as an arrow.

THE SEARCH FOR GOLD ROOSTERS

"LET'S SEE if we can get this thing out," Grandpa Yosef mutters, pounding on the shelf with the screwdriver handle until the shelf lands on the pantry floor with a loud thud. There's a flashlight on the tile floor next to him. Its beam is pointed up toward the bottom shelf of the pantry, where Grandpa's hands are searching for something. When he doesn't find what he's looking for, he lies on his back, sliding his head into the tight space between the shelf and the floor. Grandpa stares at the empty left corner of the pantry in silence.

"What's the matter?" I ask.

Grandpa continues to look blank, as if he hasn't heard me.

"What's the matter, Grandpa?"

"I can't believe this," he says, shaking his head. "I hid the box right here in this corner, but it's not there."

"What box?" I ask.

"The box with my *cocoşei*. I hid it right here," he says, pointing again at the empty corner. "Right after we moved into this house."

"Grandpa, Silviu was arrested at the Purim party last week for hiding *cocoşei* in his house," I tell him.

"Yes, I know that," Grandpa says, getting up and wiping the dust off his shirtsleeves. "That's why I'm looking for mine. We can't have them searching the house and risk getting arrested."

A wave of panic rises from my toes and travels up my spine. "What do the *cocoşei* look like, Grandpa? Tell me and I'll help you find them!"

Grandpa laughs. "They look like beautiful gold coins, Eva."

He squats so he can see my face in the dim light. Beads of sweat are glistening on his brow, and his black-rimmed reading glasses have slid down to the tip of his nose. "You've never seen a gold coin, have you?" He takes both my hands in his. "Don't worry, sweetheart, we'll find them. If they're still here, we'll find them and bury them somewhere far away from this house, where the gold coins can never be connected to any of us."

"Why did you ever keep them?" I ask, fighting my tears.

"Because they're valuable. These *cocoşei* saved my life several times during the war. They're emergency funds."

"But, Grandpa, Uncle Max said they're illegal. You can't use them anymore. Why are they so dangerous?"

"They're *gold*, Eva, and the Party says that owning any gold coins is 'capitalist.' That's why I'm looking for them." Grandpa's voice is tired. "I figured the Communists can be bribed as easily as the fascists, given the right circumstances, but maybe I was wrong. You know, Eva, sometimes money can buy you your life."

"Grandpa, they could have just as well taken your money and killed you."

"You're right. They could have, but they didn't. I thought I was shrewd, but I was just plain lucky. I always gave the fascists a reason to keep me alive. I told them that there were more *cocoşei* where those came from. It was a little game the chief of police and I played during the war. It nearly drove your grandmother insane. Every time I got picked up and interrogated, she thought it was the last time she'd see me." Grandpa smiles at the recollection. "I can't afford to play these games now. Not when your life may be at stake."

We don't find the *cocoşei*. Grandpa enlists everyone's help, except for Sabina's. He describes the box and its contents. Uncle Max takes apart the entire pantry, shelf by shelf, and then has to put it back together again. Uncle Natan looks under every mattress in all the bedrooms, despite Aunt Puica's protests that he is invading the privacy of her inner sanctum. Tata goes through the dining room breakfront and even takes the dining table apart to search its base. When Sabina retires upstairs for the evening, Grandma Iulia enters the kitchen with Grandpa Yosef. She rummages through each drawer and then takes it out so that she can look behind it in the hope that the box has somehow been taped or nailed beneath. She orders Grandpa to bring out the ladder and hold on to her as she climbs so that she can inspect the top shelves with her very own eyes.

"It's not up there, Iulia," Grandpa tries to convince her. "I know where I hid the damn thing, and I'm telling you it was in the pantry, not in the kitchen! Someone must have stolen the box, because I remember where I hid it."

"Shut up, you old fool," Grandma Iulia mutters, getting down from the ladder. "You better hope that it was stolen, because I'm not taking any chances with my children."

"Neither am I, Iulia." Grandpa sighs. "*Our* children."

"How would *you* know?" Grandma snaps.

"Where the box is hidden or whether they are my children, Iulia?" Grandpa asks, pinching her cheek.

"Don't try to sweeten me up, you old fart," Grandma says, waddling out of the kitchen.

My maternal great-grandparents Eliza and Avram Şaraga.
Date unknown (Author's collection)

Aunt Puica and my mother
in party dresses, at about eight
and ten years old, c. 1932
(Author's collection)

Grandma Iulia and
Grandpa Yosef, 1960
(Author's collection)

My mother, far right, with Aunt Puica and their aunt Cora, before World
War II. Uncle Natan looks on in the distance (Author's collection)

Grandma Hermina, before World War II
(Author's collection)

Tata reading in his room, before World War II (Author's collection)

My mother with my father's friends, c. 1949. The one on the right was in labor camps with my father (Author's collection)

Tata's army ID card, World War II
(Author's collection)

My mother in a dance recital, during World War II (Author's collection)

My parents as newlyweds. They were married during their lunch break, after which they both went back to work. Cluj, March 1950 (Gyuri Zimmermann)

My parents and me on a beach vacation in Mamaia, Romania, c. 1956 (Gyuri Zimmermann)

Aunt Puica and Uncle Max at a New Year's Eve party, 1956 (Author's collection)

Me, in a dress made of fabric brought from abroad by Mimi, c. 1957 (Gyuri Zimmermann)

Beard and Mimi at a gallery opening in Bucharest. Date unknown
(Gyuri Zimmermann)

Me in elementary school, next to a print of
Trajan's column, c. 1959 (Gyuri Zimmermann)

Mimi's portrait of me in Pioneer
uniform, 1960 (Tom Okada)

Tata's "chair out of line" was the kind of image that could get him in trouble with the Party. Photo c. 1958 (Gyuri Zimmermann)

Me in my Indian headdress,
c. 1957 (Gyuri Zimmermann)

My mother selling our belongings at Bucharest's flea market shortly before we emigrated, c. 1961 (Gyuri Zimmermann)

Tata and Beard's farewell reflected in a mirror, in a photograph taken by my father after we were granted passports, 1961. Beard's hand is over his heart in anticipation of their parting (Gyuri Zimmermann)

Mama and me, arriving in Haifa harbor, 1961 (Gyuri Zimmermann)

Tata in Istanbul, on our way to Israel, 1961 (Gyuri Zimmermann)

My parents at King Solomon's Pillars with their first car in the background. Red Sea Desert, 1962 (Gyuri Zimmermann)

Tata's self-portrait on the Staten Island Ferry, shortly after we immigrated to America, 1963 (Gyuri Zimmermann)

"EYES THAT DO NOT SEE EACH OTHER"

TWO MEN IN RAINCOATS and hats with turned-down rims show up two days later at our front door.

"Is this the residence of Yosef, Iulia, and Natan Natanson?"

I stand speechless at the door and nod. A soccer ball bounces into our foyer, and Andrei appears directly behind the two men.

"Look at my new ball!" he shouts, bounding into the house after it. "Let's go and play out in the yard." Andrei ignores the two men who are standing uncomfortably in the foyer, looking at their watches as if waiting for a train. Grandpa Yosef comes out of his bedroom to see what the commotion is all about. He extends his hand to the men in greeting as I pick up the ball and run with it into the yard. Andrei can hardly keep up with me.

We play ball nonstop until we are both dripping with sweat, and Andrei finally props himself against the yard wall and slides to the ground. His cheeks are flushed, and I am completely out of breath as well as I sit next to him.

"I've got an American Indian costume with a feathered head-dress," I tell him after a while.

"No kidding," he says. "Where'd you get it?"

"Mama and Aunt Puica made it for me with Cousin Mimi. She's a painter. The headdress is really amazing. Do you want to see it?"

Andrei nods but is too tired to get up. We sit together in silence. I am afraid to go back into the house to get my costume. I try to push the thought of the two men still inside talking to Grandpa out of my head, but I can't.

"Andrei, do you know what *cocoşei* are?"

"Sure," he says, "they're young roosters. I grew up with them on the farm. Why do you want to know?"

"Those are not the kind of *cocoşei* I'm talking about," I try to explain.

"What other kind are there?"

"Gold ones, coins," I tell him.

Andrei shakes his head. "No such bird, except in fairy tales. I suppose you're going to tell me that roosters lay eggs too."

Andrei's ball suddenly bounces off the yard wall. One of the men in raincoats is standing directly in front of us laughing.

"Too tired to play catch?" He takes off his hat and wipes his brow with a handkerchief from his pants pocket.

"No, sir," Andrei and I answer him in unison.

The men wave when they reach the yard gate. We wave back and run straight into the house. Grandpa Yosef is sitting at the dining room table sipping tea.

"What happened?" I blurt.

Grandpa continues to sip his tea. "Nothing," he says. "They just wanted to take a look at our bedroom, that's all."

"That's *all*?" I ask.

"That's all," he answers, winking at me. He cups his hand over my ear and whispers, ignoring Andrei. "They're going to allow Grandma Iulia and me to leave, because they can use our bedroom and they won't have to pay our pension anymore."

"Hey, Eva, don't you want to show me your American Indian headdress?" Andrei interrupts.

"Not now. I'll show it to you tomorrow. I've got lots of homework," I say, trying to get rid of him.

"Oh, come on," Andrei pleads.

"All right, come with me!" I grab him by the hand and pull him into our bedroom. When Andrei tries on the feathered headdress, he looks like a prince, and I decide at this very moment that I am going to marry him. "You can keep it until tomorrow if you take care of it, and promise to return it."

"It's a deal!" he says, grabbing his ball and running upstairs to his room, my headdress crowning his blond head with feathers.

THAT NIGHT EVERYONE GATHERS in excitement around the dinner table. Tata is pressing tobacco into the bowl of his pipe, and Mama brings her knitting with her. The needles make a rhythmic clicking sound.

"Can't you stop that for just one minute?" Aunt Puica says, looking at the sweater that my mother is knitting. "The sound of your needles gets on my nerves."

"Everything gets on your nerves," Mama answers.

"Children!" Grandpa Yosef says, clinking his fork against his glass. "This is no time to argue."

"Who's arguing?" Aunt Puica asks.

"Darling"—Uncle Max turns to her—"I think Papa has an announcement."

"Well, I wouldn't say it's an announcement," Grandpa Yosef begins. "It's just a hunch, but it's a good one. Given the visit we had earlier this afternoon, I believe that Iulia, Natan, and I will be granted passports for Israel soon, but we'll have to wait and see if I'm right."

Everyone starts to talk at the same time. "Do you mean you're leaving without us?" Aunt Puica screeches.

"It's not like we have a lot of choice, darling," Grandpa Yosef says.

"How dare they!"

"How dare they *what*?" Grandpa Yosef asks.

"How dare the Securitate separate our family!"

Tata snickers and excuses himself from the table. Mama runs after him, grabs him by the elbow, and starts whispering. Tata pulls her into our bedroom, where they remain for the rest of the evening.

Grandma Iulia continues to sit in silence at the dining room table next to Uncle Natan while Uncle Max shoots one question after another at Grandpa.

"Why didn't you tell them they'd be better off if they granted passports to all of us? That way they can have the entire apartment. There are two additional bedrooms, Papa."

"You want me to argue with the Securitate, Max? I was happy they didn't come here to look for the *cocoşei*."

"What about *us*, Papa? Do you expect us to live with a bunch of goy strangers in this house once you're gone?" Uncle Max's question hangs in the air.

"I expect they will let all of you go in due time as well."

"But why wait? Why not let us go now if they're going to let us go at all?"

Grandpa sighs and speaks in a patient and calm voice. "I don't know. I don't have the answer, but I believe and pray that you will join us in Israel soon."

"You'd better pray hard," Uncle Max says, getting up and leaving the room. Grandpa remains at the table sipping his tea and smoking cigarettes even after Grandma Iulia retires for the evening. I sit with him, but we do not talk. This quiet time between us is enough. I cannot imagine my grandparents leaving without the rest of us. I cannot imagine my life without Grandpa Yosef and Grandma Iulia. Uncle Natan's wheezes and snorts can be heard from his cot.

EVERY SPRING around my birthday Grandpa Yosef comes home with a large box wrapped in brown paper. He unwraps it with as much care as if the box contained something of great value, but what emerges are flat square crackers that are as dry as dust and completely tasteless.

"Matzos," he says, delighted, cracking one of the matzos and handing me a piece. I take a bite because I don't want to hurt his feelings.

"It tastes a lot better with a little butter and honey," he says, laughing. "Eat, little Leah."

Tata comes into the dining room and breaks off a piece. "And why is this year different from all other years?" Without waiting for Grandpa Yosef's answer, Tata continues, "This year in this flea-infested Communist country, next year in Yerushalaim."

"Gyuri," Grandpa says, "I didn't think you knew anything about Passover."

"Aha, but I do," Tata tells him. "During the war, between serving in the army and being sent to the *lagers*, I attended a Seder in a shtetl in Hungary where the Jews set up a table right in the middle of the main street. Anyone who passed through was welcome to join them at the table and eat. That was my first and last Seder."

"And where are those Jews now?" Grandpa asks.

Tata's smirk disappears. "You know the answer to that, Papa."

ANDREI INVITES ME to paint Easter eggs. He brings several enameled metal bowls into our kitchen, and we dip the hard-boiled eggs into different bowls of food coloring and wait for them to dry. Andrei then shows me how to paint flowers and geometric patterns on each egg.

"This is just like helping my mother with her Romanian gift boxes," I confide, but Andrei is too engrossed in admiring the eggs to listen.

"The most important part, Eva, comes now," he says, taking the most beautiful egg out of a basket he has lined with a purple cotton napkin. "Pick any one you like," he says.

I figure if he can pick a beautiful egg, then so can I, so I choose a light blue egg with pink hearts and hold it in the palm of my hand.

"Now the entire idea," he explains, "is for us to knock the two eggs together, head to head, and shout with enthusiasm, '*Cristos a înviat!* Christ has risen!' The egg that cracks the least, wins. The one that's all cracked up, loses."

"*Cristos a înviat!*" we shout in unison and crack the first two eggs.

"I win!" Andrei declares.

"I don't think so," I tell him, pointing at the cracks in his shell. "Look at how cracked your egg is."

"Yours is even more cracked," he says, peeling the shell off my egg and taking a big bite. "Here, have some," he offers, revealing crumbs of yellow yolk stuck on his front teeth. "Do you have any salt and pepper?"

I hand him the shakers from the counter. "Andrei, my grandparents are leaving for Israel."

"Oh yeah? Where's that?" he asks between bites.

"I don't know," I tell him. "It's far away. Let's knock some more eggs."

Grandma Iulia and Uncle Natan are bundled up in their winter coats even though it is spring outside. They are sitting uncomfortably at the dining room table, with two huge valises next to their chairs. Grandpa appears out of his bedroom wearing his winter fur hat.

"The armoire's completely empty, Iulia. It's time to go," he says.

"Good," Grandma Iulia answers, searching her handbag for her eyedrops. "Call a taxi. I want to be early at the train station. We still have to go through customs."

Uncle Natan starts to cough uncontrollably.

"Sabina! Please make a cup of tea with honey for Natan," Grandma Iulia calls out.

"Little Leah, come with me," Grandpa Yosef says, extending his hand and grasping mine. We go to my bedroom and out onto the terrace. Everything in the yard is in bloom. The leaves of the tree branch above our terrace spread out like a beautiful yellow-green fan. Their color is so powerful, it makes me giddy and I start to laugh.

"Eva, my little Leah," Grandpa Yosef begins, not letting go of my hands. "Look at me." I gaze up and glimpse for the first time the sadness in his deep, brown eyes.

"Here," he says, dipping his hand into his overcoat pocket. "I want you to have these." He takes out a bunch of pencils tied with a string.

"*Ochii care nu se văd se uită.* Eyes that do not see each other, forget each other," Grandpa tells me. This is a Romanian proverb I've never heard before, but it rings true despite the knot in my throat. I take the pencils.

"I want you to remember to write," he says, taking me into his arms.

LETTER FROM ISRAEL

YOU NEVER KNOW what empty is until you feel the absence of someone you love. It's more hollow than the pains of hunger and deeper than a pit. One moment Grandpa Yosef is here holding my hand and the next he is gone—and with him Grandma Iulia and Uncle Natan.

In less than a week's time the Romanian authorities assign a young gentile couple to live in my grandparents' bedroom. Given the housing shortage, they are quite happy finally to have a bedroom to themselves in a good Bucharest neighborhood. They are polite, quiet people who are out working for most of the day. They eat their main meals elsewhere and only boil water for tea and coffee on a portable burner they install in their room. When they come home in the evening, they nod a curt *bună seara*— good evening—and retire to their room. They knock before using our bathroom and carry their toiletry bags and towels with them. The wife wipes the rim of the sink before she leaves the bathroom and makes sure that the seat is down after her husband uses the toilet.

My parents never say a bad word about these people, but Aunt Puica hates them with a passion that is hard for her to contain. My father stops fighting with Aunt Puica or even paying her any mind, and my mother distances herself from her sister as well. It feels as if we are two families now instead of one, and I am the only link between them.

I have the entire dining room to myself to study every afternoon. Since Grandma Iulia is gone, Sabina no longer expects me to set the table.

"Don't tell Madame Iulia when you see her again that I've excused you from your chores. She'll never forgive me," Sabina says.

Judging from Sabina's comments, she is more confident about us getting our passports than any of us are. Later in the afternoon I take a break from reading and go to the kitchen to make tea. I find Aunt Puica standing by the stove, steaming open an envelope that has come through the mail for the gentile couple who now live in my grandparents' bedroom.

"You shouldn't do that," I say, watching the steam from the teakettle magically open the envelope.

"And who's going to tell them, *you*?" She laughs.

The letter turns out to be a long-winded correspondence from the couple's cousin in the provinces. It contains details about every family member, facts without insights. Aunt Puica tries to instill a bit of drama as she reads the letter out loud in the privacy of her bedroom when Uncle Max gets home from work, but the contents are so boring, she doesn't even bother to finish it.

"Why are you doing this?" I ask her. "What if you get caught?"

"Why? Because *they* are invading the privacy of our home, that's why! I can spy on them just as they can on us and I won't get caught," she says, resealing the envelope with her tongue. "See, I'm an expert at licking the goyim." Uncle Max snickers, and she smacks his head lightly with the back of her hand.

IN LATE JUNE we receive our first letter from Israel. The weather in Bucharest is glorious, so Uncle Max and Aunt Puica join my parents and me on the terrace. Aunt Puica rips open the tissue-thin airmail envelope.

"Be careful, Puica," Mother warns her. "You'll tear the letter."

"Don't be ridiculous," Aunt Puica retorts. She slides out the pages that reveal Grandma Iulia's large script. "I'm an expert at this."

My dear children and dearest Eva,

We arrived here one week ago, at the end of May. I would have written sooner, but I was so exhausted, I climbed into bed and slept for two days straight. Then I had to unpack since I don't want us to continue to sleep like a bunch of gypsies on straw mattresses without linens. The Israeli authorities send new immigrants wherever they are needed to help build roads and homes in new settlements. Never in my wildest dreams would I have imagined myself living in the Holy Land, next door to Nazareth, the ancient town where Jesus lived. There are thousands of Christian pilgrims who come to pray here all year round. The town is full of Arabs and tourists. We live in Nazareth Elit, the Jewish town that has recently been built on the hills surrounding the old Nazareth. It is very windy, but we have a view of the Canaan valley and on clear nights you can see the lights from Haifa twinkling in the distance. We were the first tenants in our building, and we could have chosen an apartment on any floor. I took one on the ground floor because my legs were too swollen from exhaustion to climb the stairs. It turned out to be a good decision because the iceman comes every day in the early morning and I have to meet him on the hill and carry the ice to the icebox in our kitchen by myself. Imagine if I would have had to carry a block of ice up several flights of stairs! You must be asking, Why isn't Yosef or Natan helping you?—it's because they are both out working by 6:30 a.m. Natan got a job building the new road that leads up to this town, which is so full of steep hills. He's working like a common laborer in the afternoon heat, lifting huge boulders and carrying them great distances, often without help. He doesn't complain, but I see that this is taking a big toll on him. When he's finally home in the evening, he's often too exhausted to eat supper. Yosef is the only one who's happy. He works every day in the Israeli army kitchen, peeling onions and potatoes for the soldiers, and they all love him. They feed him well, so we have one less mouth to worry about.

I miss all of you terribly and pray every day to see you and kiss you once again,

Mama

Grandma's letter is followed by one line printed in Grandpa Yosef's almost illegible handwriting. It is addressed to me.

"Eva, my sweetest girl, I miss you and kiss you and love you. Your Grandpa."

Even Aunt Puica is quiet as she refolds the letter and slips it back into the envelope. None of us comment. We sit in silence as the truth sinks in. My grandparents and Uncle Natan live in Israel now and aren't ever coming back to Bucharest, Romania.

CHRISTMAS 1960

SUMMER TURNS INTO FALL and fall into an early winter. We have very few visitors to the house, as all of our Jewish friends and family are also dealing with their own unemployment and waiting for that ever-elusive, treasured passport. We live from letter to letter. The mail from Israel takes about three weeks to arrive.

After school I spend every afternoon with Andrei, and we become even closer. He reluctantly returned my Native American headdress, but whenever he comes over to play, he can't resist trying it on and walking around as if he were Prince Charming, which of course, for me, he is. Since it is common knowledge that my grandparents and Uncle Natan have left for Israel, I assume that Andrei has accepted that I'm Jewish after all—but he never brings up the subject and neither do I. Secretly, I still dream of marrying him, though I know that this is unlikely since every fiber of my mother's being is now focused on leaving the country. At Christmastime, Mother tells me that this year we can't have a tree since it is too expensive, and "besides," she adds, "we're Jews anyway." I almost ask her why all of a sudden that makes a difference, but I don't, because I know she doesn't have the answer and I don't want to upset her any more than she already is.

I stopped going to Rabbi's house shortly after Grandpa Yosef and Grandma Iulia left. I did not find the answer to what it means to be a Jew there, only more questions. Rabbi, while kind, focused on the boys since each had to study for his Bar Mitzvah, and as Grandma Iulia had pointed out, girls don't become Bat Mitzvah around here. "You should be happy that you can read Hebrew," she told me one day when she heard me practicing out loud. But listening to the sounds of words isn't enough. I want to know what they mean, but Rabbi has no time to translate. If Grandpa Yosef were still here, maybe I wouldn't have quit. Yet not going forms a void in my heart I cannot explain to anyone because I do not understand it myself.

IT'S CHRISTMAS MORNING and I'm home alone, except for Sabina. The snowflakes dancing in the windows look like white down. Mama and Tata have gone to Beard's house since Renée is visiting from Belgium. They asked me to go with them, but I didn't feel like it. I don't know where Aunt Puica and Uncle Max have gone, and I don't care. I love having the house to myself, though I wish Grandpa Yosef were here, wearing his red Santa Claus outfit with the fake beard made out of cotton balls. I try to read, but after several pages, I stop because Grandpa's face keeps popping up in my head. The phone rings. I mark my place and walk to the foyer without rushing. I pick up the phone on the fourth ring.

"*Allo*, Eva?" Cousin Mimi's voice is so loud that I have to hold the receiver away from my ear. "Hello, Mimi." I roll my eyes as I answer her.

"Merry Christmas," she says, full of cheer. "How are you doing? I had so much fun making decorations for my tree yesterday! How's *yours*?"

I refrain from asking her why she has a Christmas tree since she's such a good Communist. I'm not looking for an argument.

"We don't have a tree this year," I tell her simply.

Mimi's voice gets louder. "Why *not*?"

"We're Jewish."

"Yes. So am I. *So*?"

"We don't have a tree because Mama says Jews don't celebrate Christmas and we can't afford one."

"That's terrible!" Mimi whines. "I called because I wanted to drop by this afternoon to wish Stefica a happy birthday. Are you going to be around later?"

"Yes. We're around," I tell her, and hang up. I had almost forgotten that Mama's birthday is the day after Christmas. Maybe it's good that Mimi called after all.

THE SNOW STICKS and even the sky turns white. I get dressed and have some hot chocolate and buttered bread for breakfast. I spend the rest of the morning reading my book on Uncle Natan's cot in the dining room. I even miss Uncle Natan hiding behind his paper and making his snorting allergy sounds. A knock at the front door startles me. I hear Sabina greeting Mimi.

"Merry Christmas, Sabina!" Mimi's voice carries from the foyer.

"Merry Christmas to you too, Doamna Mimi. Let me have your galoshes so you won't drip all over the floor."

"Eva!" Mimi shouts. "Come here to see the surprise I brought you. Hurry!"

Why can't she just come in and give me a present like any other normal person? I put on my slippers and go to the foyer. There are still snowflakes on Mimi's black beret. She gives me a great big hug and her usual lipsticked kiss, and I do my best to return her show of affection as politely as possible. I look around and don't see any presents, but I say nothing.

"Are you ready?" Mimi asks, excited. I give her a cool nod.

"Sabina, open the door!" Mimi says, taking my hand and dragging me into the hallway. Leaning against the wall at the top of the stairs is a Christmas tree that stands almost as tall as Mimi. It is fully decorated with glass balls of every color and brightly painted, hand-carved wooden people, houses, and animals. Sabina reaches into the wet branches and wraps her hand around a pinecone. The tree glistens with melting snow, and it smells so good it almost takes my breath away.

"I couldn't enjoy my tree knowing that you don't have one," Mimi says, "so I brought it over for you!"

SOMETHING WAKES ME UP in the middle of the night. It's Mama. She's sobbing. "Shhh, don't cry, Stefica. It's going to be all right." Tata's voice is muffled.

"But it isn't all right, and I'm sick of it!" Mama cries. "You have no idea, Gyuri, just how sick I . . ." Her voice breaks again with more sobs.

"I have a very good idea." Tata tries to comfort her. "You're just emotional because tomorrow's your birthday."

"No, I'm not. I don't understand why they're torturing us like this. Why don't they just let us go? It doesn't make sense. First they announce that we can apply for passports. Then when we apply, they fire us, and we can barely survive. It's been almost two years since we filed, and Mother and Father have been gone now for eight months. How much longer can we go on like this, Gyuri? What do they expect us to *do*? Die?"

"That wouldn't be a new idea, Stefica. The Germans had it first."

"Thanks for making me feel better!" Mama cries.

The rest of the night is silent.

JUST LIKE MOSES

ON NEW YEAR'S DAY Mama bakes a *cozonac*. She hasn't baked one since my birthday in April, ages ago. I follow her into the kitchen to watch her knead and braid the dough. She begins to whistle a tune as she searches the pantry for raisins and sugar.

"Grandma used to say it's bad luck to whistle in the house," I tell her.

Mama laughs. "Don't be silly, Eva. I'm happy."

"I know, but Grandma Iulia says that whistling indoors calls in the devil."

"That's the most ridiculous thing I've ever heard!" Mama says, looking up from her mixing bowl. When she sees the mortified look on my face, she stops whistling.

"Happy New Year to the Child!" Uncle Max bursts into the kitchen, takes me in his arms, and starts planting one loud kiss after another on both of my cheeks, my hands, and all over my body.

"Stop it! Your mustache itches," I tell him, pushing him away.

"She's not five anymore, Max," Mama scolds, but she's smiling.

• • •

FOR THE FIRST TIME since my grandparents and Uncle Natan left, we eat together at the dining room table as a family. Sabina brings out one dish after another. Aunt Puica has fried an entire carp that Uncle Max was able to buy by bribing a friend with connections. Tata used the extra money he made from his holiday portrait shoots to buy meat. Sabina has put the meat through the grinder, and Mother has rolled it into *mititei* and spiced it so that my mouth waters even before I taste any. There are crispy French fries, and both Tata and Uncle Max are drinking beer. I am stuffing my face and swallowing food before it is fully chewed. I'm already thinking about Mama's *cozonac* for dessert.

"Do you want the fish head or the tail?" Aunt Puica asks Mama.

"I'll take the tail since I know you're dying for the head," Mama says, trying to be nice.

"Great." Aunt Puica detaches the head of the fish with her fork, scooping it from the platter and slurping the eyes before the rest of the head hits her plate. "Delicious."

"It's all yours." My father watches her in disgust since he hates all fish and he's made a big concession for New Year's just to eat at the same table where a fish dish is served.

Uncle Max ignores all of us. He's too busy cutting his *mititei*, pouring salt on his French fries, and forking them into his mouth.

"So," my mother begins.

"So," Uncle Max answers without looking up from his plate.

"So," Mama says again as Sabina enters carrying a casserole filled with steaming cauliflower, feta cheese, and bread crumbs.

"So?" Uncle Max repeats, his eyebrows going up as he helps himself to a huge portion of cauliflower. "Mmmm, this is so good. Try some," he tells Aunt Puica, motioning to the dish.

"I've made a decision," my mother says.

"Good. Decisions are terrific, especially on New Year's," Uncle Max says with his mouth full.

Tata looks surprised as he lifts his beer glass and takes a sip.

"We're leaving for Israel," Mama announces.

Everyone, including me, stops eating and looks up.

"That's not news," Aunt Puica says, breaking the momentary silence. "We've been leaving for a long time."

"Yes." Mama's not addressing her sister, she's talking to all of us. "But now it's time that we go."

"What has gotten into you, Stefi?" Tata asks in a soft voice.

"Don't patronize me, Gyuri," Mama answers him calmly. "I've had enough and I'm going to do something about it."

"About what?" Tata and Aunt Puica ask in unison, and then laugh in embarrassment.

"About our situation," Mama answers.

Aunt Puica looks at Uncle Max. "She's gone cuckoo."

"I'm not crazy. I'm going to have a talk with the Securitate officials where we filed our application."

"Stefi." Tata tries to contain his voice. "That's not a good idea."

"Do you have a better one?"

My father gets up and starts to pace. Uncle Max and Aunt Puica are both staring at Mama.

"I don't understand why you're all so upset," Mama continues. "We were told we could leave. That was almost two years ago. We've lost our jobs and we're still waiting. How much longer is this crap going to go on?"

"As long as they want, Stefi," my father suggests.

"No. That's not acceptable."

"I'll tell you what's not acceptable. You being picked up by the Securitate isn't acceptable." Tata returns to his seat but continues to stand as he holds on to the back of his chair. "That's not acceptable to *me*, Stefi."

"Stefi," Uncle Max interrupts, "be reasonable. I never thought I'd agree with Gyuri about anything, but this isn't a good idea. You're talking nonsense. It's too big a chance to take."

"I'm taking a bigger risk living like this. I'm not stupid, Max. I'm not going to be rude or show my anger to the authorities. I will simply ask them to let us all go—or to give us back our jobs so we can at least survive."

"Whoa . . . just a minute," Aunt Puica snaps. "Max already has a job. Don't rope *us* into any of this."

"Suit yourself," Mama answers. "I won't say a word about the two of you. But I will remind them that there is a large bedroom with access to the only terrace for them to reappropriate just as soon as they let us go."

"Some sister you are!" Aunt Puica shouts. "You want to leave us with more goyim in the house? Two isn't enough for you?"

"You're the one who said you don't want to be included," my mother says, glaring at her sister.

Uncle Max sticks his two fingers into his mouth and blows a loud whistle. "Ladies, ladies!"

Tata turns to Mama. "I want to speak with you alone, Stefi."

Mama gets up from the table. Tata follows her to our room just as Sabina brings out the *cozonac*.

BUCKETS OF RAIN—SPRING 1961

THE DAY THAT MAMA goes to visit the Securitate offices is cold but sunny. She wears an open-necked white cotton blouse and an orange silk scarf with black polka dots. She takes extra time in the bathroom to apply her eye makeup and lipstick, and brush out her curls. I get a whiff of her perfume as she sits down on her bed to pull on her stockings. She slides a straight black skirt over her head and adjusts its waist before zipping it up. Then she slips on her heels and takes a look at herself in the mirror. "I'm ready," she whispers, brushing a small piece of lint off her skirt.

ANDREI IS TRAILING BEHIND me as we walk home from school. The afternoon is still crisp, and I am dying to get home to see if Mama's back. Usually he's faster than I am, but today Andrei has a hard time keeping up.

"Hey, what's the big rush?" he asks.

"Andrei, do you know what time it is?" Neither one of us owns a watch, so we rely on public clocks and asking adults.

"I don't know," he tells me, slightly out of breath. "About two thirty, I think. I'm starving."

I break into a trot, and Andrei catches up and overtakes me.

"Hey," I yell. "Wait up!"

"Hey, yourself," he yells back. "You didn't wait for me!"

I catch up with him just as we enter the yard gate. He runs up the back stairs to eat lunch at his house, and I bound up the front stairs, two steps at a time. Aunt Puica's on the telephone in the foyer. When she sees me, she pulls the phone into her bedroom and closes the door. I go into our bedroom. My parents' bed is made neatly, but neither Mama nor Tata is here. I look into the bathroom just to be sure and stick my head onto the terrace. Empty. Back in the foyer, I see the phone cord is pulled taut into Aunt Puica's bedroom, so she must still be yakking. The dining room is empty except for one plate, which Sabina has set for my lunch. I run into the kitchen hoping that Mama is feeling happy enough to bake another *cozonac*. Instead, I find Sabina in her seat near the window.

"Oh, you scared me to death, Eva. I dozed off," she says, yawning and adjusting her turban. "You must be hungry. I made you a Swiss cheese sandwich."

"I'm not hungry, Sabina. Do you know where my mother is?"

Sabina shakes her head. "No idea, Miss Eva. She's been gone since before I came downstairs this morning."

"Did she telephone?"

"You know I don't answer that thing. Go ask Doamna Puica."

"Aunt Puica's on the phone, Sabina."

"Nothing new there," she mutters.

I run back to my room. The hands on our clock point to ten minutes to three. When will Mama be back? Why has she been gone this long? Where's Tata? I grab *The Adventures of Tom Sawyer*, an old favorite, and go out to the terrace. It is chilly outside, but in the sun it's warm enough for me to spread a blanket and sit with my book. From this vantage point I can survey the entire yard through the railing. I open my book, but I can't read and watch the yard at the same time. The yard wins out. Every detail takes on a new importance. A sparrow has just landed on the branch of a tree. The tree is still bare, but when I take a closer look, I can see the beginnings of tightly knotted buds. On the yard pavement, the chalk lines of my hopscotch game are partially erased. I think back to when I last jumped around the grid, and suddenly I'm thinking about Andrei, how he is my best friend yet I haven't been able to tell him what's really on my mind. I wish I could tell him how terrified I am that my mother may be in great danger, but I've promised Mama not to talk to anyone about it, so I must keep her secret. I wish I could tell Andrei how much I want to leave Bucharest and go to Israel, where my grandparents live, yet I know no other place except here, I have no closer friend than Andrei, and the thought of leaving him and everything I am familiar with fills me with great sadness as well as great excitement and trepidation. I am tired of watching my parents in their suspended state of dread, tired of being a Jewish Communist Pioneer, tired of waiting for Mama, who has gone to a dangerous place from which she may never return. I fall asleep waiting.

Uncle Max's familiar I'm-home whistle wakes me up as he approaches the house. I'm slightly disoriented, and my eyes are still heavy from sleep. I rub them and quickly rise from the blanket and lean against the terrace railing. Uncle Max is now in the yard trailed by a small stray dog with a wagging tail that has followed him home. Uncle Max picks up a stick, and the dog bites down on it and starts to pull. Uncle Max is laughing and having as good a time as the dog.

"Uncle Max!" I shout from the terrace, and he looks up, squinting against the glare of the sun. I wave at him, and he pulls the stick out of the dog's mouth and waves back with it. "Please come up, I need to talk to you!" My voice must sound urgent, because Uncle Max instantly drops the stick and bounds up our front steps.

"What's the matter with the Child today?" he asks once he's on the terrace.

I pull him back inside and sit with him on my parents' bed. "Uncle Max, Mama went out early this morning to speak with the Securitate—I'm certain of it—and she's not back yet." My words spill out so quickly I don't know if I'm making any sense. "And Tata's not here either and Sabina doesn't know anything about it and Aunt Puica's been on the phone since I got home and I'm so worried about Mama that I don't know what . . ."

Uncle Max pulls on both ends of his mustache. He wraps his arms around my shoulders. "It's going to be all right," he promises. I shut my eyes and hold on to him. Then Uncle Max releases me and rushes out the door. I follow him to his bedroom door, where he takes off his shoes before entering.

"Puica, get off the phone right now," he says, firmly taking the receiver out of my aunt's hand and placing it back on its hook. "Stefi may be trying to reach us." Aunt Puica looks astounded, but before she has a chance to speak, the phone rings. She reaches for it, but Uncle Max answers it first.

"*Allo!* Max Albala at your service," Uncle Max says with a serious look on his face. "Stefica, I'm going to kill you! Where the hell are you?"

The rains start soon after Mama returns home that evening. She is too exhausted to do more than relate the events of her day to us, but the next day, she bakes another *cozonac*, and she fills the house with a lightness I have never felt before.

ANDREI

IT RAINS ALL NIGHT and throughout the next day. Sheets of water cascade down our windowpanes until you can't see the front yard. The gutters make gurgling sounds that rival Uncle Natan's loudest allergy attack snorts. Tata telephones that he is stuck at Victor's house and will come home just as soon as the rain stops. Mama is in the kitchen baking her *cozonac*.

Mama tries to excuse Father's absence to Uncle Max. "Gyuri couldn't sit home and wait for me yesterday. The tension of my going to the Securitate offices of the National Commission for Visas and Passports was enough to make him jump out of his skin."

"He shouldn't have left the Child to wait by herself," Uncle Max argues, swiping a fistful of raisins from Mother's mixing bowl.

"Try to understand, Max. Gyuri is a scarred person, and spending time with Victor calms him. They went through hell together in the *lagers*."

"The Child was out of her mind with worry for you, Stefi, and I don't blame her. You're lucky they didn't arrest you. *We're* lucky they haven't come to the house to interrogate all of us. Maybe they'll still come after the rain stops. You're not just sticking *your* neck out, Stefi. Remember we're all guilty by association." Uncle Max laughs dryly. "And *I'm* the one Silviu used to call reckless. Why didn't you at least call home sooner?"

Mama waits out Uncle Max's rant while kneading the *cozonac.* Eventually, she says, "I tried, Max, but the phone was constantly busy thanks to Puica. I stayed away intentionally, because I didn't want to implicate anyone."

Uncle Max's eyes bulge. "I thought you were a smart girl, Stefi. Do you think the Securitate doesn't know where you live? Don't they arrest people in the middle of the night? What's the matter with you?"

"I know all that, Max. But I figured that going to Mimi's house was the safest bet, since she and Herman are such big shots. I thought the Securitate wouldn't dare mess with them."

"Maybe. Maybe not," Uncle Max answers. "Was Mimi upset?"

"No. I called her and told her I had just been to the Securitate about our passports. She checked with Herman to see if it was all right for me to visit, and they both said 'No problem, come right over.'"

Uncle Max is surprised. "That's very brave of them. Do me a favor, Stefica, no more heroic attempts at visiting the Securitate. I just want the Child to grow up knowing her mother."

"That makes two of us, Max," Mama answers as she places the *cozonac* pan in the oven.

THE SAME TWO MEN in raincoats who came to look at Grandma Iulia and Grandpa Yosef's bedroom have reappeared in our yard. I stop in my tracks, but Andrei throws them the ball and one of the men catches it, though he doesn't throw it back. "Are your parents home?" he asks. I shake my head no. The man is clearly annoyed, but his partner tells him, "It's all right, the kids can show us around." To which the first man replies, "Good thinking, Boris. I don't want to come back tomorrow."

"Come upstairs with us," says the first man, walking toward our front steps without waiting. When he reaches the first step, he turns around and throws the ball back to Andrei.

I tug at the back of Andrei's shirt and whisper, "Please come with me."

Andrei dribbles the ball on each step and follows me upstairs.

"You must be Eva," the man who threw the ball to Andrei says to me as he enters our bedroom. I nod. The two men survey our bedroom. One of them opens the curtain that hangs between the wall and my parents' bookcase, revealing my unmade bed. He walks around the room, opens the bathroom door and sticks his head in. The other man is out on our terrace. "Hey, Liviu," he says, "come take a look. Great place to set up a table and have lunch in the sun."

While the men are on the terrace, Andrei and I sit on my parents' bed and wait. I wish Mama were home. For a moment I consider knocking on Aunt Puica's door, but I decide that's not a good idea. She might get hysterical. The men are back in the room, and one of them takes out a tape measure from his raincoat pocket while the other one goes into the bathroom.

The man with the tape measure motions to Andrei. "Hold the end so that I can measure the room." Andrei helps him out while I stand and watch them measure each wall and the ceiling height. When the other man emerges from the bathroom, he writes down in a little notebook the dimensions that his friend dictates, then they leave as quickly as they came, with a nod of their hats and no message for my parents.

Mama is dancing on air when she finds out that our room was visited by the authorities. "It's a sign that they're working on our passport file!" she tells Aunt Puica, but her sister is hardly enthusiastic. Uncle Max is surprised that this inspection comes so soon after my mother's visit to the Securitate.

"It's not over until after we have crossed the border," Tata tells us as we sit gathered around the dinner table that evening.

"The next step," Uncle Max says, "is the Letter, which, if my calculations are correct, should arrive anytime within the month."

"And the Letter states . . ." Tata urges.

Uncle Max replies across the table: "The date, the time, and the place where you must report to the Securitate offices of the National Commission for Visas and Passports in order to have an interview with the authorities who will process your passports."

"IF YOU SEE THE POSTWOMAN coming down the street, you must run and let me know immediately," I tell Andrei on our way home from school.

"How come?"

"Because she might be carrying a very important letter. My mother and father have an envelope with a fat tip ready for her, and they gave me permission to give it to the postwoman if she arrives when my parents aren't home."

"So what's in this famous letter?"

"I can't say."

Andrei looks at me, annoyed. "You want me to help you but you can't tell me what this is all about?"

I feel my cheeks flush as I shake my head. "I can't talk about these things."

"Suit yourself," Andrei says, but he is clearly hurt.

ANDREI AND I can't play in the yard because it's raining hard again. I'm so anxious about the passport letter that I ignore my homework. Instead, I'm perched behind the blackout curtain on the window ledge in Aunt Puica and Uncle Max's bedroom, where I have the best view of the yard. I wait for the postwoman, who is now late, most probably because of the downpour.

Aunt Puica is in bed engrossed in a thick romance novel and picking at her toenails until tiny red chips of nail polish fly off and land on her white sheets. The only light in the room comes from her metal-shaded night table lamp. It casts a yellow glow against the dark furniture. I press my nose against the windowpane and fog it with my breath as I listen to the rain.

A slick black umbrella appears below my window. The postwoman is leaning against the gate, the hood of her raincoat dripping water. She reaches inside a giant pouch and takes out an envelope that immediately disappears under the black umbrella. I start knocking on the windowpane as loudly as I can, and the umbrella tilts up, revealing Andrei, who is waving the white envelope at me. I bound out of the room, letting the door slam behind me.

"What do you think you are doing?" I ask Andrei before he's had a chance to catch his breath and hand me the wet envelope. I snatch the letter from his hands and run into our bedroom to find the fat tip my parents have prepared for the postwoman.

"Here, Andrei, please give this to her and tell her *thank you!*"

Andrei grabs the money like in a relay race and runs down to the yard gate again, where the postwoman is still waiting for him in the rain.

We sit together on my parents' bed and finger the damp letter. "Aren't you dying to know what's inside?" I tease Andrei.

"No," he answers. "*You* are."

I shrug. "I know how to steam open an envelope and reseal it without anyone else catching on," I tell him, but Andrei does not react. I take the unopened letter and prop it against my father's clock.

"Andrei, I am Jewish," I tell him.

"I know that," he answers.

"I'm leaving for Israel soon."

"I know that too." His wet socks are bunched around his ankles as he sits next to me, swinging his legs against mine to the sound of the rain.

TRAVELING PAPERS—AUGUST 1961

FROM THE MOMENT my parents open the letter, our lives go into fast forward. They are to report within a week to the offices of the National Commission for Visas and Passports. I'm relieved that I won't have to go, since children under eighteen travel on their parents' documents.

"Your passport will be stamped with your exit visa, and it will detail the route by which you will leave the country," Uncle Max announces at breakfast one morning. "You must sell or give away whatever belongings you have and take care of any loose ends. I wish I could tell you to liquidate your assets, but you don't have any." Uncle Max smiles. He is full of useful information because, unlike Tata, he is plugged in to the Jewish community grapevine.

Mama starts to plan everything, and Tata implements her plans without an argument. He puts in a call to one of his childhood friends who is the curator of the museum in Cluj and donates our Biedermeier chest of drawers and the ancient iron safe that has always served as my nightstand. Mama sells our armoire to the gentile couple living in my grandparents' bedroom. Our books are distributed among my parents' friends. Mama goes through all of our clothing since we are allowed only fifty kilos each of luggage, less for a child under thirteen. Jewelry of any kind is forbidden to leave the country. The one exception is a married couple's gold wedding bands. Each person over the age of thirteen is allowed one watch. On the weekend Mama goes to the Bucharest flea market and sells the clothing we are leaving behind and the few knickknacks my parents had amassed over the years.

"What are we going to do about your father's clock and your mother's vase?" Mama asks Tata.

"And what about Mimi's portrait of Eva?" Tata's voice echoes strangely in the now almost-empty room. My parents look at each other, both thinking the same thing.

"I'll see what I can do," Mama says. "I'll call Herman at the museum to see if he can pull some strings. What do the Communists need with your father's clock and your mother's broken vase?"

"You'd be surprised, Stefica, at how vindictive a lot of people can be."

"You'd be surprised, Gyurica, at how kind some people can be," Mama retorts. "I can't promise that Herman will help, but I'll ask him."

Tata sighs. "Ask," he says.

Mimi's husband, Herman, is not only kind—he is smart. He obtains the necessary papers for us to ship those items, including my portrait, out of the country legally. To be sure, these things hold no monetary value for anyone, but to us they are priceless.

THE BIG DAY has arrived. Mama and Tata are dressed in their best for their official meeting at the passport office. Even though this is the beginning of the answer to all of our prayers, I'm scared. What if something goes wrong? What if the clerks at the passport office change their minds? What if my parents don't return home from their appointment?

Aunt Puica is in her bedroom as usual, reading. Uncle Max is still at work, and Andrei is nowhere to be found.

"Sabina," I ask, sticking my head into the kitchen, "have you seen Andrei?"

"He went with his mother to the doctor," she answers. I wish Andrei had told me. I would have gone with him just to keep myself from thinking about Mama and Tata at the passport office.

AUNT PUICA'S ANXIOUS VOICE is the first sign that my parents are back. "How did it go? Did they give you your passports? What date will you be leaving? Did they tell you who will be living in your bedroom? When do they expect to move them in?"

I run into the foyer to greet my parents, and Aunt Puica is still bombarding them with questions. "What border town will you be leaving from? Is your exit visa to Vienna? Did they ask you any questions about Max and me? Did they give you any inkling of when they will issue us our passports?"

"Puica." Mama is out of breath, as if she has just run home. "Let me take off my hat and coat and then we can talk."

"What's the matter with you?" Aunt Puica snaps. "You can't take off your coat and talk at the same time?"

Uncle Max appears in the doorway. "How come no one responded to my I'm-home whistle?" he asks. "I see we have more important news to discuss. So how did it go?"

We all go to sit in the dining room. Tata docs not look pleased. Mama is exhausted but hopeful.

"Here," Tata says, retrieving two Romanian passports from his breast pocket and placing them on the table. Both Uncle Max and Aunt Puica reach for them at the same time. Everyone laughs nervously.

"We're leaving in ten days exactly," Tata says, inhaling and momentarily holding his breath. "But unfortunately, we're not going to Vienna. We're leaving by train to Sofia, Bulgaria, and then to Istanbul."

"*Istanbul?*" Aunt Puica screeches.

"Yes, Istanbul, as in the Ottoman Empire," Tata answers, smirking at her.

"Don't get cute with me," Aunt Puica growls.

"Children!" Uncle Max shouts. "*No fighting!* We've got ten days, during which I want all of us to create only peaceful family memories."

They all laugh, except for me. Ten days is a long time. We're already packed and ready to go. Sabina's entrance interrupts my thoughts.

"Sabina, come sit with us," Uncle Max says. "Soon you'll only have to take care of me and Doamna Puica."

Sabina crosses herself before sitting next to Tata.

"I was hoping we could exit through Vienna," Tata tells everyone, "but for some reason . . ." He opens one of the passports to show us. "See, they crossed out the stamped visa to Austria and *restamped* it with one to Bulgaria and then to Turkey. It makes no sense! I asked the clerk why, and all he would tell me was that we are the first wave of immigrants to test out this new route."

"Who cares?" Uncle Max snaps. "Be happy you're getting out! What difference does it make? You already went to Vienna before the war, so now you'll get to see Turkey by way of Bulgaria!"

My father rolls his eyes. "Max, this is not about being a tourist. I was hoping we could contact the American authorities in Vienna and make our way to the United States. But there is no Hebrew Immigrant Aid Society office in Istanbul, so we have no choice but to go to Israel."

Now it's Uncle Max's turn to roll *his* eyes. "Aaaha . . . America! That's another story entirely. I had no idea that you had such lofty hidden ambitions, Gyuri. Too bad you'll have to settle for Israel, land of the Jews."

My father doesn't answer. He takes out his pipe and stuffs tobacco in its bowl automatically, but he does not light up. "I don't have to answer to anyone about where I want to live, least of all to you, Max. I've paid more than my dues for being a Jew. Where we live from now on is our business."

I am stunned. *America?* Tata and Mama have never mentioned America before. I want to go to Israel and live with my grandparents again! I am so relieved someone in the passport office has changed our visas that I am sending imaginary hugs and kisses to that person as I pinch my leg under the table until it stings and gets red.

"I thought we agreed that we're not going to fight for the next ten days," Mama reminds everyone.

Sabina sighs and shakes her head. "Do any of you want tea?"

As Sabina retreats into the kitchen, Mama continues. "This is all a moot point, because we have no choice. We're leaving through

Bulgaria and Istanbul, and that's that. It's not the end of the world. I'll tell you what is bad, though. We are not allowed to take any money with us. Not Romanian lei or foreign currency. We will have to rely upon the Israeli authorities just as soon as we meet up with them in Istanbul. We also cannot take out any papers. No written material whatsoever—not Eva's birth certificate or ours for that matter, no marriage license, no diplomas, no nothing. Not even an address book with friends' phone numbers."

Uncle Max and Aunt Puica are dumbfounded. "So what the hell are you supposed to do, memorize the phone book?"

"Precisely," Mama answers.

"We have a real problem to resolve here. No papers can be taken out of this country." Uncle Max is stating the obvious. "How the hell are you going to prove your education? Or that you even exist?"

"We don't know," Tata admits.

"Good luck!" Uncle Max says. "Since we have no children, at least Puica and I won't have to prove that our child's not a *mamser*— bastard. Can any of you think of a way to legally send Eva's birth certificate abroad?"

No one fights for the next three days. Aunt Puica is quieter than I have ever seen her. I think she is worried that she will miss me, but she doesn't mention it. Mama is restless. Tata is the happiest I have ever seen him. He runs around visiting each and every one of his friends, who are thrilled for us but still cry when they come to our little room for just one more long goodbye. Beard, the film director from Tata's Studio days, takes Tata out to lunch. When they return from their outing, Tata holes himself up in the bathroom and processes some film. A few hours later he prints a beautiful black-and-white photograph of the two of them standing in front of a giant gilded mirror in a grand, ancient mansion. In the photograph, Tata is smiling faintly and looking straight into the camera, but Beard has a long, sad face, and his right hand rests upon his heart.

"That is an extraordinary photograph," Mama remarks, looking at the still-wet print.

Tata nods, pleased.

"Gyuri, what are you going to do with all your film negatives?" she asks.

Tata shrugs. "Burn them. There's no way they're going to allow me to take film out of the country when we can't even take a piece of paper with us."

"That is *not* acceptable!" Mama cries.

"What do you want me to do?" Tata's face looks so pained and helpless that Mama answers him with just one word.

"Nothing," she says.

I should have known that my mother is not the kind of person who would ever do *nothing* about anything—but I didn't. Yet Mama trusts me and no one else with her secret plan.

SABINA'S WRATH

IT IS NOT YET DAWN. Mama is getting dressed in the dark while Tata is still snoring lightly. I open my eyes and wait until the shadows in the room become discernible shapes. Mama goes into the bathroom and pees without flushing. That's not like her. She leaves the bedroom soundlessly.

I get up and rush to the bathroom, where I splash water on my face, dry myself quickly, and tiptoe out into the foyer. The light from the dining room casts giant shadows in the foyer. Mama is sitting at the dining room table, sipping coffee and going through a lot of papers. She is so intent on what she's doing that she does not notice me.

"What are you doing up so early?" I ask.

"What are *you* doing up so early?" Mama answers.

"Looking out for you," I tell her.

"Come here," she says, opening her arms. I go sit on her lap, and she kisses my head, but my eyes are riveted on the papers she's sorting through.

I pick up a yellowed piece of paper. "What's this?" I ask.

Mama smiles. "That's my marriage license to your father," she says as I start reading the document. She gently takes it out of my hands. "Eva, I'm going to ask you to keep a secret, all right?"

"Yes," I promise.

"I'll be going out now, before anyone else wakes up. I want you to be a good girl and go back to bed and act as if you didn't see me this morning. Don't tell anyone, not even Tata."

"But where are you going?"

Mama looks at me, and it is clear that she is trying to decide how much to tell me. When she finally speaks, she exudes calm and complete control.

"I'm going to ensure that these papers and your father's photo negatives get to Israel, where we will need them."

"How?" I know just as well as she does that we can't take any papers out of the country.

"By placing them into the hands of someone who will get them out safely," Mama answers simply.

Grandpa's face suddenly pops into my mind, and I'm reminded of the conversation we once had about the definition of a *sin of omission*.

"It's too dangerous for you to do that! Where are you going with these?" I ask, pointing at the papers.

Mama places her index finger to her lips. "Don't worry. I promise I'll be very careful. But you must promise me not to tell. Remember what Uncle Max said? We don't want any more fights in this house before we leave."

I watch her as she quickly selects which papers and negatives to take and which to leave behind. She places the ones she's taking in a flat envelope that she pins to the inside of her bra. Then she unrolls Tata's film that is already in acetate sleeves and winds it around her waist. She tucks in her blouse and puts a very wide belt on over her skirt. "It's a good thing I'm thin," she says, laughing. In the foyer she puts on her black overcoat and her navy blue French beret. "Bye," she says with a wave of her hand. "I'll be back before breakfast." And then she's gone.

I go back to bed. The light from the terrace is beginning to fill our room. The sound of Tata's clock is as reassuring as ever, but the clock is no longer resting on the Biedermeier chest. It is now standing on top of our luggage.

WHEN I WAKE, I find Mama having breakfast with Tata in the dining room. I give her a great big hug, and she holds on to me tightly before releasing me and offering me a cup of hot chocolate.

"I'm going to meet with Victor today," Tata says. "He's got a connection that can arrange for me to get permission to take one of my cameras with me. If we can pull that off, it will come in very handy for freelance work in Israel."

Mama nods and smiles. "Good luck," she tells him.

Since we are so close to our departure date, Mama allows me to skip school. "The less your school friends know about our leaving for Israel, the better," she says, and I agree. Except for saying goodbye to Claudia, and of course to Andrei, I have no desire to explain anything to anyone. I am so anxious about Mama's safety that I cannot wait for us to leave. Each morning I cross off another day on the calendar next to my bed. There are only four days left. I wonder how long it will take for us to travel to Israel. I am going to see Grandpa Yosef and Grandma Iulia again! This morning, as every day this week, I wait to see Andrei off to school.

I run to the foyer as soon as I hear the sound of the front door latch, but instead of hearing Andrei's cheerful "Good morning," I am met by a man with a stone-cold face who didn't bother to knock.

"I am looking for a woman," the man says without introducing himself. "She is about five feet tall, with curly brown hair and light eyes—most likely blue, but could be green. Do you know anyone who fits that description?"

I freeze and stare up at him. He is describing my mother, who I know is in our bedroom, but something tells me not to call her.

"Just a moment," I tell him, and run to get Sabina. I find her in the kitchen drying a skillet with a dish towel, grab her by the hand, and barely have time to breathe into her ear, "There's a bad man in the foyer who says he's looking for someone that sounds just like my mother."

Sabina adjusts her turban before greeting the man. "*Bună dimineața*—good morning," she says in a casual, almost bored manner as she continues to wipe the skillet. "The girl here says you're looking for someone?"

"Yes," the man answers, his tone impatient. "A woman in her mid to late thirties, slender, curly hair, pretty. She was observed entering and leaving the Israeli Consulate earlier this morning, and I am here to ask her some important questions."

Sabina stops wiping the skillet and sets it on the counter. "I don't know anyone who looks like that, and neither does this child. You must have the wrong address," she says in her heavy provincial accent, then turns on her heels.

The man is visibly annoyed. "No, I have the correct house. The woman I'm looking for was followed here by my colleague very early this morning."

"Your colleague must have given you the wrong information," Sabina tells him.

"Is the lady of this house at home?" he asks.

"I don't think so," Sabina says.

"Very well then. I shall have to come back and speak with someone who has enough brains to give me some answers. Please inform all the occupants of this house that the woman I'm looking for was wearing a black overcoat and a navy blue beret, exactly like these." The man points to my mother's coat and beret that are hanging on the coat rack.

Sabina's eyes harden. "Ah, I see you must be looking for Doamna Stefi, but you have no business here because she is leaving the country this week for Israel. That might explain why your colleague saw her at the consulate. But she doesn't look anything like the way you described her."

"She may not leave for anywhere until after I've had my talk with her," the man says, turning to go. "You can be sure of that."

"Just a moment," Sabina says, spitting in her palms. "I don't think so. Let me tell you something, Mr. Comrade. Don't you come into this house threatening my mistress, because I promise you I will flatten your face flatter than the flattest pancake with this skillet and your mother will feel sorry she ever gave birth to someone as ugly as you. And don't think that I'm afraid to do it! I was born and raised here on a farm that you and your Party made poorer. I *am* the *Proletariat* you all brag about so much, and I swear that there are no better, kinder people than these people I have been working for for more than five years. Now get out of here and don't come back!" Sabina spits in her palms again and adjusts her turban. Then she grabs my hand and pulls me into the kitchen.

• • •

THE SECURITATE MAN comes back the next day. By now, however, Sabina has told my parents everything about her encounter with him, and they've prepared a story everyone agrees upon. Mama tells him that her parents live in Israel and that her mother is gravely ill. We have no way of contacting her parents to let them know that we will be coming, since they have no phone. And once we are in transit we won't be able to send letters and await a reply, which is why she had to go to the Israeli Consulate before our departure. The Securitate man seems to buy Mama's story. He calls the National Commission for Visas and Passports to check that my grandparents have indeed emigrated to Israel. Once that information is confirmed, he leaves our house, but not before going into the kitchen and spitting in Sabina's face. "Jew lover!" I hear him call her. When he emerges from the kitchen, there are red welts on his cheeks from Sabina's hand.

ACROSS THE FRIENDSHIP BRIDGE—SEPTEMBER 1961

OUR TRAIN IS LEAVING tonight at ten. Everything is packed and ready to go. I look around our room and notice that I left my turquoise toiletry box with my Hebrew book and my mezuzah next to my bed. Also, the American Indian headdress is still hanging on a nail, its feathers fanned out against the white of the wall. I grab both and leave the empty room.

I take the toiletry box into Aunt Puica's bedroom and hand it to her. "Please give this to Uncle Max after we're gone," I ask her.

She doesn't question me about the contents of the box. "Come sit with me, Evişoară," she says, patting her bed. Aunt Puica is still in her robe, and I am wearing three layers of undershirts and two sweaters—"so that you'll have more room in your luggage," Mama insisted.

"I'm not going to the station with you," Aunt Puica starts. "I can't watch that train take you away, you understand?"

I nod. She rolls up her robe sleeve and takes off her watch. "Here, I want you to have this," she says. "It was the first present Max ever gave me."

"I am not allowed to wear a watch because I'm too young," I remind her.

"That's okay, sweetheart. They probably won't check under all those layers, but if they give you a hassle, let them keep it. I do hope you can take it to Israel with you, though."

"I will do my best," I promise.

"And one more thing," she says, laughing and crying at the same time as she wipes her nose with the back of her sleeve. "When your train crosses the border from Romania into Bulgaria, please spit on their famous *Friendship Bridge* for me."

I FIND SABINA in her room upstairs. She looks so different without her turban. Her long and scraggly hair has turned gray, and it's parted in the middle. There are spots where I can see her scalp.

"Sabina, we're leaving," I tell her, tiptoeing into the room. She takes me in her arms and holds me for a long time. "Tell your grandparents and Uncle Natan that I love them and miss them," she says. "And may God watch over you always," she whispers, crossing herself.

ANDREI IS MY LAST GOODBYE at home since Uncle Max will be taking us to the train station. I knock on Andrei's door, and he sticks his head out and says, "I'll meet you on the terrace in a few minutes."

Outside, a sliver of a moon hangs in the dusk sky and a few stars have made their appearance. The autumn air is cool and crisp. I place my American Indian headdress on my head and wait for Andrei. When he joins me, he is holding a package wrapped in brown paper.

"Andrei, you know I can't take anything with me," I tell him.

"This you can take," he answers, unwrapping the brown paper and revealing my favorite type of Hungarian salami, from Sibiu. "Oh, and I also brought you dessert," he says, presenting me with a bar of dark chocolate.

"This must have cost a fortune!" I embrace him, and then we both pull away uncomfortably.

"Don't worry about it," he says.

"I'm going to miss you," I say, looking down into the darkness that has descended upon the yard.

"I'm going to miss you too," he answers, taking my hand.

"Here, I want you to keep this." I take off my feathered head-dress and place it on his head.

THE CUSTOMS OFFICIALS have searched our luggage and discovered Aunt Puica's watch on my wrist during the body check. "Let the girl keep it," one of the clerks says to the other. "That watch isn't worth much." So I get to keep the watch. When they find the Hungarian salami, they pierce holes through it with knitting needles to make sure that we have not hidden any jewelry inside. They break the bar of chocolate into pieces for the same reason. None of us cares. The train is hurtling forward into the cold night air toward Bulgaria.

We stop in Giurgiu, the last town on the Romanian border. Even though we have an entire compartment to ourselves, it's tight quarters. My father stands up to stretch. Mama has fallen asleep. "Where are we?" she asks, yawning, when she wakes up. She looks out the window at the barren station.

"We're almost out of here," Tata answers.

"Fifteen minutes!" The conductor's voice comes through so loudly over the sound system that I have to cover my ears. "This train will depart in fifteen minutes. Please be sure to be back on board by eleven fifteen sharp."

"How about a family photo at the Romanian border?" Tata suggests. I can tell that my mother doesn't feel like posing right now, but she humors him. "Get up, sweetheart," she says, taking my hand. We step off the train and wait for Tata on the platform. When he doesn't join us after a few minutes have passed, Mama gets impatient. "Stay here," she tells me. "I'm going to see what's holding him." A moment later she reappears, grabs my hand, and pulls me back onto the train.

"What's wrong?" I ask.

"Your father can't find his camera bag." She looks ashen.

Tata doesn't speak. He continues to rummage through all of our belongings, including my valise.

"Try to remember when you last had it," Mama tells him.

Tata keeps looking at his watch.

"We've got seven minutes before this train crosses the border," he says, ignoring Mother's advice. "I'm going to talk with the conductor."

Tata runs to the front of the train. He is back in our compartment four minutes later. I checked the time on Aunt Puica's watch.

"They found my camera bag in Bucharest on the train platform!" he announces. "There's nowhere for them to ship it and I'm not even going to consider that as an option, because it will get stolen—guaranteed. Stefi, I must go back to Bucharest and get it. I spoke with the station chief there, and he swore that he'll hold on to it for me. Of course, I promised him a huge tip. I'll have to call Max and ask him to come to the station with the money."

"Are you crazy, Gyuri? You want to go back to Bucharest for *a camera*? You'll buy another one when we get to Israel!" Mama shouts.

"No!" Tata says. I know by the look on his face that there is no arguing with him. "We have no money. That camera is my only means to make a living. I'm going back to Bucharest to get it. You and Eva wait for me in Sofia at the train station. I promise, I'll join you as soon as I can."

Tata steps off the train without so much as a goodbye kiss. Less than one minute later, the locomotive starts up again and transports my mother and me out of Romania with a puff of white steam against the night sky and the wail of a long whistle.

NEW FRIENDS IN SOFIA

MAMA DOES NOT DISCUSS Tata's decision to go back to Bucharest for his camera. We are both worried about how long we will have to wait for him in Sofia and whether the Hungarian salami and the chocolate that Andrei has given me, our only food, will last until we are reunited and on our way to Istanbul.

"You know, Eva, just before we left Bucharest, my friend Livia telephoned and asked me to call a friend of hers who lives here in Sofia, and say hello. She gave me her friend's number, but I didn't write it down since we couldn't take anything written with us. I told Livia that I would try to memorize her friend's number, but honestly, it just didn't seem that important at the time. I wish I knew her friend's last name so we could look her up in the Sofia phone book."

"Try to remember the number, Mama" are the last words I murmur before the sound of the train lulls me to sleep.

When I wake up, my mother is engrossed in conversation with a man who is sitting across from us. They are speaking French, but the man peppers his conversation with Romanian words spoken in a heavy accent I do not recognize. Neither of them notices that I'm awake, so I close my eyes quickly and then only half-reopen them, so that I can observe their conversation through my lashes.

The man is unnervingly handsome. His black hair is thick and slicked back, his skin is olive, and his brown eyes are enormous. He is well dressed in a light gray suit with a deep blue silk tie. His hands express concern as he speaks. I am relieved when I notice a gold wedding band on his left hand. I don't know if it's because they're speaking in French or if it's just my imagination, but I detect a bit of flirtation in Mama's voice. I decide to let them know that I'm awake just as the train pulls into the station at Sofia. It is five thirty in the morning.

Our luggage is unloaded onto the platform by a *hamal* whose hand is out, expecting a tip. Mama looks on with gratitude and embarrassment as our new friend pulls out his wallet and tips the *hamal* in Bulgarian currency. More words in French are exchanged as our handsome friend reaches into his pocket for his card and hands it to Mama before he's whisked away to a waiting black limousine.

We watch the commotion as passengers are met by family members who embrace them, others hail taxis, and the remainder rush to make connecting trains. Mama and I form a solitary island in the Sofia train station. Perched on top of our valises, we watch the multitude rush by. I envy their sense of purpose and their focus on a destination.

Mama breaks off a piece of Andrei's chocolate and hands it to me. "Here," she says. "It's too early for salami. Think of this as a cup of hot chocolate while it melts in your mouth."

I don't think about hot chocolate, I think about Andrei. He is probably in school right now, listening to Comrade Popescu's

boring math lesson. I wonder if he allows himself to drift and
think of me as I'm thinking of him. One day shortly before we left,
one of Mama's friends came to the house to bid us farewell. She
asked, "What will you miss the most after you're gone, Eva?" and
without hesitation, my answer was "Nothing. I will miss nothing,
because while I have good friends here, I will make new ones
wherever I go." Now that Andrei's dark chocolate is melting in my
mouth, I miss him so much already, I would trade this chocolate
just to see him one more time.

Mama gets up from the valise, goes to the phone, and dials.
She got some change for phone calls from our handsome friend. I
leave our luggage to go talk to her. "Are you calling the man we
met this morning?" I ask.

Mama turns around as her fingers press down on the telephone
receiver lever. "No, I'm trying to reach my friend Livia's friend,
but her number is constantly busy. Don't leave our luggage unattended. Get back there now!"

I return to our luggage and sit down. I wish I had a book, but
since books are prohibited as printed material, mine were left behind in Bucharest. I wonder when Tata will reappear. Mama comes
back from the telephone looking defeated. "Let me have a piece of
chocolate," she says, sitting down on her valise. As she savors the
chocolate, she checks her watch for the time. It is eleven thirty. She
goes to the ticket booth and tries to speak with the clerk. I hear
Mama trying to explain our situation to him in French, but he
clearly does not understand. He answers her in Bulgarian. Mama
starts to gesticulate, but that doesn't help. She finally gives up and
rejoins me.

"Are you sure you have the right number for Livia's friend?" I ask.

"I've got as right a number as I'm ever going to remember, Eva. I wish whoever is on that phone would stop yakking and pick up."

I yawn. It's hot and I'm very thirsty. My mother won't leave our luggage, so I have to find the bathroom by myself. It isn't very clean, but there is a sink with running water. I perch myself on the sink ledge and let the water run until it's cold. I drink without touching the faucet and the water tastes great. When I get back, Mama has left our luggage unattended and is on the phone again trying to reach her friend's friend. I stand guard by our valises. By two p.m. we are both famished, since we were too nervous to eat a proper dinner before leaving Bucharest. Mama hands me the salami, and, since we have no knife, I bite into it.

"Save some for dinner," she cautions, nibbling on her own tiny bite.

I chew slowly, wishing for a piece of bread to go with the salami, which is delicious but spicier than usual. After lunch I'm exhausted. I place my head on Mama's shoulder and fall asleep. This time, what wakes me is my mother standing up and stretching her arms above her head.

"I'm going to call that man from the train I was speaking with this morning, Eva. I must have the wrong number for Livia's friend, whoever she may be, or the phone is out of order, because it's still busy." Mama checks her watch and I check mine. It is 5:20 p.m. We've been in this station for nearly twelve hours. Mama walks over to the telephone again, and after just three minutes she returns smiling.

"I got him," she announces. "He's sending a car out to pick us up."

I glance at her and say nothing. I wonder how Tata will feel about this, but we have no choice. Tata should have thought about his decision to go back to Bucharest before leaving us stranded with no money and no food in a foreign country. I'm furious with him.

THE SAME BLACK LIMOUSINE that met the handsome man this morning picks us up. The driver is a uniformed chauffeur who holds the car door open and helps us with our luggage. He speaks only Bulgarian, but he clearly knows about us because he shows us the same card my mother received earlier in the day.

At the house, Vasily, Mama's handsome friend, greets us and introduces us to his wife, Ana.

"Welcome to Sofia," she says in English, extending her hand to Mama, who shakes it vigorously and answers her in French.

"I'm so sorry I'm not fluent in English," Mama apologizes in French and stands there tongue-tied until Vasily intervenes by translating.

Our room is bright. There are fresh roses in a vase on the dresser across from the bed.

"How do you like Sofia so far, Eva?" Mama asks me, pleased with herself. When I don't respond, she stops unpacking and sits next to me on the bed. "We are so lucky, Eva. Can't you see just how lucky we are? When Vasily telephoned the train station, he was told that they don't expect another train from Bucharest for at least three days! He said we are welcome to stay with his family. What would we have done in that station alone and with no money?"

Mama is right, but my stomach hurts. I run to the bathroom, but nothing comes out. When I return, Mama opens my valise and takes out my gauzy white blouse with Romanian embroidery, a gray skirt, and white knee-highs to go with my only pair of black shoes. She combs my hair and pins it off my face before we join the Bulgarians for dinner.

The table is set with a white lace tablecloth, china, crystal, and silverware. A vase with daisies and purple bellflowers is resting on the sideboard. Vasily lives with his in-laws. He tells Mama that he is an actor with the Bulgarian National Theater and that he travels to Bucharest often. His wife is a painter, just like Cousin Mimi. His father-in-law has white hair and a mustache and is extremely polite. The maid brings out a soup terrine, and the mother-in-law ladles the white broth into each bowl. Suddenly, I miss eating with Grandpa Yosef and Grandma Iulia, and a lump rises in my throat, but I swallow and push back my tears.

"The soup is traditional," Vasily's wife tells Mama. "It's cold milk with cucumbers and other raw vegetables. Try it," she says, motioning at me.

I bring a spoonful to my lips and stop. My stomach feels like it is about to come out of my nose. Mama's knee knocks mine under the table. She smiles charmingly at our hosts and whispers to me in Romanian, "Drink it." And so I swallow down the soup. The rest of the meal is better. There is beef stew and steamed potatoes garnished with butter and dill weed, foods I am familiar with. Dessert is a home-baked apple cake and grapes. I eat just enough that I won't offend our hosts.

THREE DAYS LATER, Tata arrives at the Sofia train station with *țuică*—strong Romanian plum liquor—on his breath. He is close to collapsing from physical and emotional exhaustion, but he is smiling as he gets off the train with his camera hanging around his neck like a trophy. His only other luggage is the camera bag, filled with lenses since we brought his valise with us to Sofia. He is still wearing the same pants and shirt he had on when we left Bucharest.

"Gyuri," Mama says after a restrained public embrace, "I'd like you to meet our Bulgarian friends." Tata shakes hands with Vasily. During our ride back to their home, Tata's eyes glaze over as Mama tries to explain what has happened to us since we last saw him.

"Forgive me"—Tata speaks in French so that Vasily can understand—"I have not slept in three days. Once I got my camera back, it was just a matter of waiting for the next train to Sofia, but it took this long, and the customs authorities would not allow me to go home since I'm emigrating. The stationmaster was kind enough to let me take naps in his office, but drinking *țuică* with him was part of the deal."

Mama slips her hand into Tata's. He smells so bad I wish I could open the car window. Luckily, the driver must have read my mind.

My PARENTS ARE ANXIOUS to leave for Istanbul as quickly as possible, but erratic and unreliable train schedules prevail for another week. I am constipated, and Mama is worried about me. She reminds me that we are doubly lucky to have found our Bulgarian friends, who continue to treat us as honored guests. On the night before our departure, Vasily's father-in-law asks to have a word with my father in private.

"What did he want?" Mama asks anxiously when Tata returns.

"He didn't *want* anything, Stefica," Tata tells her. "He *offered* us the option to stay in Bulgaria."

Mama is speechless. "I don't understand," she finally says.

"It's hard to understand kindness when you're not used to it, isn't it?" Tata remarks. "Stefica, did it occur to you that most Bulgarians don't drive around in chauffeured limousines? It just so happens that the old man is a big-shot minister in the Bulgarian Communist Party, and he can make things happen. He offered us housing, jobs, the works, despite the fact that he is well aware that we're Jewish. All we have to do is say yes."

"What did you tell him?" Mama panics.

"I accepted his offer, of course," Tata answers, taking out his pipe.

Mama looks blankly at him. As she opens her mouth, she gets red in the face trying to control her voice. "Very well then. You can stay here and find yourself a new Bulgarian wife to go along with your new Bulgarian job and apartment." She yanks her suitcase and mine out of the closet and starts to throw our clothes in.

Tata can't contain himself. "Get a hold of yourself, Stefica. I was joking!" When he sees the doubt in her face, he repeats, "I'm *joking*! I thanked him very much for his offer and explained that we must join your parents in Israel. Your mother is not well and needs you. He understands and respects my decision."

"*Your* decision?" Mama asks.

"*Our* decision, Stefica, since I love you so much, I read your mind."

THE BOSPORUS STRAIT

IN ISTANBUL, my parents act like birds that have just been released from a cage. They pull me out of bed each morning so we can visit as many places as possible. The Israeli authorities put us up in a cheap hotel and give us enough pocket money to last exactly seven days. On our final day we are to take a train to Ankara and then on to Izmir, the port city where we will finally board a ship for our voyage to Israel.

We walk everywhere in order to save money. In Kapalicarsi, the Grand Bazaar, I am overwhelmed by how many vendors and stores there are. Wherever I look I see vibrant color, even more luscious than the colors Cousin Mimi squeezed out of her oil paint tubes. Mama buys me my first piece of jewelry—a silver ring with tiny blue pieces of turquoise—in a crowded stall where people are elbowing each other. She bargains until she wears the vendor down to what she has to offer, which isn't much.

Tata takes us on a short boat ride through the Bosporus Strait and points to the places where the tension between the European side of the city and the Asian side can be demonstrated geographically. "This is where Europe and Asia meet, greet, and part ways so quickly it makes your head spin!" Tata says, trying to impress us.

We visit Hagia Sophia and the Topkapi Palace, both in a single day, and it is hard to take it all in: the awesome architecture of the ancient church, the sultan's wealth at Topkapi, the sounds of birds calling as they float above the Golden Horn in the twilight.

I have my first sip of Coca-Cola, an American drink that is as brown as Romanian cough syrup and almost as sugary. I long for one of Grandpa Yosef's homemade raspberry syrups with seltzer. In the afternoon, we feast at an inexpensive restaurant that serves chunks of roasted lamb on skewers and pilaf. We dip our meat in sauces laced with aromatic spices I never knew existed. On our way back to the hotel, Tata buys black tea and gooey baklava from a street vendor who wears a red fez and balances his silver tray full of steaming glass cups on one hand. At dusk, the cobblestoned road turns a slate blue in the golden light that permeates the city. We pass a woman whose face is hidden under a long black veil. She floats down the street like a ghost, her robes trailing in the breeze as she turns the corner.

On our last day in Istanbul we visit the Blue Mosque. At the door we are asked to take off our shoes. Once we are inside, a hush descends. We are surrounded by blue and white tiles and a soaring cupola. An eerie chant rises from somewhere outside. "It's the call to prayer," Tata whispers. This is the first time I have entered a house of prayer other than Rabbi's hidden room back in Bucharest. I wonder what a synagogue looks like.

THE TRAIN RIDE from Ankara to Izmir seems interminable. There is standing room only as more and more people come aboard.

Tata has found an almost empty compartment that everyone is avoiding. He sits down across from a woman who is very ill. She is shivering uncontrollably under her blanket despite the stifling heat.

"Malaria," Tata explains, and smiles. "You can only catch it from carrier mosquitoes. I had it twice myself, in the *lagers*."

I believe him, but I'm annoyed at his show-off bravery, so I remain outside with Mama and the rest of the crowd. It is so hot that the very air we breathe feels like it has been boiled and is turning into steam. I am dying of thirst. Tata uses his last Turkish coins to buy a bottle of water. Though it turns out to be quite hot, the three of us gulp it down, grateful for every drop. This is the first time we've ever had to pay for drinking water.

By nightfall Mama and I are so tired from standing that we collapse next to Tata in the compartment where the woman with malaria is still shivering. There is an acrid smell coming from her body. Tata opens the upper window, which is so dirty you can't see through it. Suddenly, a million stars appear in the night sky. I place my head in Mama's lap, and she runs her fingers through my hair. The last thing I see before drifting off is the sliver of a moon rising.

HAIFA HARBOR—OCTOBER 1961

WHERE DOES THE WATER in the sea come from? I don't bother asking Tata because I know what he would say. He would tell me that all the rivers and streams flow down from the mountains through the valleys and the deltas and eventually spill into the seas. He would explain that clouds in the sky cause rainstorms and snowstorms that also contribute water to rivers, streams, lakes, the seas, and the great oceans. He would talk about melting glaciers, climate change, and the tilt of the earth. *All this water,* I tell myself as I gaze at the blue expanse from the top deck of our ship. Water reaching beyond the horizon, beyond the rush of rivers and the cascading mountain streams, beyond the swell of the great oceans, water that sometimes evaporates into thin air and then pours down from the heavens again. Where does all of it really come from?

On the ship I feel like a rootless emigrant for the first time. Suddenly I hear Romanian spoken by a few other Jewish families with children, but we do not socialize. We keep each other at bay, since they are from the provinces and we are from Bucharest, every family a world unto itself, revolving around its own fears, needs, hopes, and dreams. The Israelis have paid for our passage. Our quarters are in a communal sleeping hall in the bowels of the ship. The portholes reveal that we are housed below the waterline. We sleep in single cots or bunk beds, each with a straw mattress and an army-issue blanket. There are no accommodations for couples. Each person is assigned a bed, and mine is a top bunk; Mama sleeps beneath me, and Tata is a couple of beds away. Our sheets are clean, but the pillows are hard.

To reach the dining room, we have to walk down several long and narrow passageways that are dimly lit by fluorescent bulbs, casting blue shadows on the walls, and up the stairs to the second deck. Long pipes run along the ceilings, and when I look up, I notice several black tails scurrying above. "Rats," my father says, squeezing my hand. "There are no ships without rats. Remember that, Eva." A shiver goes down my spine and lodges in my belly.

In the dining room there are beautifully set round tables decorated with flowers. The tourists onboard have cabins, some with private terraces and a view of the sea. They're all having a good time—speaking in French, English, German, even some languages I do not recognize—laughing, getting dressed in fancy clothes for dinner, ordering drinks, and gorging themselves on desserts. We eat in the same dining room, but we live in another world. The tourists act like we are invisible.

I spend most of my time on the upper deck, looking out at the horizon. We sail from Izmir through the Aegean Sea. On the first day the waves swell and turn ultramarine, reflecting the sky. There are storm clouds everywhere, and the sea is choppy. One of the Turkish sailors offers me a fruit I've never tasted before. "Delicious," he says, handing it to me. I bite into it just as my father appears from below. "That's a fig," the sailor tells me, looking at my father for his approval. When Tata smiles, the sailor asks me, "Do you like it?" I nod and savor the fruit's delicate flavor.

On the second morning the storm intensifies. We are making our way through thousands of Greek islands, some as tiny as a single rock protruding through the water's black surface. The ship sways fiercely from side to side. I am terrified of the raging sea, which feels like it's about to swallow us up. At breakfast there is no one in the dining room, except for my father, who is enjoying his food. I sit next to him and watch him eat as the boat tips enough to make our water glasses tilt and our silverware rattle. Back on deck, we have to hold on to the railing while the ship rolls. A giant wave splashes the top deck and sprays both of us. The water is frigid. My stomach feels queasy. I notice several other passengers on deck, one of them rushing to the railing and vomiting overboard. Tata smiles, grabs my hand, and points. "Keep your eyes on the horizon and you won't get sick," he says.

Mama arrives, looking for us. She is wobbly as she waves. I reach out to grab her extended hand, but she turns around and vomits. The smell makes me so sick that I throw up as well. Tata keeps smiling calmly and looking out to sea.

The weather gets better once we are in the Mediterranean. The sun reappears on the third day, and everyone's spirits lift. We stop in Cyprus to allow some tourists to disembark and others to come onboard, but we do not leave the ship.

WE SAIL INTO Haifa harbor at dawn. The sun is so bright it feels like a ball of white light rising against the clear blue of the sky. All of the immigrants are gathered on deck with their luggage. Two Israeli officials have set up a folding table in the middle of the deck, and there is already a line forming. Tata hands me a pair of red-framed sunglasses. Everything looks so much better without the glare from the sun. Mama leaves the line to talk to one of the other immigrants, a man who has just finished speaking with the Israeli officials. She returns and whispers to Tata, whose gaze is focused on the head of the line. "They're separating white-collar workers from blue-collar. White-collar people go to live in central towns and get better housing."

Tata answers her without taking his eyes off the Israeli officials. "Don't worry. We're both white-collar."

I slip free from Mama's hand and go to the railing. People in the port are milling about like ants in slow motion. Passengers from our ship have already begun to disembark. Some look completely disoriented as they gather their belongings and take their first steps on Israeli soil. Others, met by relatives, are shouting in joyful recognition as they embrace.

From behind my new sunglasses, my eyes roam the crowd, searching until they rest on a man in a short-sleeved blue shirt. His hands are cupped in front of his eyes in binocular fashion, and he is focused up at the ship's deck. It is Grandpa Yosef, and next to him is Uncle Natan, his thick eyeglasses reflecting the glare. My arms shoot up, and I start waving wildly. I take off my glasses and continue to wave until Grandpa Yosef points and waves back in recognition. There's a rush of air into my chest like one of the giant waves I witnessed during the storm, except this time I'm flooded with joy.

I run back just in time to join my parents as they meet with the Israeli officials. I can hardly keep myself from telling my parents that Grandpa Yosef and Uncle Natan are waiting for us.

"What is the child's name?" the Israeli asks.

"Eva," Mama answers.

"This is Israel. In Israel she must go by her Hebrew name," the official tells my parents.

My parents do not respond. The official stamps a bunch of papers and then announces matter-of-factly, "From now on she will be Haya. Welcome to Israel, Haya." He looks up from his papers for the first time and smiles.

ACKNOWLEDGMENTS

I am lucky. There are so many amazing people who have sustained me in miraculous ways throughout the writing of this book to whom I owe far more than gratitude. To Frances Foster, my publisher and genius editor: your wisdom and kindness have exceeded my expectations. To Leigh Feldman, agent extraordinaire, for recognizing the merit of this book and fostering its growth. To Charles Baxter, bless you for helping an unknown writer! To Lisa Graff, for your insightful editorial advice. To Jay Colvin, for your flawless eye in the design of this book. To Richard Tuschman, whose jacket design is visual poetry. To Margaret Ferguson and the amazing FSG team, for minding every detail, big and small. To Victoria Wells Arms, for your editorial help and enthusiasm at the beginning, when I needed it most. To my steadfast first readers: Dee Birch, Ron Collins, Gary Derish, Molly Donahue, Penny Burrow Marwede, Sylvia Peck, Pauline Rothstein, and Yael Shapiro—for your friendship and candor. To Mark Chimsky-Lustig, for your unwavering friendship and sound advice. To Peg Walz, always a "tender button." To Lisa Haliday, for encouragement on my first draft. To Susan Conceicao, my best friend, for insight on the last draft. To Sandy Serebin, for offering your country home as a writer's sanctuary. To Karen Quinn, friend and trailblazer. To Rabbi Andrea Myers, Julie Standig, and Peter Albu, for help with Jewish research. To Rodica Belea for checking my Romanian language accuracy. To Ana Calmanovici and Max Albala for providing missing photographs. To Anna Perez, for trays filled with sustenance. To my teachers: Dr. Gerald Epstein, Dr. Elizabeth Barrett, and Denise Linn, for your love, support, and wisdom. To Monica Thakrar and my Soul Coaching sisters, for being the first to call me Haya. To Marvin Schneider, for repairing my father's clock, and for your kind soul. To my Rodeph Sholom family, thank you for your prayers, your songs, and your continued presence in my life. To Susan Muller-Hershon, for being the sister I've always wanted. To my beautiful cousin Claudia, for your belief in me. To Mathilde Greenfield, for the strength of your presence. And to Alice Okada, for your unmatched grace.

Most of all, I owe this book to my daughter, Mika, who asked about the past ardently enough to compel me to write about it, and to my son, Jacob, whose advice during the writing process proved indispensable. Last but always first, to my husband, Tom, my anchor and best friend. Without you, I would not have persevered.

Although I never met Rabbi Moses Rosen, of blessed memory, Chief Rabbi of Romania, 1948–1994, I am humbled to have discovered almost fifty years later his heroic undertaking. Rabbi Rosen suffered great personal risk and endured much criticism for "brokering deals" between the anti-Semitic Communist regime and the State of Israel. In the end he persevered in orchestrating the mass exodus of almost 400,000 Romanian Jews to Israel. My family and I are indeed lucky to be among those he saved. It is a great gift that he gave us, and I am eternally grateful.